Making Law in the United States Courts of Appeals

When presented with opportunities to make law, how do judges respond? In this book, Professor Klein addresses this question by examining the decisions of circuit court judges in cases not clearly covered by existing precedents. Specifically, he considers whether the actions and characteristics of their colleagues influence the choices of circuit judges to adopt particular legal rules. In addition, he asks whether and why circuit judges attempt to decide legal issues as they think the Supreme Court would in their place.

Using evidence drawn from quantitative analyses of several hundred cases, as well as interviews with two dozen circuit court judges, Klein finds that judges give serious attention to the work of colleagues, whether on their own court or other circuits. The actions, prestige, and expertise of these other circuit court judges are important factors in their decision making. However, while Supreme Court precedents factor heavily in circuit judges' rulings, expectations as to how the Supreme Court might decide in the future appear to have little effect on their actions. These findings speak to ongoing debates about judges' motivations and behavior, suggesting that both legal and policy goals influence judges.

David E. Klein is an assistant professor of government and foreign affairs at the University of Virginia.

D1367124

Making Law
in the United States
Courts of Appeals

DAVID E. KLEIN

University of Virginia

CAMBRIDGE
UNIVERSITY PRESS

PUBLISHED BY THE PRESS SYNDICATE OF THE UNIVERSITY OF CAMBRIDGE
The Pitt Building, Trumpington Street, Cambridge, United Kingdom

CAMBRIDGE UNIVERSITY PRESS
The Edinburgh Building, Cambridge CB2 2RU, UK
40 West 20th Street, New York, NY 10011-4211, USA
477 Williamstown Road, Port Melbourne, VIC 3207, Australia
Ruiz de Alarcón 13, 28014 Madrid, Spain
Dock House, The Waterfront, Cape Town 8001, South Africa

http://www.cambridge.org

First published 2002

Printed in the United Kingdom at the University Press, Cambridge

Typeface Sabon 10/13 pt.   *System* QuarkXPress [BTS]

A catalog record for this book is available from the British Library.

Library of Congress Cataloging in Publication Data
Klein, David E., 1970–
Making law in the United States Courts of Appeals / David E. Klein.
p. cm.
Includes bibliographical references and index.
ISBN 0-521-81023-X (hbk.) – ISBN 0-521-89145-0 (pbk.)
1. Appellate courts – United States. 2. Judicial process – United States. I. Title.
KF8750 .K59 2002
347.73'24–dc21   2001052622

ISBN 0 521 81023 X hardback
ISBN 0 521 89145 0 paperback

Contents

v

Tables

Acknowledgments

I am grateful to a number of people and institutions who helped to make this a better book than it otherwise would have been. Prominent among them are the twenty-four circuit judges whom I cannot name here but who gave generously of their time to a graduate student and project they knew nothing about. (Many more judges were gracious enough to grant my request for an interview, but I was unable to work out the logistical details with them.)

The Ohio State University provided crucial assistance in the project's early stages through a Graduate Student Alumni Research Award. The University of Virginia helped me to complete the analysis and writing of this work through a Sesquicentennial research leave, Summer Research Grant, and Rowland Egger grant.

In the course of the work, I ran into some tricky methodological issues. Kevin Rask, Donald Richards, and Christopher Zorn kindly helped me work through them.

Darby Morrisroe provided able research assistance and collaborated in the development and validation of the measure of judicial prestige described in Chapter 4.

Eric Newman and my mother, Sheila Klein, provided valuable editorial advice. My wife, Tina Rask, helped with some of the most tedious work, including checking citations.

William Landes, Mary Mattingly, Richard Posner, Donald Songer, Isaac Unah, and Stephen Wasby each read some piece of this study in an earlier version and provided valuable suggestions.

Elliot Slotnick and Gregory Caldeira read a substantial segment of the final product in an earlier incarnation. Harold Spaeth and an anonymous reviewer read one or more complete drafts of the current version. All four of them provided many helpful comments and suggestions.

I owe the most to Lawrence Baum. From the beginning, he has helped with theoretical, methodological, and presentational issues, reading and responding to different pieces of the work more times than I can recall. His advice and encouragement have been invaluable.

Because convention bars me from blaming any of the aforementioned for the book's shortcomings, I am tempted to blame my daughter Julia, whose quick fingers and curiosity about keyboards sometimes threatened disaster. But the truth is that it is easier to do good work when one's home life is as happy as Tina and Julia have made mine. I appreciate their support, as well as that of the other members of my family whose interest and confidence have made it easier to keep going.

Law Making in a Hierarchical Judicial System

On June 10, 1996, the U.S. Supreme Court handed down its decision in the case of *Whren v. United States*.[1] Whren and a co-defendant, accused of federal drug law violations, had been convicted in District Court and, after appealing to the U.S. Court of Appeals for the District of Columbia Circuit, had lost there too. At both courts they had requested that the drugs found in Whren's car be excluded from evidence at their trial, contending that the arresting police officers' purported basis for stopping them – a minor traffic infraction – was in fact a pretext, employed because the officers wished to search for drugs but had no probable cause to do so. Their argument now failed for a third time. According to a unanimous Supreme Court, "the District Court found that the officers had probable cause to believe that petitioners had violated the traffic code. That rendered the stop reasonable under the Fourth Amendment, the evidence thereby discovered admissible, and the upholding of the convictions by the Court of Appeals for the District of Columbia Circuit correct" (819).

When viewed as a single Supreme Court case or even a series of cases involving a single defendant, these events probably seem unremarkable. In reality, though, they constitute only the final chapter in a complex, intriguing legal saga involving numerous defendants and courts. The first chapter began eleven years earlier, on June 5, 1985.

Early that morning, two men driving along Interstate 95 in Florida were stopped by a trooper from the Highway Patrol. The trooper called for a drug dog, which, sniffing the exterior of the men's car, signaled the

---

[1] 517 U.S. 806 (1996).

presence of drugs. A search of the car's trunk uncovered a kilogram of cocaine. The two men were arrested and charged in federal court with conspiracy to possess cocaine with intent to distribute.

At the trial, the trooper testified that he had become suspicious immediately upon seeing the defendants. He thought that they fit a drug courier profile, in that they were both young men, were in a car with out-of-state tags, appeared to be driving overly cautiously, and avoided looking at the trooper as they drove by him. He followed their car for about a mile and a half, observed it cross about six inches into the emergency lane and then back to the center line, and pulled it over. As Whren would later do, the defendants argued that the stop was unreasonable under the Fourth Amendment and asked that the seized cocaine be excluded from evidence at the trial. In their view, the trooper had used a trivial violation as a pretext to undertake a search for which he had no justification.

After the district court judge denied their motion to suppress the evidence, the defendants appealed to the U.S. Court of Appeals for the Eleventh Circuit. For the most part, the circumstances and arguments must have seemed drearily familiar to the three judges hearing the appeal. Drug cases had come to occupy a substantial portion of federal court dockets, and the particulars of this case were not unusual. Nor was the defendants' argument novel. The concept of "pretextual stops" had emerged as a ground for invalidating searches in a number of courts.

Nonetheless, the law in this area was not fully settled. In a series of cases beginning with *Scott v. United States*,[2] the Supreme Court had made clear that when evaluating Fourth Amendment claims, judges were to disregard police officers' intent and instead consider only whether searches or seizures were "objectively" reasonable. The Eleventh Circuit judges had to decide if and how judges could determine whether a stop was pretextual without reference to officers' intentions. No precedents from the Supreme Court, their own court, or even another court of appeals spoke directly to the question, and it was not an easy one.

Their solution was to announce this rule: "[I]n determining whether an investigative stop is invalid as pretextual, the proper inquiry is whether a reasonable officer would have made the seizure in the absence of illegitimate motivation."[3] The judges argued that their test was objective, in the sense that it asked not about an individual officer's thinking

---

[2] 436 U.S. 128 (1978).
[3] *U.S. v. Smith*, 799 F.2d 704 (11th Cir. 1986).

but about the typical behavior of officers in similar situations. This approach instantly became authoritative law for all federal courts in Florida, Georgia, and Alabama, the states of the Eleventh Circuit. But it did nothing to resolve the legal problem in any other federal circuit, all but one of which would be called on to decide the same issue in the next nine years.

The Fifth Circuit was the next to confront it, just a few months later. Without much discussion, the three-judge panel cited and adopted the rule from the Eleventh Circuit.[4] Any possibility of a national consensus disappeared shortly afterward, however, with another decision of the Fifth Circuit, this time sitting en banc.[5] By an 8–6 vote, the full court ruled that as long as police officers had observed some offense for which they have the authority to stop drivers, a stop would be considered valid, even if the offense was minor and it was unusual for the police to stop someone for it. Interestingly, although the dissenters approvingly cited the two cases just discussed, the majority failed even to mention them.

Other circuits were now faced with two alternatives, sometimes referred to as the "would" rule (Eleventh Circuit) and the "could" rule (Fifth Circuit). Over the next three years, three more circuits weighed in, with the Seventh and Eighth Circuits adopting the "could" rule[6] and the Tenth Circuit adopting the "would" rule.[7] Throughout this time, as circuit courts grappled with the difficult issue and confusion grew, the Supreme Court remained silent, even though in three of the cases litigants asked it to grant certiorari and issue a definitive ruling on the question.

In fact, the Supreme Court did not speak for another six years, denying four more petitions for certiorari before granting Whren's in 1996. During this time, six more circuits decided the issue. One, the Ninth, adopted the "would" rule.[8] Four others adopted the more permissive standard of the Fifth Circuit.[9] The Sixth Circuit wavered, first inclining against the "would" rule, then adopting it, and finally, in an en

---

[4] *U.S. v. Johnson*, 815 F.2d 309 (5th Cir. 1987).
[5] *U.S. v. Causey*, 834 F.2d 1179 (5th Cir. 1987).
[6] *U.S. v. Trigg*, 878 F.2d 1037 (7th Cir. 1989); *U.S. v. Cummins*, 920 F.2d 498 (8th Cir. 1990).
[7] *U.S. v. Guzman*, 864 F.2d 1512 (10th Cir. 1988).
[8] *U.S. v. Cannon*, 29 F.3d 472 (9th Cir. 1994).
[9] *U.S. v. Hassan El*, 5 F.3d 726 (4th Cir. 1993); *U.S. v. Scopo*, 19 F.3d 777 (2nd Cir. 1994); *U.S. v. Whren*, 53 F.3d 371 (DC Cir. 1995); *U.S. v. Johnson*, 63 F.3d 242 (3rd Cir. 1995).

banc decision, rejecting it for a variant of the "could" rule.[10] The Tenth Circuit revisited the issue, now choosing to adopt the "could" rule en banc.[11]

By the time of the Supreme Court's *Whren* decision, matters stood as follows: In Alabama, Alaska, Arizona, California, Florida, Georgia, Hawaii, Idaho, Montana, Nevada, Oregon, and Washington state, the U.S. Constitution barred police from stopping suspects unless a reasonable officer would have stopped them for the same offense. In almost every other state of the union, the Constitution allowed police to make a stop as long as the suspects had technically violated some law.[12] For nine years, suspects had been accorded more protection by the Constitution in some states than in others. For ten years, in some states, police had been constrained and evidence suppressed on the basis of a rule that the Supreme Court would unanimously reject when it finally considered it.

THEORETICAL ISSUES

This story of the development of a legal rule, while by no means typical, highlights an important truth and raises a host of questions about the dynamics of law making in large court systems. The truth, well known but often overlooked in the media and even in serious scholarship, is that lower court judges play a major role in the development of legal doctrine. Issues reach them first, and higher courts might not address those issues for years afterward if in fact they ever do. Furthermore, in many systems courts of equal authority are not bound to heed, or even take note of, one another's decisions when deciding their own cases, even where they are constructing legal policy from the same statutes, constitutional provisions, or higher court precedents.

As a result, even if a particular court is just a single mid- or low-level component of a large system, it may well possess the power to affect legal policy independently and substantially. In a hierarchical structure, its best opportunities to do so arise when it confronts issues not yet resolved by a higher court. The research described here is motivated by curiosity about how judges react to these opportunities. Do they feel con-

---

[10] *U.S. v. French*, 974 F.2d 687 (6th Cir. 1992); *U.S. v. Ferguson*, 989 F.2d 202 (6th Cir. 1993); *U.S. v. Ferguson*, 8 F.3d 385 (6th Cir. 1993).

[11] *U.S. v. Botero-Ospina*, 71 F.3d 783 (10th Cir. 1995).

[12] The only exceptions were the four New England states making up the First Circuit, which had not ruled on the issue.

strained by the courts around and above them? In what ways, and why? More specifically, as they consider unsettled issues, do they attempt to determine how a higher court would rule in their place and decide accordingly? How much attention do they pay to other judges of equal authority who have addressed the same issue? Do they tend to follow the leads of these judges? What factors make them more or less likely to do so?

These questions form the central focus of this study. The answers will in turn generate deeper questions. For example, if we found that judges did attempt to anticipate the Supreme Court's reactions, we would naturally wonder why they did. Such questions go to the core of judicial decision making, have long been debated, and are critically important. The results of this study will not speak as directly to them as to the central questions, but they will allow for some inferences. I discuss these in the final chapter of the book.

In my search for answers, I have chosen to study the twelve regional U.S. Courts of Appeals. Also known as circuit courts, they form the middle level of the American federal judicial system, above the district (trial) courts and below only the Supreme Court. Where the Supreme Court has not already spoken, each court of appeals sets the law for all federal judges within its jurisdiction. For all but one of the circuits, the District of Columbia, this jurisdiction covers at least three states. In a typical year, the courts of appeals together decide more than a hundred times as many cases as does the Supreme Court. In short, the circuit courts are tremendously important and undeniably worthy of attention.

Even so, the questions confronted in this research have been surprisingly unexplored, and there is little existing knowledge on which to build. Furthermore, the present study, though theoretically grounded and carefully conducted, is, inevitably, imperfect. For these reasons, conclusions will have to be drawn with some caution. Realistically, I aim to produce an accurate broad picture of the policymaking role of courts of appeals in the federal system along with highly credible evidence as to the details and, in doing so, to contribute to broader debates over the factors influencing judges' decision making.

Caveats notwithstanding, I will not hesitate to discuss interesting implications of the study's findings. In considering these implications, it is important to keep in mind that the courts of appeals constitute just one set of courts among many. What we learn about them here should have relevance for other sets as well, in the United States and in other countries. Two interesting examples that come to mind are U.S. state courts under federal law and European national courts under European

Union law. In both cases, individual courts of equal authority serve very different constituencies and proceed under no obligation to respect each other's views. They are bound by the rulings of only one court (the U.S. Supreme Court and the European Court of Justice, respectively). Unless judges in different jurisdictions have far less in common than I imagine, the behavior of those in the other systems should mirror that of circuit judges to some extent. At the same time, though, unique circumstances and institutional arrangements of each system may produce important differences. Thus, the study will not allow for confident inferences about other legal systems, but it should generate insights and questions for scholars interested in them.

Similarly, because circuit judges are not unique, any conclusions about internal and external influences on their behavior will cast at least some light on the actions of other judges. For example, by the final chapter we will have encountered substantial – albeit mostly indirect – evidence that legal goals affect circuit judges' decisions. In that chapter I argue that the same conclusion probably applies to most kinds of courts in most situations.

EXISTING RESEARCH

Twenty years ago, the claim just made about the state of our knowledge would have been unsurprising. Writing in 1981, J. Woodford Howard had the following to say: "Beyond general impressions . . . knowledge of the functions and operations of circuit courts is largely intuitive and fragmentary. . . . Courts of Appeals remain among the least comprehended of major federal institutions" (xvii). Now, the neglect of the circuit courts seems a thing of the past. Howard's book itself constituted a major advance, and the study of circuit courts has continued steadily since. Political scientists have substantially furthered our understanding of the factors at work in circuit judges' decision making while legal scholars concerned with issues of caseload and capacity have devoted considerable attention to circuit rules and procedures. We now understand circuit courts far better than we once did.

Yet, precisely because there was so much to be learned, studies have almost invariably taken a broad view, asking how courts operate and how judges behave *generally*. Most of the work of circuit judges involves the application of settled legal rules. Information about their actions in typical situations does not permit firm conclusions about their behavior in those special cases where they can actively shape the law.

As a clarifying example, consider the question of whether circuit judges try to decide unsettled issues of law as they think the Supreme Court would. Researchers have developed a highly credible body of evidence showing that circuit judges and other lower court judges are generally (though not perfectly) responsive to the policies announced by their superiors. They tend to comply with and otherwise adjust their decision making in response to precedents from higher courts (Gruhl 1980; Stidham and Carp 1982; Johnson 1987; Songer and Sheehan 1990; Songer and Haire 1992). Furthermore, their decisions typically track ideological trends in higher courts (Baum 1980; Songer 1987; Songer, Segal, and Cameron 1994; Rowland and Carp 1996; but see Sheehan, Hurwitz, and Reddick 1998). But because the relationship between higher and lower court decision making is not perfect and the studies do not isolate and examine cases not covered by higher court precedents, we cannot conclude anything about decision making on open issues. The findings of substantial but imperfect responsiveness are entirely consistent with the possibility that lower court judges adhere faithfully to higher court precedents – and so appear responsive in the bulk of their cases – but ignore their superiors entirely when deciding new questions. For instance, if the Supreme Court became increasingly conservative in the area of search and seizure, so would the precedents governing the cases that came before circuit judges. If the circuit judges followed those precedents, we would expect to see a conservative trend in their decisions, regardless of whether they tried to decide cases as the Supreme Court would.

Naturally, one can look for insights in research not specifically focused on the courts of appeals. I do so extensively in this study. But little work is directly relevant. Political scientists interested in judicial decision making have overwhelmingly tended to concentrate on individual judges' votes on case outcomes. While some studies of judicial behavior give close attention to the part that judges and courts play in developing legal doctrine (e.g., Shapiro 1965, 1970; Landes and Posner 1976; Canon and Baum 1981; Epstein and Kobylka 1992; Glick 1992; Wahlbeck 1997), these remain rare.

DESCRIPTION OF THE STUDY

In the research presented here, I add to the small store of such studies by focusing on the announcement and treatment of new legal rules. New legal rules are defined as either: (1) rulings on issues not previously

addressed by the Supreme Court or any federal court of appeals; or
(2) unprecedented approaches to issues that previously had been
addressed in other ways. (Clarifications and examples are given in
Chapter 3.)

The study is based primarily on an examination of U.S. Courts of
Appeals cases decided between 1983 and 1995 in the areas of antitrust,
search and seizure, and environmental law. The full set of cases consists
of those announcing new legal rules and subsequent cases for which the
initial ones are relevant precedents.

The analysis of cases is supplemented with information from interviews with two dozen circuit court judges. The interviews provide theoretical grounding for hypotheses about judges' behavior, tests of some
of the hypotheses, and additional context for understanding the various
findings. Judges were asked about, among other things, their motivations, work styles, workload, attitudes toward and usage of precedent,
and other judges' reputations.

I believe the two sources of data complement each other well. The
analysis of cases provides for relatively rigorous, objective, and complete
tests of hypotheses. It has limitations, though: chiefly a narrow focus,
a tendency to identify commonalities among judges while obscuring
differences, and some imprecision in the measurement of concepts. The
interviews deliver contextually rich insights into dynamics generally,
rather than just in three fields of law; reflect on the validity of the
assumptions underlying my explanatory hypotheses; and reveal intriguing and significant differences among judges.

The picture of circuit court law making that emerges by the end of
the study is not a simple one, but a few themes do come through rather
clearly. One theme is the independence of circuit court judges. Their
work does not appear to be closely supervised by the Supreme Court,
nor does it seem that they try very hard to anticipate the Court's reaction when making their own decisions. They do not adhere slavishly
to precedents from other circuit judges, and circuit conflict is fairly
common. Their decision making appears individualistic, with ideology
playing an important role. Yet there are also strong currents running in
the other direction, toward uniformity. Different courts agree considerably more often than they disagree. Agreement probably arises in part
from similar political values and shared standards of decision making,
but it does not happen just by chance. Circuit judges pay serious attention to one another's views and are sometimes influenced by what others
have done or even by who they are. Ultimately, it appears that their con-

fidence and self-reliance are tempered by respect and a sense of participation in a shared enterprise.

The construction of this picture begins in the next chapter, where
I draw on existing research and the interviews to develop assumptions
about judges' motivations. These are used to derive hypotheses about
the factors affecting circuit judges' decisions on unsettled issues of law.
Broadly, I hypothesize that the judges will more often adopt than reject
the rules of their colleagues and that the likelihood of adoption will vary
with their own attitudes and the actions and characteristics of the judges
deciding before them. I do not take a position as to whether or not they
are likely to anticipate the Supreme Court's response when making their
decisions. Strong arguments can be made in either direction, and I adopt
a neutral perspective to ascertain whether the weight of evidence favors
one or the other.

Chapter 3 introduces the cases used in the quantitative analysis.
I explain how they were chosen, provide preliminary descriptions of
circuit judges' behavior in those cases, and summarize the Supreme
Court's reactions to them. Chapters 4 and 5 are devoted to tests of the
hypotheses about interactions among circuit court judges. The case
analysis, which plays the primary role in the hypothesis testing, is presented in Chapter 4. The interviews, discussed in Chapter 5, provide
further tests and additional information. Chapter 6 examines the influence of possible Supreme Court reactions, using only the cases. In
Chapter 7, I discuss the implications of the findings.

2

Theory and Hypotheses

Although judges on intermediate appellate courts enjoy considerable independence, their decisions are not made in legal or institutional vacuums. In many instances, the issues before them have been addressed previously by judges of equal authority. Even if not, there are always the precedents and possible reactions of a higher court to be considered. The aim of this study is to gain a better understanding of how and why these other judges' decisions – actual or anticipated – affect judicial resolutions of contested legal issues. Although my specific concerns are atypical, at heart this is an examination of judicial decision making. For this reason, I construct the theoretical framework for the study from the vast literature on judicial decision making in political science and legal studies.

THEORETICAL FRAMEWORK

I follow Baum (1997) by focusing on what this literature teaches us about judges' motivations, or goals. Other approaches are possible and might be preferred by some scholars. Gibson (1983) is not alone in believing that "[j]udges' decisions are a function of what they prefer to do, tempered by what they think they ought to do, but constrained by what they perceive is feasible to do" (32). Nevertheless, there is good reason to begin with an emphasis on goals. Judgeships – particularly on appellate courts – are highly prestigious, desirable, and competitive positions. Undoubtedly, most people who become judges work hard to gain the office, devoting substantial portions of their professional lives to the quest. It would be strange if the motives that brought them there were not reflected in their behavior as judges, especially in that aspect of behavior at the core of the judicial function – decision making. Furthermore, although at first glance Gibson's formulation appears to sharply distinguish goals – what judges prefer to do – from the other two elements, goals may actually be implicated in all three. There are very few inherent limitations to the judicial power of decision making. Constraints of feasibility are most likely self-imposed and instrumental, expressed something like this: "Given what I wish to accomplish, such an action would be unwise." Even what judges "think they ought to do" can be influenced by goals. We may sometimes internalize norms to the point where we follow them unthinkingly, but often we adhere to them because we desire the respect and good opinion of others or ourselves. In short, even under a more complex view of decision making, goals appear pervasive.

As Baum shows, the roster of goals that might influence judges' behavior at one time or another is long and diverse. Some goals, though, are more likely than others to be relevant in particular situations. For the framework of this project to be manageable and productive, the number of assumptions must be limited. Therefore, I sought to distill from the decision-making literature a few goals that are fundamentally important generally and particularly likely to be relevant to judges on the courts of appeals. As an independent gauge of their importance, I asked the interviewed judges how much they mattered. Based on my reading of the literature and the judges' responses, I assume that all circuit judges wish to do at least one (often more) of the following:

• Promote policies consistent with their policy preferences
• Reach decisions that are legally sound
• Maintain coherence and consistency in the federal law
• Limit the time spent deciding any one case

Scholars skeptical of a heavy emphasis on goals might take issue with this list. In particular, they would probably argue that legal soundness is better understood as a constraint, whether in terms of what judges can do or in terms of what they should do.[1] This perspective appears to be widely shared. Yet it seems to rest on an assumption that judges' only genuine desire is to shape public policy. The strictures of legal correctness may be important to judges, but only so far as obedience furthers

[1] For some clear examples, see Howard (1981), Gibson (1983), George and Epstein (1992), Wahlbeck (1997), and Epstein and Knight (1998).

the policy goal. I reject this assumption. For one thing, legally sound decision making might help judges achieve other goals, like the respect of the legal profession or career advancement. For another, it seems highly likely that at least some judges find the search for good answers to legal questions intrinsically rewarding. The opportunity to engage in this activity differentiates judging from other occupations in legislatures, executive offices, or the private sector far more clearly than any disparities in prestige or policy influence. It is quite possible, then, that rather than simply appearing as an obstacle to policy making, the challenge of reaching decisions supported by legal reasoning actually attracts judges to their profession.

Support for this view comes from Sarat's (1977) interviews with forty-eight county court judges. Sarat concluded that they could be categorized by the types of incentives that led them to become judges. Of the four categories he constructed, the "game" incentive was the most common. According to Sarat, the judges in this category

derive their satisfaction from the activities and behaviors which are associated with judging. They enjoy these behaviors in and of themselves and not because they associate them with the achievement of particular substantive results. Judging is a difficult and challenging vocation, and these people get pleasure out of overcoming the difficulties and meeting the challenges. They see value in the rituals and rules which govern the operation of courts and seek to master and apply those rituals and rules. (pp. 376–7)

Judge Posner (1995:131) has expressed a similar view. After arguing that judges yield to such influences as feelings about litigants or lawyers and the desire for advancement "less often than the suspicious layman thinks," he explains:

[T]he utility they derive from judging would be reduced by more than they would gain from giving way to the temptations that I have listed. It is the same reason why many people do not cheat at games even when they are sure they could get away with cheating. The pleasure of judging is bound up with compliance with certain self-limiting rules that define the "game" of judging. . . . It is by doing such things that you know you are playing the judge role; and judges for the most part are people who want to be – judges.

I find these ideas compelling and so begin by treating both legal and policy considerations as important goals, rather than assuming in advance the primacy of the latter. It is important to emphasize that I do not propose to set out or test a "legal model" of decision making in the sense Segal and Spaeth (1993) use the term. That is, I do not attempt to show that from knowledge of relevant texts, precedents, and rules of interpretation one could generate accurate predictions of judicial decisions. It is true that such a model is more likely to be successful if judges take legal goals seriously, but one is still left with the problem of constructing the model. As I discuss later, judges themselves appear to have great difficulty explaining why they view some positions as more legally plausible than others. The obstacles facing a researcher who wishes to operationalize legal soundness are necessarily at least as high, and they are not overcome in the research presented here.

In this sense, the assumption I test here is more limited than it might be. In another sense, though, it goes beyond the kind of model just described. Even if we found that we could predict judges' decisions from texts and rules, we could not be sure that legal *goals* were at work or even that the decisions reflected the judges' own legal views. They might go along with what they take to be more easily acceptable positions in order to protect their courts' legitimacy and so preserve their policy-making power (Knight and Epstein 1996; Epstein and Knight 1998) or to avoid calling unfavorable attention to themselves. The claim explored in this study is that judges act as they do in part because they wish to make legally sound decisions, not simply that considerations of legal correctness enter into their decisions.

The validity of this assumption, like the others, will be tested by the performance of the hypotheses derived from it. Aside from judges' statements, I will not provide any direct evidence to support it. What other evidence there is will come from observations of behavior or relationships that would be difficult to explain if the assumption were incorrect.

Whatever goals judges care about, there are different ways in which they might pursue them. In recent years, scholars have become increasingly interested in the question of whether judges act strategically – that is, whether they take into account the possible behavior of others in deciding what actions are most likely to further their interests (see Baum 1997, ch. 4). Although the question is as interesting in the context of this study as in any other, I take no position on it.

One reason is that I do not have clear expectations. Researchers have uncovered evidence of strategic behavior, especially at the Supreme Court (Murphy 1964; Maltzman and Wahlbeck 1996; Wahlbeck, Spriggs, and Maltzman 1996; Epstein and Knight 1998), and it certainly seems reasonable to suppose that circuit judges act strategically at least occasionally. Yet judges, like all human beings, possess cognitive limitations that generally prevent them from giving thorough consideration to all possible options when called on to make decisions (Fiske and Taylor 1991). These limitations, which are reinforced by the time constraints imposed by heavy caseloads, make it impossible for judges to act strategically all the time.

The more important reason is that the study explores generally uncharted territory. I have no expectation of developing a comprehensive model. The analyses presented here are complicated even when only the four primary goals are considered. Adding tests of strategic behavior would likely generate more confusion than insight.

Even so, certain findings will cast some light on the issue of whether or not circuit judges act strategically. I will note them and discuss their significance as they arise.

In the next two sections I draw on the decision-making literature and my interviews with judges to justify the foregoing assumptions. The final section of the chapter is given to the generation of hypotheses from these assumptions.

JUDGES' GOALS: THE LITERATURE

The notion that judges act to further their policy preferences was advanced by early scholars of judicial behavior in both law[2] and political science (Pritchett 1948; Schubert 1965; Rohde and Spaeth 1976) and has gained considerable currency over the past few decades. The attitudinal model – as it is called – is firmly rooted in theory and strongly supported by empirical data, especially at the Supreme Court level.[3] It is now established almost beyond doubt that justices' policy preferences frequently drive their voting decisions.

Of course, the environment in which circuit court judges operate differs somewhat from that of the Supreme Court. As Segal and Spaeth (1993) note, the Supreme Court's docket is composed almost entirely of difficult cases, where the law is unclear; the Supreme Court is not bound by the rulings of, nor can it be reversed by, a higher court; and Supreme Court justices rarely possess ambition for higher office. While opportunities for justices to promote their policy preferences abound and disincentives are few, the same is not true for lower court judges.

---

[2] See Fisher, Horwitz, and Reed (1993), especially the essays in Chapter 6.

[3] Support comes from works too numerous to list. Segal and Spaeth (1993) and Spaeth and Segal (1999) provide the most definitive exposition and testing of the attitudinal model.

Nevertheless, the differences should not be overstated. Like Supreme Court justices, judges on the Courts of Appeals are not electorally accountable. Furthermore, as the judges interviewed for this study attest, not all cases that reach the circuit courts are governed by precedent from the Supreme Court or the circuit.[4] Finally, as Llewellyn (1951) explains and illustrates, the judge who wishes to distinguish an apparently controlling precedent can often do so without much strain. Of course, the judge then runs the risk of reversal and any attendant embarrassment or damage to career prospects. But the Supreme Court hears very few appeals; apart from egregious cases of disregard for precedent, the risk of reversal will normally appear moderate, at worst. In short, circuit judges frequently encounter cases where their policy preferences are likely to come into play and where the costs of heeding them are acceptable. These considerations and a number of empirical studies point to the same conclusion: Circuit judges' policy preferences affect their decision making.[5]

As with political scientists, it has become common for judges writing about the decision-making process to admit that personal values enter into some decisions (Friendly 1961; Newman 1984; Edwards 1991). Some even argue in defense of such subjective considerations. Writing in 1959, a Louisiana appellate judge noted that "Although a great preponderance of an appellate judge's caseload ... involves routine application of precedent and word-logic, fairly soon in the life of the new judge the moment comes when he realizes that there are some cases in which he (or no one) can find 'the law.'" In such cases the judge should "decide on the basis of what is best for the community ... that is, on the basis of policy considerations" (Tate 1959:62–3). More recently, Judge Wald (1992) of the D.C. Circuit wrote:

So what, if any, judicial philosophy should a judge adopt? The closest approximation I can espouse is something that some of my colleagues roundly denounce: a pragmatism that decides cases on the merits, what Judge Posner calls "practical reason," that takes all the circumstances including precedent, real-world significance and institutional relationships with the other branches into consideration, tempered on occasion by compassion. (181)

---

[4] This is, of course, especially true for the types of cases analyzed here – those dealing with new doctrines.

[5] See, for example, Goldman (1975); Howard (1981); Johnson (1987); Songer and Haire (1992); Songer, Segal, and Cameron (1994).

Where most judges differ from many political scientists is in their belief that they should and do try to make good law, meaning (at least) something other than law consistent with their own policy views. The following quotation from Judge Newman (1984) is representative:

I am not so naïve to deny that some judges in some cases permit personal predilection to determine the result.... I do assert, however, that the facile description of "result oriented" decision making must be applied with caution, for its wholesale invocation is simply false. The ordinary business of judges is to apply the law as they understand it to reach results with which they do not necessarily agree. They do this every day. Distasteful statutes are declared constitutional and applied according to the legislators' evident intent; unwise decisions of administrative agencies are enforced.... (p. 204)

Even judges who view the influence of subjective considerations as legitimate place limits on it. Shortly after the excerpt quoted previously, Judge Wald continued: "For our citizens to have confidence in the courts' decisions they must be convinced that judges are impartial as to litigants, including the state, and that we are not embarked on personal ideological crusades. That is the closest I have been able to come to a judicial philosophy" (1992:181–2). She thus joins a number of other writers with realist perspectives who over the years have suggested that some methods of arriving at solutions are more proper than others (see, e.g., Cardozo 1921; Levi 1948; Posner 1990b).

Political scientists give some credence to the notion that judges try to make good law. Arguments or evidence that legal accuracy matters to judges can be found in works as diverse as Becker (1966), Brigham (1978), Johnson (1987), Lawler and Parle (1989), Swinford (1991), Epstein and Kobylka (1992), and Unah (1998), among others. In recent years, "new institutionalists" have forcefully defended this view against "attitudinalist" attacks.[6] But many scholars take a skeptical view, disparaging judicial lamentations that personal predilections must yield to the dictates of the law.[7] I agree that skepticism is called for but believe it should be a tempered skepticism (even at the Supreme Court level). For even if we were to accept the notion that judges freely publish outright lies, we would still have to confront the issue of why they do so. Logically, it must be to impress or satisfy an audience – an audience in all probability composed of the legal community. But if the legal community is the intended audience, it must place some value on the legal

---

[6] See Gillman and Clayton (1999), Clayton (1999), and other pieces in the same volume.
[7] See, for example, Segal and Spaeth (1993).

soundness of decisions. (Otherwise, why bother with the protestations?) Judges, of course, come from that community, and it is hard to imagine that none of them shares its values. This is not to argue that judges make objectively good law or even that such a thing exists. What this reasoning suggests is that the desire to produce good law should be considered a significant motivation.

The third assumption – that judges wish to further the coherence and consistency of law – is familiar from judges' opinions and introductory legal textbooks. As Merryman (1954) notes, consistency helps not only potential litigants, who can undertake actions with greater certainty about outcomes, but also judges themselves, whose work becomes easier as an area of law becomes more settled. In addition, consistency can be of indirect benefit to judges insofar as it bolsters the integrity and legitimacy of the judicial system (Johnson and Canon 1984:37–8). Research demonstrating the importance of intercircuit conflict as a determinant of the Supreme Court's certiorari decisions (Ulmer 1984; Caldeira and Wright 1988; Perry 1991) also highlights the value of consistency. It suggests that even judges who cared nothing for consistency in itself might adopt it as an instrumental goal to avoid reversal by the Supreme Court. More important, it provides strong evidence that some federal court judges (the justices) care about reducing conflict as an end in itself. If some federal judges care, it is likely others do, too.

Finally, the comments of one judge interviewed for this project suggest that consistency can win the approval of other judges:

> I think you should measure circuit excellence by the uniformity of the law it promulgates. . . . There are lots of good judges all over – some who make no effort to get attention, others who do lots to. I evaluate by asking if the circuit stays fairly current and generates a coherent, consistent, cohesive body of law.

Taking all these points into account, it seems highly likely that at least some judges value coherence and consistency.[8]

The fourth assumption about judges' goals would seem hardly to need defending. Most people value leisure time, and there is little reason to think judges are different. Furthermore, considerations of justice and convenience for the parties argue in favor of prompt resolution. And even if judges preferred to dawdle over cases, their workloads would not allow them to do so. Even prior to the period studied here, judges sometimes

---

[8] The distaste with which judges regard one type of inconsistency – intracircuit conflict – is well illustrated by the efforts of the large Ninth Circuit to avoid it (Hellman 1989).

complained of time pressures. Judge Oakes (1975) recounted how, as a law review editor, he looked forward to becoming a lawyer in order to have more time to study cases in depth and, as a lawyer, looked forward to judging for the same reason. He continued:

When I became a judge, I dreamed that I was once again a law review editor and had the time to do the research that really needs to be done in every single case that we have, to get to the underlying rationale of each principle of law. . . . We work in time frames and with the pressure of statistics. We cannot always articulate all of the major, let alone the minor premises. (pp. 2–3)

Since Judge Oakes wrote these words, time constraints have tightened dramatically. Between 1972 and 1992, the number of appeals per year filed in the Courts of Appeals rose from 13,694 to 43,481, a 218 percent increase, while the number of active judges grew by only 57 percent (Federal Judicial Center 1993). In such circumstances, even judges who care little about promptness as an end in itself must try to dispose of cases quickly to avoid being swamped by their caseloads. Proof of this is seen in circuits' efforts to control caseloads through shortcuts such as omission of oral argument, screening of cases by staff attorneys, and affirming of trial court decisions without comment (see, e.g., Mathy 1985; Richman and Reynolds 1996; Gulati and McCauliff 1998).

JUDGES' GOALS: INTERVIEWS

To further probe the validity of the assumptions, in interviews I asked judges whether the posited goals were important to them. Before turning to the results, I must briefly describe the interviews.

Overview

The interviews were semi-structured and consisted entirely of open-ended questions about judges' motivations, decision making, and related matters. (The text of the model questionnaire is presented in Appendix B.) They ranged in length from about one-half hour to an hour and a quarter, averaging about forty-five to fifty minutes. Twenty-four active and senior judges[9] were interviewed, ten from the Sixth Circuit (com-

---

[9] Senior judges can be thought of as semi-retired. Many of them continue to participate regularly on panels (they generally do not sit in en banc cases). All of the senior judges interviewed were still involved in deciding cases, and a number of them had been on active status at some point during the period examined here.

prising Michigan, Ohio, Tennessee, and Kentucky) and the other four-teen from various circuits in the eastern half of the United States.[10] All the judges who participated were promised anonymity. Little would be gained from identifying a judge's race, sex, or other background characteristics, especially as claims about subgroups cannot be generated from this sample. Accordingly, I generally present the judges' comments without additional information.

The interviews have some limitations that should be taken into account as results are considered. The most important is that judges' perceptions may be flawed. It is very difficult for people to step outside themselves and analyze their own behavior and beliefs, especially in the rather artificial context of an interview. There is a kind of chaotic, spontaneous quality to everyday thinking that probably gets refined in recollection. Respondents may be unaware of certain thoughts or thought processes or forget about them over time.

Furthermore, people will not always be comfortable describing their thoughts or actions to a stranger, particularly if that stranger plans to report them in a book. Decades of skepticism from legal realists, political scientists, and the media have made the legitimacy of their decision making a point of some sensitivity for many judges. It would not be surprising if some of them were less than perfectly frank in describing their own approaches.

The judges' answers may have been influenced by the emphases of my questions. Because of the breadth of the issues discussed, I frequently had to focus on specific factors. For instance, I might ask: "Do you care who wrote an opinion or what circuit it came from?" The judge might respond affirmatively even though this factor mattered less than some others. Even worse, a judge might answer "yes," not because a particular factor ever had influenced that judge, but because it seemed reasonable that it might.

No two interviews were precisely the same. Questions asked of some judges were not necessarily asked of all. The same question might be worded a bit differently or change position from one interview to another. The judges were not presented with fixed alternatives, and so their answers were not always directly comparable. Nor is it likely that they all understood the same questions in the same way.

---

[10] Specifically, of the other fourteen, five are from the Third Circuit, four from the Seventh, two from the First, two from the Eleventh, and one from the Fourth.

The final limitation of the interviews is the sample. It is not random, so precise findings from the sample cannot properly be generalized to the universe of Court of Appeals judges (or, obviously, to the larger universe of all judges). This is not to say that inferences about other judges are impossible, only that they must be cautious and nonspecific. For instance, if I find that six of the twenty-four judges consider a particular goal important, I can be almost sure that some other judges feel the same way. What I should not suppose is that 25 percent of them do.

Naturally, the interviews possess strengths as well. Judges may not be able to explain their own behavior perfectly, but they know more about it than anyone else and thus are excellent sources for insights that could otherwise escape the researcher. In addition, their comments can reveal nuances and complexity difficult to capture in quantitative analyses.

Taken together, these considerations suggest the following strategy for analyzing the surveys: As much as possible, judges should be allowed to speak for themselves, with interpretations offered only cautiously, so that readers can draw their own conclusions. Accordingly, I will quote extensively from the interviews and only occasionally present summary information. (Quotations are taken from notes made during and immediately after the interviews. While I could not record everything the judges said with perfect accuracy, I am sure that all of the quotations are accurate, with the possible exception of the occasional minor word.)

Judges on Goals

Questions from the interviews fell into three main categories. In the first were those that inquired into judges' motivations. The second set of questions was directed at identifying the elements of several key concepts, such as "prestige" and "good law." The final group focused on intercourt dynamics. Only the first set is important for this chapter.

For the most part, questions about motivations were straightforward. For questions about coherence and consistency and legally sound decisions, I was able to use language quite similar to that used earlier in this chapter. To ask about limiting the time judges spent on cases, I focused on a closely related goal, the desire to decide cases promptly. Inquiring about the goal of good policy required more subtlety, because of the suspicions that might be raised. My approach was to begin with the more innocuous questions about promptness and coherence/consistency and then move to policy preferences. For that goal, I asked how important it was that the outcome of a case seem just or good. This approach carried a cost: It got at the concept of interest only indirectly. Still, as expected, most of the judges appeared to interpret the question the way it was meant. A few did not, but this seemed a reasonable price to pay for greater candor.

The goals of promoting desired outcomes and making legally sound decisions are best discussed together, in that they are often seen as conflicting. Political scientists, especially, seem to regard them as mutually exclusive; legal models of decision making compete with the attitudinal model. Not surprisingly, a few judges took the same line. Here are three judges' reactions to the question about the goal of good/just outcomes:

Terribly unimportant, completely off the scale. This is just an invitation to not do what the statutes say. There are many cases where I wouldn't have voted to pass the statute, but my job in a democratic society is to make sure the majority wins, not that my view of justice does.

I just happen to think that's a wrong objective. Lots of times I write and just hate the opinion, but if it's what the statute, regulation, Supreme Court, or [my] Circuit requires, I can't do anything about it. It seems to be almost by definition that if that's an important objective you're close to ends justifying means decision making. Ends never justify the means. . . .

In a recent case I was on two of us really hated the result but thought the statute clearly dictated it. We got a letter from another judge (not on the panel; we had circulated the opinion) who said, "I agree that's what the statute says, but I think that's a bad result. Can't you come up with a way to get around it?" My belief is a flat no. If you don't like the statute, see your congressman.

Well, I think you have to be clinical. Hard facts make bad law. You have to intellectually discipline yourself to understand that we'll sometimes get results we don't like at the gut level, but the law goes that way and there's no intellectually honest way to go the other way without hurting consistency.

As might be expected, these judges were not alone in claiming that legal soundness is very important. I have attempted to classify each judge's valuation of a goal along a five-point scale ranging from very important to not at all important. These classifications are approximate, generated by comparing judges' responses with their colleagues' responses and their own responses to other questions. They are shown in Table 2.1. Of the twenty-two judges whose responses I could confidently classify, fifteen seemed to view "legally correct" decisions as very important while the rest considered it important. What may be more surprising is that most of the judges (fourteen) seemed to view the goal of achieving "good or just outcomes" as at least important, with six

TABLE 2.1. *Judges' valuations of goals*

Goal	Very Important	Important	Moderately Important	Not Very Important	Not Important	N/C
Good/Just Outcomes	6	8	3	3	3	1
Legally Correct Decisions	15	7	0	0	0	2
Coherent, Uniform Law	5	7	7	2	1	2
Prompt Decisions	10	6	6	0	0	2

Note: Coded from interviews. For each goal, $N = 24$. N/C = No codable response.

considering it very important. Only six adjudged it not very important or not at all important.

Because the two goals are often seen as conflicting, we can array judges along a continuum by the relative weight they accord to considerations of outcome and legal correctness. Some judges, such as the ones just quoted, deny any legitimacy to the former and so can be placed at one extreme. There may be judges at the other extreme – discounting legal correctness entirely – but they did not appear among those I interviewed. Most fell toward the middle of the continuum. To illustrate, I will quote at length from several interviews, arranging them in roughly ascending order of weight given to considerations of outcome. In cases where I include a single judge's reactions to both goals, the comments are together.

I'd say that's a secondary consideration, because I don't view my role as simply doing what I view as good and just in a particular case. I see a specific role with specific limits on my authority. It doesn't leave much room for justice and right. But there are instances when that can come into play.

Of course, if within applicable precedent you can choose one or the other, you will take the one that leads to the good outcome – if precedent allows. . . . In appeals, you just deal with them as individual cases, try to apply good legal principles to particular cases. Some judges have a pretty definite ideological turn of mind; they may overcome it if they're conscious of it. If you've been here as long as I have, and as you get older, I think you tend to get more skeptical – about parties too. There are no particular litigants I'm trying to help. I'm trying to follow the law, even if it's not the law I would write. I think a high percentage of judges will reach a result they don't want to if the law goes that way.

[A good outcome] is great when it can happen and agonizing when it can't. There are many cases (a small percentage, though) where you can make good happen. I would say that more often than I like to think, you can't do anything. We have a case now where the judge below did a great job in a hideous trial and I would love to affirm, but I think we'll have to reverse. I don't think justice is being done, but hopefully it will be more proper now. . . . A legally correct decision is a form of justice, a systemic kind of justice. It doesn't give the unfortunate individual solace but it's better than judges ruling by what they ate in the morning.

There are judges who would answer [the question about outcomes] by saying that's a primary premise. But I couldn't say that entirely accurately. . . . Sure, substantive justice is important, and if I were God and not constrained by law I would be more comfortable. Our court is just a piece of the action; our authority is pretty strongly circumscribed.

As an intermediate court, we're very constricted. Often our personal inclinations are at odds with the result that must flow from the cases. Then you have to decide if the result is one you can live with or if your disagreement is so fundamental that you can't. An example is the death penalty. I haven't had to decide yet, but I don't know what I'll do when I'm faced squarely with the question of whether it's cruel and unusual. I just don't know. I'm fundamentally opposed to organized killing – doing it systematically with the blessing of society. Yet the Supreme Court has written a lot on it. When I'm faced with a concrete case, I don't know how I will come down.

[A good outcome is] very important. . . . There are three cases in my career I've really enjoyed. [The judge then related a story about a disability claimant denied benefits for eight years.] The SSA [Social Security Administration] was right on the technicalities, but we were able to find one regulation they overlooked. Just the one we needed to rule for the claimant. [I was unable to record the details of the second story, but the judge was "outraged." The third story concerned a poor black woman whose mortgage was foreclosed by the Federal Housing Administration.] I said to the U.S. attorney, "I assume you spent a good deal of money on this case." The U.S. attorney said, "Yes, Judge, we prepared very thoroughly," and so on. And I said, "You did all that because this woman wanted to talk to a bureaucrat for fifteen minutes?' All three cases went for the individual. Things like that make you feel good at the end of the day. It beats all antitrust, international law. It's good when you know people have the right to complain about their government and have something done about it. . . .

There's a wide misconception in the public about the freedom a judge has. We're hemmed in. Within certain bounds, we can move around a bit. But there are some cases where we're very hemmed in. Even the ones where I took a personal interest [the earlier stories], I researched the cases thoroughly and had to find law to support my position.

I do approach my work from the old adage Earl Warren had on his desk: "Is this fair?" I always approach my work this way, although sometimes I don't have a choice.... The two most important parts of what we do is see if there's an error so unjust that it warrants a new trial and see that nothing very stupid happened.

[Ensuring a good/just outcome is] very important. I'd put that way up top. We're here to do justice, primarily.... I guess the art of judging consists in trying to produce just results within the constraints of legality.

If we are prepared to accept the judges' claims, two points emerge clearly from this long set of quotations. The first is that most of the judges are committed to deciding cases in accordance with some notion of legal soundness.[11] Even those who admit to caring deeply about outcomes do not feel free to ignore the law. The second is that the judges also care about the consequences of their decisions, with many of them believing it legitimate and even important to consider outcomes in deciding cases.[12]

Turning now to the other two goals, by my estimation, five of the twenty-four judges thought it very important to promote consistency and coherence in the law. Here are examples of their remarks.

That's just a crucial thing. The only time you're not thinking about that is when your circuit hasn't spoken and you disagree with the other circuit and want to call the issue to the Supreme Court's attention.

I think that's the principal one. Next to resolving the dispute before us, it's the most important thing we have to do.

Seven judges saw this goal as important, with another seven viewing it as moderately important. Here are two examples from the latter category:

---

[11] In most of the interviews I asked the judges if they could explain what a legally correct decision was. They generally were unable to do so very intelligibly. A few were not even willing to try. Nevertheless, what they were able to communicate suggested that they view legal soundness rather broadly, certainly as more than faithful adherence to precedent. A legally correct decision might "follow a good text on the subject," "follow decisions that are binding and the conventions we should follow in interpreting statutes and cases," involve "logic and reasoning, sometimes just plain common sense," rely on "honest fact reporting," and so on. Judges' views on this subject are explored at greater length in Chapter 5.

[12] Incidentally, their candor in discussing this gives us added reason for taking their other statements at face value.

Well, it's important, but not a priority item. The priority item is: What is the justice of a particular case? Stated more simply, did the district judge make a mistake? That's our only purpose for being here.

Well, it is important. I look to see what principles undergird the position of one party or the other, what is being advanced, if they have seeds of what I consider to be positive social and redeeming aspects, not detrimental. To promote precedent simply because it is precedent is not sufficient. We need to reexamine the precedent. I come out of a tradition where precedent for so many years was used to perpetuate injustice. I see precedent as important, but we shouldn't use it when it perpetuates injustice.

Finally, three judges thought this goal not very important or not at all important. Here are the comments of two of them:

Well, I'm not interested in a certain area of law; I'm interested primarily in what the law is in the circuit. Sometimes that law is not coherent and consistent, sometimes it's not what I think it should be. I can't do much about it as a senior judge. I'm not a judge like Friendly who I hear is able to bring an unraveled mess into a coherent ball.

Since this is absolutely impossible (logically and axiomatically) I don't worry overmuch about it. It's Arrow's theorem – judges are as much subject to it as are legislators. Something has to give, and it's coherence.

It seems clear that this goal belongs among the assumptions of the model. It is just as clear that it varies widely in importance from one judge to another. Some see it as critical, others as one among several goals, and others as merely secondary.

The judges disagreed less about the importance of speedy decision making. Ten of the twenty-four seemed to think it very important to decide cases quickly. One judge saw it as "terribly important to the parties." According to another, "It is probably the reason I became a judge." Three judges summed up the case for promptness nicely:

It is very important for a number of reasons. First, litigants are entitled to prompt decisions, although still well thought out and so on. Also, there's a personal reason. If a case is old, I have to go back and refresh myself.

That's a very high priority. The principal reason: the huge caseload is such that the incoming flow is relentless; you get buried. Also, as a case gets colder I don't get any smarter. There are some judges who don't get opinions out fast. That's a burden on everybody.

Now that I don't carry a full load, I'm a nut about that. I think that's very important, not just for the litigants, but for the other judges. If I sit on an opinion for eight months before I get it to the other judges on the panel, they may have forgotten the case, and the clerks who worked on it may have left. I think cases' opinions should go out in four or five months at most.

No judge appeared to view promptness as less than moderately important. Those least concerned about it said things like: "I don't think this can be a primary driving force. . . . We just make an effort to be timely"; or "It's an important consideration but we can't always accomplish it." A few judges pointed out that speed is more important in some kinds of cases than in others.

Interestingly, several judges spontaneously addressed the tradeoff between speed and quality. As one said, "I'd generally rather produce a B+ opinion early than an A opinion late." Another took a similar view, opining that "[p]erfect justice takes far too much time." A judge who had come to the federal bench recently from a state supreme court said, "There's an avalanche of stuff here, high volume. At some point, about all you can think about is not 'Is it just or fair?' but 'Have I made any bad mistakes?' Later maybe I'll be able to look at other things more, but being new now, I worry."

Not all would make the same choice. One said, "Given the choice between producing a much better opinion and finishing it promptly, I would generally choose the better opinion, especially if it's to be published." In the words of another: "Obviously, justice delayed is justice denied. . . . Still, I think we have to take the time it takes to truly decide a case."

Still, the fact that so many of the judges care about deciding cases promptly and the stated willingness of a few to sacrifice a bit of quality to speed are reasons to think that judges keep their eyes open for shortcuts. This is not to suggest that their decision making is often sloppy, but it means that they do not ponder cases as deeply and thoroughly as they could if they heard only ten or twelve cases a year or were willing to spend many months on a single case.

As is evident in several of the foregoing quotations, the various goals can come into direct conflict. It is not always possible for judges to reach desired outcomes through reasoning they view as legally sound. The desire for consistency must sometimes yield to the need to limit the time spent on a case. Hence, by the time a decision is reached, often one goal will dominate the others. This simplified final result should not blind us to the complex of motivations with which the judge first approached the decision. If, as the interviews suggest, many judges care about several different goals, each goal may have its effect at some time in some circumstances.

HYPOTHESES

The reviews of existing research and judges' own statements have provided support for the four basic assumptions about judges' goals. The next task is to derive hypotheses about how judges decide unsettled issues of law and why they decide as they do. This final part of the chapter is divided into three sections, corresponding to the three central questions of the project. The first two sections focus on the responses of other circuit judges once a panel has announced a new legal rule: How favorably are the new rules treated, and what factors affect this treatment? The third section considers the decision making of all the judges in this study, including those on the initial panel. The primary question there is how large a role the Supreme Court's ideological position plays in circuit judges' decision making. I also discuss one factor that might condition the Supreme Court effects.

Frequency of Adoption and Rejection

Weighing the goals' various implications leads to a firm prediction about the incidence of rule adoption and rejection: *Judges should more often adopt than reject other judges' rules.* One assumption points unequivocally to this conclusion, and two others clearly favor it. Only one of the four assumptions has ambiguous implications.

The goal with the most obvious implications is that of maintaining consistency in the law. If judges value coherence and consistency, they should avoid introducing confusion through their decisions. There are probably many ways in which confusion can arise, but one of the most egregious is through the creation of inter- or intracircuit conflict. When different circuits produce conflicting legal rules, the troubling consequences can include inconvenience to multistate actors like businesses and government, unfairness to litigants who are treated differently solely as a function of where they live, and greater difficulty in making decisions or predicting those decisions for judges and potential parties in other circuits.[13] The problems caused by intracircuit conflict are similar,

---

[13] For an excellent example of a set of intercircuit conflicts and the problems caused by them, see Haire and Lindquist (1997).

though, naturally, not as far reaching. We expect judges concerned about consistency to avoid these consequences by adopting rules already laid down by other judges.

The goal of producing legally sound decisions should also encourage rule adoption. Judges in search of convincing answers to legal questions would be foolish to ignore the work of fellow professionals. They may not always be influenced by what their colleagues have written, but such influence as occurs is surely more often positive than negative. In those cases where their views are not swayed one way or the other, similarities in training and professional socialization should ensure that they see many issues the same way. In other words, judges interested in legally sound decisions should probably reach the same conclusions more often than not even if they work independently; active consideration of one another's arguments should make agreement even more likely.

So should the desire to save time. One of the easiest ways of reaching a decision is simply to copy what another has done. While it seems unlikely that many judges take their responsibilities this lightly, it is not hard to imagine them beginning with a presumption in favor of existing approaches. Of course, another way of saving time is to keep one's research to a minimum, and doing so may result in ignorance of other judges' work. But there is no reason why ignorance should lead more often to conflicting solutions than to similar ones. The net effect of this goal should be to encourage favorable treatment of precedents from other judges.

An objection could be lodged against the reasoning in the previous two paragraphs. It might be stated this way: "You seem to assume that judges are faced with just two options, adopt or reject. But in actuality the range of choices is far greater. The real question is what rule to adopt – the one chosen by the first court or one of any number of others the judges could come up with. (Think of the actual and possible alternatives to strict scrutiny for identifying violations of the Equal Protection Clause.) When the question is put this way, the likelihood that the first rule will be followed by other judges seems rather slim." The logic of this objection strikes me as valid, but I believe its premise is clearly unsound. Judging from the rules included in this study, a simple pair of alternatives is, in fact, the norm. Most of the rules can be understood as answers to yes-or-no questions. (For instance: Is a hospital legally capable of conspiring with its staff? Do judges have the authority to issue search warrants authorizing video surveillance of private buildings? Do the criminal provisions of the Resource Conservation and Recovery

Act apply only to owners and operators?) Even when they cannot, the set of *plausible* alternatives is often quite restricted. In extremely few of the instances studied here did more than two approaches vie for acceptance.

This fact has consequences for the final goal as well. Judges' policy preferences vary widely, and we might expect the pursuit of them to generate equally widespread disagreement over legal rules. But this can occur only if the range of alternatives is sufficiently broad. Unless the policy preferences of rule-announcing judges are systematically different from those of other judges (an unlikely possibility), then as the number of issues with only two possible answers increases, the baseline rate of adoption must approach 50 percent. When we consider the additional point that respect for others' precedents may enhance the long-term prospects of one's own (Landes and Posner 1976:272–3), it begins to seem doubtful that the policy goal drives adoption rates very far below 50 percent.

In sum, three of the goals encourage adoption of other courts' rules, while only one discourages it. Unless the one goal of furthering policy preferences is able to overwhelm the other three, adoptions should out-number rejections.

Factors Affecting Treatment of Parallel Precedents

If judges care about furthering their policy preferences, they should be more likely to adopt other judges' new legal rules when they think doing so will lead to policy outcomes they support. Because we can never know what every judge thinks of every legal rule confronted, this hypothesis is not directly testable. Fortunately, it is well established that in most areas of law both judicial decisions and judges themselves can be ordered along a liberal-conservative dimension (Pritchett 1948; Schubert 1962, 1965; Rohde and Spaeth 1976). Rather than focus on specific policy agreement, we can follow the conventional practice of speaking in terms of ideo-logical proximity, as follows:

(H1) *The probability of adopting a relevant precedential rule should be greater, the more compatible the ideological direction of the rule is with the ideology of the deciding judges.*

Assuming that judges are concerned about making good law leads to the hypothesis that when considering nonbinding precedents, they follow those that they believe to be legally sound. Unfortunately, in this form the hypothesis is not very useful. The problem is that "legal soundness" is extremely difficult to conceptualize. Even the judges interviewed struggled unsuccessfully to explain what the concept meant to them. It is even more difficult for an outsider to define. Still, we can attempt to get at the concept indirectly.

One way – perhaps ideal – would be to evaluate the opinions in which new rules are announced. In their studies of compliance with Supreme Court decisions, Tarr (1977) and Johnson (1987) attempted something of this sort, coding the opinions in terms of clarity and simplicity. However, these variables made more sense in their analyses than they would here, as they should matter more to a court trying its best to follow a binding precedent than to one weighing the merits of a persuasive precedent.

More helpful for our purposes would be a variable measuring the quality of legal arguments in an opinion. It may be possible to identify in the abstract certain aspects of opinions that make them more or less persuasive. For instance, Schaefer (1966) has written that "an opinion which does not within its own confines exhibit an awareness of relevant considerations, whose precedents are concealed, or whose logic is faulty is not likely to enjoy either long life or the capacity to generate offspring" (11). Operationalizing these concepts presents a greater challenge.

In a study of state wrongful discharge cases, Walsh (1997) proposed opinion length as a measure of quality and found that courts with longer average opinions were more likely to be cited by their fellows. While I am not entirely convinced of his measure's validity, it is certainly credible in the context in which Walsh employs it. Unfortunately, that would not be true in the present study, which, unlike Walsh's, covers a large number of legal issues. Differences in length of opinions across issues almost certainly reflect the relative difficulty of those issues, not just the care with which judges have addressed them.

In the end, I have been unable to discover a satisfactory way of measuring opinion quality. Consequently, the approach adopted here looks not to opinion characteristics but to the characteristics and behavior of judges, as explained below.

Previous studies of intercourt dynamics have found that courts and judges differ considerably in the extent to which their decisions are cited by others (Mott 1936; Merryman 1977; Friedman et al. 1981; Caldeira 1985; Walsh 1997; Kosma 1998; Landes et al. 1998). The fact that certain judges and courts are cited more than others does not necessarily mean that they have a greater impact on their colleagues' decisions. But it does suggest that their colleagues think their views worthy of attention. And there are good reasons to think that more respected judges could actually influence the decisions of other judges, especially if the latter are concerned with legal soundness. For one thing, unless the reputations of prestigious judges are undeserved, their opinions are likely to display particular insight, logic, craftsmanship, or some other similar quality and so be more persuasive than the average opinion. That is, prestigious judges probably have greater ability to convince other judges of the accuracy or wisdom of their positions through superior opinions. Alternatively, judges currently confronting an issue might be moved not by the arguments of earlier judges but by their reputations alone.[14] Research in social psychology suggests that "sources of greater status or prestige influence the receivers of their messages," even leaving aside the content of the messages (Brembeck and Howell 1976:258).

The influence of prestigious judges should be enhanced by the goal of deciding cases quickly. Psychologists have found that people employ different methods of information processing in different situations. Where they are highly motivated to reach a correct decision and where doing so would not be too burdensome, they typically engage in "systematic processing." When one of these conditions is not met, they are likely to use "heuristic processing." Under heuristic processing, people look to simplify decision making through reliance on cues – "any variable[s] whose judgmental impact is hypothesized to be mediated by a simple decision rule" such as "experts' judgments can be trusted" (Eagly and Chaiken 1993:327).

Cue taking has received little attention in judicial research, and that primarily in the area of docketing decisions.[15] Legislative scholars, however, have studied it more closely, finding that legislators frequently rely on cues in making decisions (Fiellin 1962; Matthews and Stimson 1975; Hurwitz 1988; Kingdon 1989). While judging and legislating are different activities, it seems likely that judges, too, sometimes rely on cues. Thorough consideration of alternatives can demand too much time and mental energy of judges, even if they wish to reach legally sound decisions. In such situations, they might choose to follow the lead of respected judges as shortcuts to the desired end.

---

[14] According to Macey (1989): "Well-known jurists such as Henry J. Friendly, John Harlan, and Richard Posner are distinguished for their love of the law as well as for their reasoning ability. Their name on an opinion has a signaling effect that magnifies its value" (111).

[15] See Perry (1991) for a review. I am aware of only one major study examining the use of cues in decisions on the merits: Segal (1986) found some evidence that they matter.

All of the above reasoning leads to the following hypothesis:

(H2) The probability that judges will adopt a precedential rule should increase with the prestige of the judge initially promulgating the rule.

If the influence of prestigious judges results in part from cue taking, evidence of it might well be more visible in situations where cue taking is particularly attractive, namely where reaching a sound decision without a great expenditure of time is especially difficult. Such situations might arise from the difficulty of the case or the inexperience of the deciding judge. The possibilities will be discussed more thoroughly in Chapter 4. For now,

(H2a) The effect posited in H2 should be greater, the more difficult a case is to decide.

General prestige is not the only characteristic of judges that could affect how others react to their rulings. The logic just outlined also implies that judges with special expertise in a particular area of the law will be influential. As Unah (1998) argues in his study of specialized judges, experts often enjoy greater familiarity with and a deeper understanding of the relevant issues and materials. For this reason, they might offer more attractive solutions and more compelling arguments than their colleagues. Or, for the same reason, their colleagues might look to them for cues. Here, again, work in social psychology and legislative politics provides empirical support for intuitions (see, e.g., Petty and Cacioppo 1981:235–7; Kingdon 1989).

Thus:

(H3) The probability that judges will adopt a precedential rule should increase with the expertise of the judge initially promulgating the rule; and

(H3a) The effect posited in H3 should be greater, the more difficult a case is to decide.

Although it is the author of the initial opinion who is most likely to influence later judges, other judges on the original panel might exert some pull as well – particularly if they write a dissent. A dissenting opinion could alert later judges to possible weaknesses in the majority opinion. As one of the interviewed judges put it, "Sometimes I look at the dissent. If there's a dissent and the majority doesn't address its point well, I begin to see a rat." The idea that a dissent can affect later judges' responses to a decision receives some – albeit mixed – support from Johnson's (1979, 1987) research on lower court compliance with Supreme Court decisions and Pacelle and Baum's (1992) study of responses to remands.

A dissent might be associated with later judges' rejection of a rule for another reason as well. Some legal questions are harder than others. In cases where no solution is clearly legally best, the chances that a judge will dissent from the majority decision are greater. So, of course, is the likelihood that panels will disagree with one another.

For both these reasons, I hypothesize that

(H4) *the probability that judges will adopt a rule should be lower if the court announcing the rule is not unanimous in supporting it.*

As already noted, the goal of promoting coherence and consistency in law should encourage judges to adopt other judges' rules. But the goal's pull should not be felt as strongly at all times. Rather,

(H5) *the probability of adopting a rule should vary positively with the strength of support for that rule among circuits already having considered it.*

The relationship should take this form because the cost of disturbing a consensus grows as the consensus becomes stronger. Examples should help clarify the point. Imagine that four circuits already addressing an issue have split evenly, two in favor of a particular rule, two opposed. In this instance, little could be lost by the current court's decision to reject the rule. But if the situation is just slightly different – say, a 3–1 split in support of the rule – the potential costs become significant. In this situation, parties may have begun to view the minority circuit position as anomalous – perhaps even as a mistake that might be recognized and remedied – and to plan and behave accordingly. A decision by the current court to reject the majority rule would not only reintroduce confusion where it had started to fade but would also penalize those who had tried to conform with the dominant legal position. These effects would be further magnified if the previous circuit lineup were 4–1, even more if it were 4–0.

The goal of legal soundness should encourage the same relationship between support for a rule and later courts' reactions. Other things being equal, the strength of support for a rule among judges who have considered it would seem to be a fairly good gauge of the rule's soundness. Consider the case of a judge who must choose whether to adopt or reject a particular rule. It is easy to imagine her beginning with a presumption against it if she finds that it has been rejected by four circuits in a row, just as it is easy to imagine her leaning toward adoption if she finds that all three circuits to consider it have followed it. In fact, the circuit lineup could serve as a useful cue for judges who are unable to give full consideration to the issue or who find the different alternatives equally persuasive on the merits. As with the other cues identified previously, this one should be particularly valuable where reaching a decision requires greater cognitive effort. Therefore,

(H5a) *The effect from H5 should be greater, the more difficult a case is to decide.*

Anticipating the Supreme Court

I ask two questions about how circuit judges might take into account the Supreme Court in making their rulings. First, do they try to decide an issue as they think the Supreme Court would if it had the chance? Second, if they do so, is it because they fear having their decisions reversed by the higher court? Unlike in the previous section, no hypotheses are offered here. This is because "yes" and "no" seem about equally plausible answers to either question. Not only can one arrive at different answers depending on which assumption about judges' goals one begins with, but even a single goal may allow for different answers.

Consider first the goal of producing legally sound decisions. Most judges would agree that legally sound decision making requires faithful adherence to the precedents of higher courts. But there are different reasons for thinking so. One way of viewing respect for precedent is as a relatively simple, reliable method for deciding cases as the higher court would. Law is made from the top down, and lower court judges best fulfill their function by keeping legal doctrine moving in the direction the higher court means it to go. Judges who think this way will probably try to decide as the higher court would even when it is not so easy to predict its reaction.[16] Other judges might see precedent as simply a piece of binding law, no different from a statute or a clause of the Constitution. Under this view, just as judges have no obligation to consider how the current Congress might choose to deal with a particular problem, they need not consider how the Supreme Court would do so. If answers to the problem cannot be found in existing precedent, judges must turn to such considerations as logic, sound statutory or constitutional construction, or predictions of the social consequences of a decision.

Yet another understanding of vertical precedent is suggested by Kornhauser (1995). He argues that in a system of equally competent

[16] See Caminker (1994) for a normative argument in favor of such anticipatory, or predictive, decision making, even where it might seem to conflict with adherence to existing precedent.

judges who share the goal of maximizing the number of "correct" decisions (however defined), the argument for adhering to higher court precedents rests on that court's greater freedom to specialize and give intensive consideration to important cases. Obviously, this logic cannot extend to issues the higher court has not yet had a chance to consider. What the higher court might do should count for less than what an equally competent judge thinks after actually considering the issue.

The goal of maintaining consistency in the law does not yield predictions that are any more definite. Conceivably, decisions based on the anticipated response of the higher court might be seen as furthering that goal. Such decisions would be more in line with the expectations of litigants and the legal community, insofar as those groups tried to read where the High Court was heading. Additionally, because anticipatory decisions are more likely to survive an appeal, they should produce less instability over time in a court's own jurisdiction. Yet an attempt to anticipate a higher court might produce inconsistency of another sort. This could occur if the higher court's recent rulings have broken with established rules. Pushing further in this direction would accelerate the growth of confusion and uncertainty. Anticipatory decisions might also bring a court into conflict with parallel courts that have already addressed an issue.

The goal of limiting the time spent on a case proves no more helpful. To the extent that this goal matters, lower court judges should choose whichever course is easier. But surely this will differ from case to case. At times the signals coming from the High Court may be so frequent and consistent that predicting the Court's reaction is less time consuming than thinking through one's own view of an issue. But at other times or for other issues, signals may be few and contradictory. When this is the case, judges should eschew anticipatory decision making.

When we consider the goal of furthering one's policy preferences, the picture at first seems clearer. Judges surely do not define desirable policy in terms of what the Supreme Court would do. And because the opportunities for lower court judges to shape policy directly are limited, they might be expected to seize them when they arise, deciding as they wish to, not as the higher court would. Yet the choice is not quite so simple. When a circuit court establishes a rule, it sets policy only for the federal judges within its circuit. The result of a reversal by the Supreme Court, by contrast, is a rejection of the circuit judges' favored policy, not just for the federal judges in their circuit but for all judges, federal or state, in the entire country. Judges who care about affecting policy may act strategically, adopting policies they would otherwise oppose in order to avoid such an outcome (Cameron 1993; Songer, Segal, and Cameron 1994; McNollgast 1995; Baum 1997).

As this discussion shows, if circuit court judges do engage in anticipatory decision making, it may be because they wish to avoid having their decisions overturned by a higher court. Although it means leaving the theoretical framework for a moment, it is worth pointing out additional considerations that might lead judges to avoid reversal. Two identified by Caminker (1994) are:

(1) fear that their professional audience, including colleagues, practitioners, and scholars, will disrespect their legal judgments or abilities; (2) fear that a high reversal rate might reduce opportunities for professional recognition and advancement (including promotion to a higher court or appointment to judicial or other commissions) (77–8, footnotes omitted)

Thus, there is good reason to think that fear of reversal could be an important influence on judges' behavior.

Again, however, there are also reasons to think otherwise. Avoiding reversal is not an end in itself. In certain situations, judges may doubt that avoiding reversal would actually serve other ends well. For instance, appearing overly cautious might cause damage to a judge's reputation and career prospects. Even if it did appear to further certain goals, those goals might be less important than others at the time. Thus, a judge who felt strongly that a particular answer was legally right might choose the risk of reversal over the certainty of making bad law.

Although this discussion does not lead to confident hypotheses about either anticipatory behavior or the fear of reversal, it does generate one clear prediction about the intersection of the two. For judges solely concerned with making good law, the possibility of reversal should be irrelevant. Therefore, the greater the extent to which anticipatory decision making is driven by the goal of legal soundness, the smaller should be the observed link between the likelihood of reversal and judges' decisions.

This one hypothesis aside, I am simply not sure what to expect of the relationship between a higher court's projected decisions and a lower court's actual ones. Posner's (1990b) discussion of what he calls "the prediction theory" illustrates the theoretical difficulties well:

The judge of a lower court can predict how a higher court would decide his case in exactly the same way that lawyers in the case can predict how that judge (or higher judges) will decide it. . . . But why should judges conceive of their function in [these] terms, even if it is feasible for them to do so? Not all judges do conceive their function thus. Some decide cases in accordance with their own view of the law and, by doing so, court reversal. Reversal is after all not *so* painful. Yet most judges are highly sensitive to being reversed, and for them the prediction theory makes good sense to follow.... Most judges try to avoid being reversed, and this commits them to the prediction theory.... The theory has greater explanatory force than its critics allow, but it is unusable in areas of profound legal uncertainty. (224)

In other words, deciding as one thinks the higher court would makes sense for some judges in some circumstances but is least likely to influence their decisions in unsettled areas of law. Fear of reversal may be an important motivation, but on the other hand it may not.

If logic does not allow us to choose sides on these issues, neither does existing evidence. In his mail survey of federal circuit court judges, Howard (1981) asked them how important the anticipated response of the Supreme Court was when they confronted cases with unclear precedents. Twenty of the thirty-five judges rated the anticipated response as either "Important" or "Very Important." However, this consideration ranked behind six others in the judges' ratings. Of the eighteen federal district judges who responded to similar questions from Kitchin (1978), ten felt they were very or moderately likely to follow the anticipated response of their court of appeals, while the other eight found this unlikely. Nine thought it very or moderately likely they would anticipate the Supreme Court, and nine thought this unlikely.

Reddick and Benesh (2000) provide clear evidence that circuit court judges sometimes issue decisions that are more consistent with the Supreme Court's current views than with its precedents, even to the point of explicitly refusing to apply a precedent, on the grounds that it no longer enjoys the Supreme Court's support. However, they are not able to say whether the judges they studied acted as they did because they thought the Supreme Court would decide that way or simply ruled as they wished to, justifying their actions through references to trends in the Supreme Court.

Aside from these studies, I know of no other published empirical evidence bearing directly on the question of anticipatory behavior.[17] Evidence as to fear of reversal is similarly scarce. Howard (1981) asked his judges how much they worried about reversal. If their answers are

---

[17] As discussed in Chapter 1, investigations of trends in higher and lower court decision making are related to, but cannot answer, the question.

to be believed, they did not worry much (139–40). But perhaps their answers should not be taken at face value. As one of the judges claimed, "[E]verybody minds it. Don't believe that business about 'I don't mind a bit' – at least from any judge who is any good" (140).

Another study came at the same question from a different direction. Cross and Tiller (1998) examined circuit court review of agencies' statutory interpretations in the wake of the Supreme Court's *Chevron* decision.[18] *Chevron* is generally viewed as directing lower courts to accord substantial deference to agency interpretations. Cross and Tiller uncovered a "whistle blower" effect in their cases: Judges were more likely to defer to interpretations that ran contrary to their own ideological leanings if there was an ideological split on the panel. In other words, a panel composed of three liberals was more likely to overturn a conservative agency interpretation than one made up of two liberals and a conservative. As the authors note, this finding at first seems attributable to fear of reversal. Judges in the majority appear to realize that if they were to follow their own preferences, the other judge might dissent, signaling a possible violation to the Supreme Court. Nevertheless, they conclude that this interpretation is untenable. The cases they studied were decided between 1991 and 1995, a period when the Supreme Court was clearly conservative in its leanings. Since liberal decisions had a smaller chance of surviving Supreme Court review, liberal judges should have been more constrained than conservative judges by the presence of a potential whistle blower. In fact, however, the authors found the opposite.

Van Winkle (1997) has provided what is probably the most persuasive evidence that fear of reversal can affect judges' behavior. He examined search and seizure decisions in the U.S. Courts of Appeals in the early 1990s, at which time all circuits had a majority of conservative judges. Controlling for case facts, he found that the likelihood that liberal judges would vote to find a search unreasonable increased with the number of liberals on the panel with them and the narrowness of the ideological divide on their circuit. He also found that liberal judges were less likely than conservative judges to dissent when they were outnumbered on a panel. Other interpretations are possible, but it is reasonable to view these findings as reflecting efforts to keep from being reversed by the circuit en banc, in part by avoiding unwanted attention. However, it is difficult to say how large a role the fear of reversal plays in their

---

[18] *Chevron U.S.A. Inc. v. Natural Resources Defense Council, Inc.* 467 U.S. 837 (1984).

decisions and impossible to say whether it has an influence as they decide unsettled issues.

Because I do not have clear expectations about anticipatory decision making, I adopt a somewhat unusual approach to analyze it. That approach is described and presented in Chapter 6. The questions about circuit judges' reactions to one another's rules are investigated in a more traditional manner in Chapters 4 and 5. The interviews provide the data for Chapter 5, but Chapters 4 and 6 contain quantitative analyses of circuit court decisions. Before turning to these analyses, it is necessary to describe the cases and legal rules on which they are built. This is the task of the next chapter.

3

The Cases

At the heart of this study is an analysis of several hundred cases decided in the U.S. Courts of Appeals in the 1980s and 1990s. This chapter introduces these cases and the legal rules involved in them. First, I explain how the cases were chosen and discuss possible biases arising from the sample selection method. Next comes some information about the legal rules, meant to give the reader a more concrete sense of the types of issues contested in the cases. I then describe the Supreme Court's reactions to the new rules, showing that circuit judges had a substantial independent impact on legal policy. The chapter ends with the focus back on the circuit judges' decisions, presenting an overview of their responses to one another's precedents. Here the key questions are how often early opinions are cited and how often their rules are adopted in later cases.

SAMPLE SELECTION

The cases were drawn from three areas of law: antitrust, search and seizure, and environmental law. These fields meet four major criteria. First, they are broadly representative of the work of the federal courts, encompassing statutory and regulatory as well as constitutional law. Second, they have widespread impact; decisions in these fields matter, often to a large number of people. The third and fourth common characteristics are that the fields are neither so immature that the courts of appeals are unfettered by Supreme Court precedent nor so settled that they lack discretion in decision making.

Within each field, I identified cases announcing new legal rules between 1984 and 1991.[1] As previously noted, new rules are defined as either: (1) rulings on issues not previously addressed by the Supreme Court or any federal court of appeals; or (2) unprecedented approaches to issues that had previously been addressed in other ways. (Rules in the second category include rejections of earlier rules, but only where the rejected rule is replaced with a novel formulation.) The first category – into which all but a few of the rules fell – would not seem to need any elaboration, but an example of a rule in the second category might be helpful. The example concerns the evidence necessary to prove an illegal "tying" arrangement.

Tying arrangements exist where a business conditions the sale of one item on the purchase of another – for instance, a computer manufacturer refuses to sell desired hardware to a customer unless the customer agrees to buy software as well. They are, in some circumstances, illegal under U.S. antitrust statutes.[2] A party that considers itself injured by a tying arrangement may prove an antitrust violation in court under either of two standards – per se or rule of reason. Under the former, an arrangement that meets certain initial criteria will be judged illegal without further analysis. A plaintiff who fails to establish a per se violation may still prevail under the rule of reason by presenting more extensive evidence of a different sort.

Prior to 1984, circuit courts had performed rule of reason analyses in numerous tying cases. But in that year, in a confused and confusing decision,[3] unanimous as to outcome but divided on rationale, the Supreme Court muddied the distinction between the two standards and left unclear how the rule of reason should be applied to tying cases. One issue raised, but not settled by the decision, concerned plaintiffs' need to show that defendants possess "market power." This element – a demonstration that the seller has sufficient control in a particular market to force buyers to purchase products they do not desire – was traditionally required under the per se rule. Following the Supreme Court's decision, the question arose whether failure to show market power also doomed a plaintiff's rule of reason analysis. The first circuit to address this question answered it in the affirmative, thus producing a new rule.[4]

---

[1] There are two exceptions. Because I was able to find fewer new rules in antitrust than in the other fields, I elected to include two antitrust rules announced in 1983.

[2] Sherman Act, 15 U.S.C.A. secs. 1–7; Clayton Act, 15 U.S.C.A. secs. 12–27.

[3] *Jefferson Parish Hospital District No.2 v. Hyde*, 466 U.S. 2 (1984).

[4] *Amey v. Gulf Abstract and Title*, 758 F.2d 1486 (11th Cir. 1985).

To identify cases in which new rules were announced, I read through casebooks, law review articles, and research supplements such as the *American Law Reports* (ALR) and *West's Federal Digest*. Other cases came to my attention as I read court opinions. All cases meeting the definition just given and succeeded by at least one case from another circuit clearly involving the same legal rule have been included in the case analysis. A list of the new rules and cases involving them is in Appendix A.

The succeeding cases were located through the use of *Shepard's Citations, West's Federal Digest,* and LEXIS citation and keyword searches. Deciding whether a later case was closely enough related to the original typically presented little difficulty, as in most such cases the issue in question was explicitly addressed and the precedent-setting case or another succeeding it was cited and discussed. I did not second-guess judges in any of these cases. If they took sides on an issue, the case was counted, regardless of how cursory their discussion of the issue was or whether their treatment of it might be considered dicta. How they arrived at their position and whether they actually needed to take one are immaterial; what matters is the position they took.

The only occasions for judgment arose when a court confronting a case apparently similar to earlier ones mentioned those cases only in passing or neglected them and the shared issue altogether. In such instances, I proceeded by first framing the precedential rule as the answer to a question. I then considered whether, with unrelated issues left aside, asking and answering that question in the present case could affect the case outcome. If not, the present case was discarded; if so, it was added to the series of cases for analysis.

To help illustrate the selection process, I will describe two cases included for analysis even though the judges did not cite an earlier case or carefully discuss the rule from that case. The first is *U.S. v. Alcan Aluminum Corporation.*[5] Under the Comprehensive Environmental Response, Compensation, and Liability Act (CERCLA), the federal government may sue to recover the costs of cleaning up a hazardous waste site provided, among other things, that the cleanup costs are "not inconsistent" with the Environmental Protection Agency's national contingency plan (NCP). In an earlier case, *U.S. v. NEPACCO,*[6] the Eighth Circuit had ruled that if a defendant wishes to avoid reimbursing the

[5] 990 F.2d 711 (2nd Cir. 1993).   [6] 810 F.2d 726 (8th Cir. 1987).

government on the ground that its costs were inconsistent with the NCP, the burden of proof rests with the defendant. However, in the *Alcan* case, a panel of the Second Circuit wrote the following:

> Before entering upon an analysis of the merits of this appeal it will be helpful to set forth an overview of CERCLA. In bringing an action under this Act, *the government must establish that*: (1) . . . and (5) the costs incurred conform to the national contingency plan under § 9607(a)(4)(A) as administered by the EPA. (Emphasis added, citations omitted, 719–20)

The judges did not cite the *NEPACCO* decision, nor did they devote any real discussion to the question of where the burden of proof should lie. Furthermore, the fifth item in their list may not even have been necessary to their decision. But because this item clearly contradicts the rule from the Eighth Circuit, it has implications for intercourt dynamics and the development of federal law. Hence, it was included for analysis.

In *U.S. v. Macdonald*,[7] the Second Circuit created a new rule in the area of search and seizure. At the time of its decision, courts generally recognized an "exigent circumstances" exception to the requirement that police obtain a warrant before searching a residence. For instance, a court might uphold a warrantless search because police reasonably believed that evidence was about to be destroyed. The exception had limits, though. A warrantless search in response to exigent circumstances might not be upheld if the police caused the exigent circumstances themselves. The Second Circuit's innovation was to rule that the police officers' contributions to the exigency are irrelevant if their actions are otherwise lawful. The case of *U.S. v. Johnson*[8] also involved exigent circumstances, but the *Macdonald* decision was not cited and its ruling was not addressed. The Eighth Circuit panel in *Johnson* invalidated a search because the police had created the exigent circumstances they relied on to justify the search. Yet all of the actions specified by the court appeared to be legal. Had the Eighth Circuit judges asked the question covered by the *Macdonald* rule (Can legal actions impermissibly create exigent circumstances?) and given the answer required by *Macdonald* (No), they would almost surely have upheld the search. Thus, the two cases are related, and *Johnson* is included in the analysis.

---

[7] 916 F.2d 766 (2nd Cir. 1990).   [8] 12 F.3d 760 (8th Cir. 1993).

Potential Biases

Two final points will complete this description of the sample selection. First, because the research was begun in 1995, no cases decided since that year are included. This also means that the sample includes no rules for which a second relevant case did not arise by 1995. Neither exclusion seems likely to bias the analyses in any significant way.

Another exclusion was more important. If a circuit ruled repeatedly on the same issue in the same way, I stopped counting that circuit's rulings after the second consecutive case. The reason for this is that judges tend to cite rulings from their own circuit quite liberally – far more frequently than is strictly necessary. According to my coding rules, any statement of position on a rule should count as an adoption or rejection of the rule, even if made in dicta. But including repeated rulings from a single circuit could distort the findings. For example, imagine that a panel of the Fourth Circuit were to announce a rule and the rule were to be rejected by another circuit but cited approvingly by five additional panels of the Fourth Circuit. Including all of the Fourth Circuit decisions would badly overstate the popularity of the rule and the amount of inter-judge agreement. Furthermore, if self-citation is not distributed evenly across rules and circuits, a failure to weed it out might exaggerate or obscure relationships between characteristics of the initial judge or opinion and the reactions of other courts. Whichever decision is made – to include all decisions or not – some distortion is unavoidable. I believe the choice made here creates far less distortion than the alternative would.

Before turning to the data, it is important to consider other, more important, possible sources of bias introduced through the selection system. To start, it should be noted that the original selection of rules for analysis was not strictly random. Rather than picking cases from a known population, I simply included all the cases I could find. While it seems reasonable to assume that my own errors of omission were nonsystematic, we probably cannot assume the same about the sources consulted. Because I had to rely mainly on secondary sources, it is likely that the sample underrepresents legal rules that provoked no controversy and so went unnoticed by writers of the law review articles and research supplements. The underrepresentation is almost certainly slight, given the comprehensive scope of the supplements. Nevertheless, this potential bias should be borne in mind as results are considered.

Continuing with the discussion of new legal rules, recall that the sample excludes issues arising in only one circuit. This choice was motivated by the study's focus on courts of appeals as elements of a national system. Issues so unusual or local in nature that they arise in only one circuit are of little interest from this perspective. The problem is that there is no foolproof way of identifying every case in which a certain legal issue might be relevant. To some extent, the researcher is forced to rely on judges' descriptions of the problems facing them. But judges might overlook an issue or, worse, purposely ignore it to avoid having to cite or discuss an unadmired precedent. Consequently, the sample may underrepresent strange, poorly written, or otherwise weak or forgettable rules. Even for rules that were included, the search process probably failed to discover some cases for which those rules were relevant precedents. To the extent either type of omission occurred, the result will be an overestimate of judges' recognition of one another's rulings and their willingness to follow them. However, in the analysis of circuit court–Supreme Court interactions, no significant bias should result.

One last source of bias must be considered. Most unpublished circuit court opinions were not available on LEXIS for some of the years covered here, some still are not, and only six are included in the case analysis. While the great majority of unpublished cases involve the routine application of settled law, not all deal with trivial matters, as evidenced by the fact that the Supreme Court sometimes votes to grant certiorari in such cases. Moreover, unpublished decisions represent a significant portion of circuit courts' output. If unpublished decisions differ in some way from published decisions in their treatment of precedent, then an analysis limited to the latter may produce biased results.

This possibility is not overly worrisome. The nonroutine nature of the cases in this study guarantees that most will be published. There is some risk that courts will refuse to publish in order to conceal conflicts they have created (Gardner 1975). However, it is hard to believe that this could happen with any frequency, primarily because it makes little sense. Presumably, the motivation to conceal would be a desire to avoid being reversed (by the circuit en banc in a case of intracircuit conflict, or by the Supreme Court in a case of intercircuit conflict). But, of course, a conflict-creating decision might be affirmed. And, by the rules of the circuits, unpublished decisions have no precedential value. So judges who engage in these types of tactics trade a chance to shape circuit or national law for the certainty of determining one case outcome. Such a tradeoff may sometimes appear attractive, but surely not often. More important, it is far from clear why refusing to publish an opinion should make reversal less likely. Even if the judges agree to hide a conflict from readers of the *Federal Reporter*, the parties can still see it and request a rehearing en banc or petition the Supreme Court for certiorari, thus leaving the judges no better off than had they published. In short, I see little reason for concern about the exclusion of unpublished opinions.

Because the selection process was flawed, some potential biases were unavoidable. It is necessary to keep them in mind as results are considered, and I will refer to them at appropriate times. But it is also important to recognize how slight they probably are. For inferences about the incidence of rule adoption by circuit judges, the biases introduced run in opposite directions (toward underestimates of rule adoptions and underestimates of rule rejections). My suspicion is that the likelihood of underestimating rejections is greater, but the countervailing tendencies ensure that the bias will be limited. As for the hypotheses about why rules are adopted or rejected, because the selection process may be correlated with the dependent variable, the most likely effect of the selection bias, if there is any, is to depress estimates of relationships, thus providing conservative tests (see King, Keohane, and Verba 1994:130–7). Finally, the sample selection problems seem unlikely to be related to the decision as to whether or not to anticipate Supreme Court reactions, so that analysis should be unaffected.

OVERVIEW OF CASES AND RULES

The search for new rules yielded a total of 81, announced in 62 cases. (Some cases produced multiple rules.) Twenty-three rules were in antitrust, 27 in search and seizure, and 31 in environmental law. In addition to the original 81 rulings, the rules generated 300 codable subsequent rule treatments (in 225 cases), for an average of about 3.7 per series.

Frequency of Appearance

The rules varied greatly in fertility, with the number of subsequent cases ranging from one to eighteen. The modal series contains just one subsequent case, while the median series contains three.

The variation between series seems rather striking. Some of it can be explained by the relative frequency of different circumstances. For example, a ruling that the EPA may regulate internal waste treatment waters[9] produced only one subsequent case, while the pretextual stop rule discussed in Chapter 1 led to eighteen. The disparity is almost certainly due to the fact that contestable traffic stops are far more common (and more commonly litigated) than the regulation of internal waste treatment waters. In addition, several series of cases were truncated by definitive rulings from the Supreme Court, while others were cut short by congressional legislation or changes in regulations or behavior by agencies that overrode rules or rendered them moot before they had time to spread. Still, some mystery remains. I will come back to this point in the discussions of citation and adoption.

Scope of Impact

The number of cases in which a rule arises gives some sense of its significance or the scope of its impact – how many people are governed by it, how much commerce it affects, and so on. We can get a more direct, though also more impressionistic, reading of the rule's importance by looking at its content. A few of the rules listed in Appendix A are rather limited in reach. Examples are the rule that jockeys may be subjected to random drug tests and the rule governing the killing of animals of a threatened species under the Endangered Species Act. But these types are overwhelmingly outnumbered by rules with a broad impact. Just about every rule from the antitrust and environmental cases appears to cover transactions and behavior potentially involving many millions of dollars in the aggregate. This is even true of a few of the search and seizure rules. Among the others, it is hard to find more than a couple that would not touch the lives of hundreds or even thousands of individuals over a several-year span.

Issue Difficulty

The fact that a legal question is important does not necessarily make it hard to decide. A precedent from the Supreme Court, while not directly on point, might still provide an easy answer. This seems to have been the case, for example, with the rules that it is impossible for two companies under common ownership to conspire in violation of the Sherman Act and that a canine sniff of an automobile from the outside is not a search

---

[9] *Texas Mun. Power Agency v. Administrator of the U.S. EPA*, 836 F.2d. 1482 (5th Cir. 1988).

under the Fourth Amendment. If the issue is one of statutory interpretation, the contested provision or the legislative history behind it might speak to the question with reasonable clarity, if not quite explicitly. The rule that CERCLA imposes strict liability on current owners and operators appears to belong in this category.

I cannot offer any precise estimates of issue difficulty in the cases studied here, only impressions based on the length and nature of the discussions devoted to the rules in the courts' opinions. My sense is that most of the issues – probably about two-thirds – could be considered moderately difficult: The weight of argument favors one side, but reasonable judges could disagree. Of the remainder, very difficult cases, where the sides are evenly matched, appear to be about twice as common as easy ones.

Ideological Implications

To learn something about the policy implications of the rules and to prepare for the analyses of judges' decision making, I coded each rule as either liberal or conservative. Under conventional practice in judicial politics research, the ideological direction of a case outcome is defined in terms of the party favored by it (Spaeth 1997). Adapting this practice to my needs was a simple matter. I began with the same definitions and coded a rule as liberal or conservative according to whether it makes liberal or conservative outcomes more likely. In search and seizure cases, liberal rules are those that favor criminal defendants. Liberal rules in antitrust cases favor parties attacking what they perceive as anti-competitive practices.[10] In environmental cases, liberal rules benefit parties seeking greater environmental protection. Four environmental rules – involving the application of criminal provisions – were problematic. Three of them concerned scienter requirements, and one dealt with the right to a jury trial. In these four instances I departed from the general coding scheme, scoring as liberal those rules benefiting defendants, in the

---

[10] This coding scheme follows Kovacic (1991) in all but one respect. While I did not deviate from the rule described above, in cases involving certain types of immunity Kovacic coded pro-defendant outcomes as liberal, noting that in such cases defendants presented First Amendment claims. He readily admitted the difficulty of classifying these cases, and I find his argument unconvincing – though on intuitive, not logical, grounds. My doubt is reinforced by his finding that Carter and Reagan appointees both ruled in liberal directions (according to his coding) in a large majority of these cases, in almost precise opposition to their behavior in all other antitrust cases.

TABLE 3.1. *Ideological direction of new rules, by field*

Field	Liberal	Conservative	N
Antitrust	30.4%	69.6%	23
Search and Seizure	37.0	63.0	27
Environmental	74.2	25.8	31
Total	49.4	50.6	81

TABLE 3.2. *Ideological direction, all decisions, by field*

Field	Liberal	Conservative	N
Antitrust	39.8%	60.2%	103
Search and Seizure	33.6	66.4	137
Environmental	69.5	30.5	141
Total	48.6	51.4	381

belief that defendant rights liberalism trumps environmental protection liberalism. The pattern of judges' votes in these cases confirms my suspicion: Liberal judges voted more often for defendants.

Table 3.1 displays the percentage of new rules in liberal and conservative directions, broken down by field. No one familiar with federal court law making in the 1980s and 1990s will be surprised by the strong tendency toward conservatism in search and seizure and antitrust. The high rate of liberal decisions in environmental law was less foreseeable. At this point I can only speculate about its causes. My sense is that it can be traced to a combination of factors: The judges authoring the environmental rules were slightly more liberal than those in the other fields; the legal arguments in favor of liberal positions might have outweighed the judges' conservative inclinations; and ideological considerations may generally be less salient in environmental cases. These ideas will be explored further in the next two chapters.

The frequencies of liberal and conservative rulings for all cases are shown in Table 3.2. The unit of analysis here, as throughout this study, is not the case outcome but the court's treatment of the rule in question. A liberal treatment is either an adoption of a liberal rule or a rejection of a conservative rule; a conservative treatment is the opposite. There are a few interesting differences between this table and the previous one:

Apparently, later courts decided in a more conservative fashion in search and seizure and environmental law and, especially, more liberally in antitrust.

Still, the broad pattern remains the same. The general thrust of circuit court policy making was to make life harder for criminal defendants and antitrust plaintiffs while encouraging environmentalist litigants. But how much did these decisions really matter? Did they establish the law in a real sense or simply act as temporary markers until the Supreme Court spoke? To find out, we must examine the Supreme Court's reactions to these decisions. I pause here to do so before continuing with details about circuit judges' reactions to one another's rules.

SUPREME COURT REACTIONS

Howard's (1981) survey of circuit court litigation led him to conclude that "[c]ourts of Appeals are mini–Supreme Courts in the vast majority of their cases." (58; see generally 75–82). Of decisions rendered by the Second, Fifth, and District of Columbia Circuits between 1965 and 1967, 20 percent were appealed. The Supreme Court granted certiorari in 9 percent of the appeals. Thus, just 1.8 percent of the circuit courts' decisions were reviewed by the Supreme Court. Only 1.3 percent of their decisions were actually reversed. In their update of Howard's work, Davis and Songer (1988–9) found even lower levels of review. The Court in 1986 reviewed fewer than 1 percent of the decisions from the Fourth, Eleventh, and D.C. Circuits. More than 99.5 percent of their decisions were left undisturbed by the Supreme Court. Because these studies did not distinguish routine cases from those involving unsettled law, we cannot draw any firm conclusions about the circuits' autonomy in policy making. Yet, as Howard argues, if we can assume that more than 1.9 percent (or .5 percent, using the more recent numbers) of the circuits' cases have significant policy implications, then we can safely conclude that the Courts of Appeals play an important role in developing the federal law.

Data from the present study can provide more direct evidence. Out of 273 cases in which certiorari could have been requested (that is, excluding panel decisions reheard en banc), a petition was filed in 121, or 44.3 percent. The Supreme Court granted the petition in 11 cases – 9.1 percent of the requests and 4.0 percent of the total cases. It reversed the court of appeals five times, affirmed four times, and partially affirmed and partially reversed in the other two cases. The rate of appeal to the

Supreme Court was considerably higher than in the studies just cited. And while the percentage of petitions granted was about the same as Howard's, it was far higher than was typical for the Supreme Court in the mid-1980s to mid-1990s. Still, in absolute terms, the proportion of cases reviewed and the proportion disturbed by the Supreme Court were quite small.

As interesting as these numbers are, they do not tell a full story. The focus of this study is the legal rule, not the case. It is more interesting to ask how often new rules were reviewed by the Supreme Court and to what effect.

The dataset comprises eighty-one series of cases involving new rules. In seventy of those series (86.4 percent), at least one case was appealed to the Supreme Court. Clearly, the Court was provided with ample opportunity to oversee the policy making of the circuits. Determining how it responded is a bit trickier. The Court could choose to hear a case without reviewing the particular rule of interest for this study. Furthermore, the Court might address the rule in the context of a case not included in the study, either because the Court simply reached out to decide the issue in a case where it had not previously arisen or because the case, as one of several from the same circuit, was among those purposely omitted from my sample.

To gather information about the Supreme Court's reactions, I examined every one of its cases decided by the end of 1998 that either (1) was an appeal of one of the cases from the dataset; (2) cited one of the cases from the dataset; or (3) came up in a LEXIS word search of terms broadly related to the rule in question. In thirteen instances the Court clearly adopted or rejected the circuit court rule. The Court's treatment of the rule was favorable in nine cases, unfavorable in four. (The thirteen rules and the Supreme Court's reaction to them are described in Table 3.3.) In sum, the Court rejected 4.9 percent of the rules in this study, approved 11.1 percent, and did not review the other 84 percent.

Even in those areas where it did become involved, the Court's action was not always swift. The length of time from the initial announcement of a rule to the Supreme Court's decision ranged from fourteen months to nine years and four months. In nine of the thirteen instances, at least three years passed before the Supreme Court spoke; in six instances, at least five years. It is difficult to avoid the conclusion that in developing legal rules in unsettled areas of law, the Courts of Appeals are largely left to themselves.

TABLE 3.3. *Rules reviewed by the Supreme Court*

Circuit Court Rule	Supreme Court Reaction
Maximum resale price maintenance is not per se illegal under the Sherman Act if prices are nonpredatory. *Jack Walters and Sons Corp. v. Morton Building, Inc.* 737 F.2d 698 (CA7, 1984).	Adopts rule in *Atlantic Richfield Co. v. USA Petroleum Co.*, 495 U.S. 328 (1990).
For lawsuit to qualify as sham (and so be unprotected by Noerr-Pennington doctrine), suit must be baseless. *Omni Resource Development Corp. v. Conoco, Inc.* 739 F.2d 1412 (CA9, 1984).	Adopts rule in *Professional Real Estate v. Columbia Pictures,* 508 U.S. 49 (1993).
If lawsuit is successful, it cannot be considered sham under the Noerr-Pennington Doctrine. *Columbia Pictures Industries v. Redd Horne, Inc.* 749 F.2d 154 (CA3, 1984).	Adopts rule in *Professional Real Estate v. Columbia Pictures,* 508 U.S. 49 (1993).
Defendant has no constitutional right to jury trial in civil action brought by federal government alleging violations of Clean Water Act. *U.S. v. Tull* 769 F.2d 182 (CA4, 1985).	Rejects rule in *Tull v. United States* 481 U.S. 412 (1987).
Person in car is "seized" for purposes of the Fourth Amendment when police deliberately place a roadblock in front of the car. *Jamieson v. Shaw,* 772 F.2d 1205 (CA5, 1985).	Adopts rule in *Brower v. County of Inyo,* 489 U.S. 593 (1989).
For manufacturer's termination of distributor to be illegal per se under Sherman Act, must be pursuant to price maintenance agreement with another distributor. *Business Electronics Corp. v. Sharp Electronics Corp,* 780 F.2d 1212 (CA5, 1986).	Adopts rule in *Business Electronics Corp. v. Sharp Electronics Corp.*, 485 U.S. 717 (1988).
In determining whether investigative stop is invalid as pretextual, proper inquiry is whether reasonable officer would have made seizure in absence of illegitimate motivation. *U.S. v. Smith* 799 F.2d 704 (CA11, 1986).	Rejects rule in *Whren v. U.S.,* 517 U.S. 806 (1996).
Police chase does not constitute seizure unless there is restraint on individual's freedom to leave accomplished by means of physical force or show of authority. *Galas v. McKee* 801 F.2d 200 (CA6, 1986).	Adopts rule in *Brower v. County of Inyo,* 489 U.S. 593 (1989).
Noerr immunity does not apply to lobbying of private model-code association, even where government usually adopts its standards. *Indian Head, Inc. v. Allied Tube and Conduit Corp.* 817 F.2d 938 (CA2, 1987).	Adopts rule in *Allied Tube and Conduit Corp. v. Indian Head, Inc.*, 486 U.S. 492 (1988).

Circuit Court Rule	Supreme Court Reaction
RCRA does not waive federal government's sovereign immunity: not subject to civil penalties imposed by states. *U.S. v. State of Washington*, 872 F.2d 874 (CA9, 1989).	Adopts rule in *U.S. DOE v. Ohio*, 503 U.S. 607 (1992).
To be responsible as operator under CERCLA, parent company must be actively involved in activities of subsidiary; general authority or ability to control is not sufficient. *U.S. v. Kayser-Roth Corp.* 910 F.2d 24 (CA1, 1990).	Agrees with rule in *U.S. v. Bestfoods*, 524 U.S. 51 (1998).
Control of decisions about hazardous waste specifically is not necessary for parent company to be responsible as operator under CERCLA. *U.S. v. Kayser-Roth Corp.* 910 F.2d 24 (CA1, 1990).	Rejects rule in *U.S. v. Bestfoods*, 524 U.S. 51 (1998).
CERCLA authorizes recovery of attorney's fees in private response action. *GE v. Litton Industrial Automation Services*, 920 F.2d. 1415 (CA8, 1990).	Rejects rule in *Key Tronic Corporation v. U.S.*, 511 U.S. 809 (1994).

To complete the picture, we can consider how well the decisions of the individual circuits on these issues matched the Supreme Court's eventual decision. The thirteen rules considered by the Court implicated 62 (15.9 percent) of the 391 decisions in the dataset. The Court agreed with 37 (59.7 percent) of these decisions. Considering only circuit positions (rather than the decisions of all individual panels), by the time of the Supreme Court's decision 30 of 47 (63.8 percent) were consistent with the position it ultimately took. On 4 of the rules, the circuits were evenly split. The Supreme Court went along with the majority of circuits in 6 of the other 9.

The rate of agreement between the two levels of courts is somewhat striking, especially given the fact that the Supreme Court tends to reverse the decisions it agrees to review (see Segal and Spaeth 1993:194–5). This sample of Supreme Court decisions is too small to support confident inferences, but it at least suggests that the Court's typically high rate of reversal may disguise broad agreement with lower courts about what the law should be.

More interesting for this project is what the substantial agreement tells us about the connection between circuit court and Supreme Court decision making. I can think of three plausible explanations for the agreement: (1) Because they are similarly trained and work from the same legal materials, justices and circuit judges more often than not see things the same way; (2) the justices are influenced by the decisions of the lower court judges; (3) the circuit judges successfully anticipate how the Supreme Court would decide the issues currently before them. (Naturally, these possibilities are not mutually exclusive; all three may be correct.) While testing explanations 1 or 2 would take us into Supreme Court decision making and, so, outside the scope of this work, the third possibility is the subject of Chapter 6.

That issue aside, the message of this part of the study seems clear: Through the cases analyzed here, the Courts of Appeals played a substantial role in shaping federal law. Not only did they have numerous opportunities to rule on important issues before the Supreme Court did, but they typically enjoyed the last word as well. And their influence was not limited to trivial issues. A glance at Appendix A reveals a fair number of other legal rules seemingly just as significant as those the Supreme Court chose to review. Nor can the High Court's inaction be attributed to its reluctance to spend time on easy or consensual issues. Twenty-six of the rules not reviewed by the Court engendered inter-circuit conflict.[11]

CIRCUIT JUDGE RESPONSES

As already explained, cooperative behavior in circuit courts – especially between circuits – is essentially voluntary. Judges generally need not pay attention to what other judges have decided, nor must they decide their cases the same way. Even within circuits, where one panel's ruling is considered binding on another, means of enforcement are limited. Thus, before turning to the question of why circuit judges react as they do to parallel precedents, it makes sense to ask how they react.

The key variable of interest is a later court's adoption or rejection of the rule in question. Fortunately, adoptions and rejections are often clear and explicit. But in some cases they are not, and a judgment is required. Viewed a certain way, the judgment might seem like a difficult one to make. As legal scholars have long noted, the level of generality at which

---

[11] Hellman (1995, 1998) has argued carefully and at length that many circuit conflicts are not consequential enough to require the Supreme Court's intervention. I do not measure conflict severity here and do not take a stand on this issue.

a legal rule operates is always open to question. No two cases are precisely the same, and judges often evade predecessors' influence by showing where the facts of the cases differ in significant ways, explaining why the rule previously laid down must be narrowly construed, and dismissing more general formulations as dicta. In short, a rule as stated by one court may differ from the rule as interpreted by another. Consequently, it is impossible to say in absolute terms what constitutes the vital legal rule of a decision.

The foregoing might seem to imply that there is no firm ground on which to build an analysis. If this study were motivated by a lawyer's need to determine the precise state of doctrine or by a desire to evaluate judges' faithfulness in following precedent, this might well be true. But the study is motivated by an interest in the way judges shape policy. From this perspective, what matters is not some abstractly proper rule but the actual rule as stated by the precedent-setting court. That court, for whatever reason, has chosen to advance a particular policy. What interests us is whether other courts cooperate to establish that policy and why they react as they do.

The fundamental coding question, then, is whether the current court's decision follows the legal rule as stated by the precedent-setting court. I first ask if the issue covered by the rule is addressed in the current case. If so, is the issue handled as required by the rule? If the answer to the second question is Yes, the current court's treatment of the rule is coded as favorable, or adopting; if No, it is coded as unfavorable, or rejecting. If the issue is not addressed, the coding is slightly more complicated. Decisions inconsistent with the rule present no real problem for the analysis. Although they do not offer explicit alternatives, they undercut the rule by establishing conflicting precedents. Thus, they are treated as rejections of the rule. On the other hand, where a court happens to reach the required outcome without actually discussing the question the rule is meant to address, its decision adds nothing to the rule's stature. Naturally, it does not detract from it either. The logical choice was to exclude the handful of such cases from the analysis.

Obviously, rules have less chance of being adopted in later cases if they go unnoticed. Further, as was just noted, they can be bolstered by later cases only if they are explicitly recognized in them. Thus, whether a ruling is actually cited by other courts is another important aspect of how it is treated, even if less significant than whether it is followed or rejected. I will briefly discuss citation patterns before returning to the more central issue.

Citations

Table 3.4 displays the frequency with which the initial case was cited in subsequent cases, broken down by field. There are some differences across fields, with environmental cases being cited most consistently, antitrust cases least. Because this pattern will reappear when we examine adoption rates and the two rates are probably related, I will discuss the differences at that point. For now, we can concentrate on overall citation rates.

The initial case was cited just under 77 percent of the time by later courts. This figure does not necessarily mean that 23 percent of the time judges took no note of the precedential rule. Sometimes they cited an intervening opinion instead of the initial one. This happened, for instance, when the intervening opinion stated the rule more clearly than the first or, especially, when it was from the same circuit as the judges now deciding. Where the intervening opinion had itself cited the initial case (or cited an opinion which cited that case, and so on), there was at least a citation connection between the current case and the first. If we look at citation connections, the rate increases to almost 85 percent. The full frequencies are shown in Table 3.5.

At first glance this rate certainly seems high enough. Yet, considering that the analysis includes only cases for which the first was a relevant precedent, we might have predicted that it would be even closer to 100 percent. As it happens, in 15 percent of the cases, the deciding judges evinced no awareness that another court had stated a rule meant to cover an issue now before them.

My impression from the interviews is that the judges would be surprised by these numbers. I did not ask a question specifically about citation, but several judges volunteered the opinion that they rarely missed relevant cases from other circuits, and no judge said anything much to

TABLE 3.4. *Frequency of citation of rule-announcing case in subsequent cases, by field*

Field	Citation	No citation	N
Antitrust	70.0%	30.0%	80
Search and Seizure	73.6	26.4	110
Environmental	84.6	15.5	110
Total	76.7	23.3	300

TABLE 3.5. *Frequency of citation connections, by field*

Field	Citation connection	No citation connection	N
Antitrust	75.0%	25.0%	80
Search and Seizure	83.6	16.4	110
Environmental	92.7	7.3	110
Total	84.7	15.3	300

Note: Citation connection occurs where rule-announcing case is cited or later case citing the rule-announcing case is cited, and so on.

the contrary. As some pointed out, they have clerks to do legal research for them, and in the age of LEXIS and WESTLAW, related cases are not all that hard to find.

The numbers speak clearly, though: Precedents are frequently overlooked. (Interestingly, Lindquist [2000] reached the same conclusion in a study of conflicts resolved by the Supreme Court. The panel creating an intercircuit conflict failed to cite the relevant precedent in fourteen of the eighty-eight cases where it could reasonably have been expected to be aware of the precedent.) My research was not designed to interpret this particular finding, but it does suggest a few plausible explanations. To start, lawyers and judges may not always be on the lookout for legal rules. As I read many opinions, it became apparent that judges often care more about resolving a particular dispute than giving a clear statement of the legal rules governing it. This point was brought home in the following exchange from an interview:

DK: Does the judge or circuit an opinion comes from matter to you?

Judge: Not to me personally. It might influence some judges. I'm interested in the facts and how they are reasoned.

DK: Does that vary for different types of cases?

Judge: No, I don't think so. You and most people tend to put lots of emphasis on the law, but facts are so important. . . . Different facts govern a lot of how you go. Of course you look to the law, but. . . . [The judge did not complete the thought.]

It may be that lawyers share this emphasis in some cases and so attempt to fit facts within existing rules rather than press for the adoption of new rules. Their briefs are an important source of information for judges, since clerks may not always have the time or inclination to go much beyond them in their research. If relevant citations are omitted from briefs, judges may never see them.

Briefs may be incomplete for other reasons, too, including strategic decisions to ignore particular issues and shoddy research. Marvell (1978) found widespread dissatisfaction with briefs among the appellate judges and clerks he interviewed in the 1970s. The judges I interviewed were perhaps even more critical. Here are some of their comments.

> Still, in 10 percent of cases you miss a decision by your own circuit. [DK: Why?] Lawyers didn't bring the cites. . . . The worst thing about judging is the low quality of the lawyers. In most cases I go back to my own cases, and often I won't find the cites in the briefs.

> The briefs do a miserable job. The practice of law is very time-consuming and there are many times where the stakes of a case don't encourage investment.

> Briefs are very, very unreliable. The quality of appellate advocacy, I think, is declining. More and more lawyers write poorly.

> No, they're not good – I guess they usually identify the most important cases, but not all the pertinent ones.

Some judges offered dissenting views. Here is one:

> On the whole, the parties do a very good job. The law clerks are very thorough with their electronic research now. I'm relatively confident when I get working on a case that all important authorities have been brought out. Also, we all read *Law Week*.

This judge was in the minority, however, and the findings here suggest he was being generous.[12]

Citation patterns may at times have more to do with rules and judges than with lawyers. For example, new rules may have particular trouble getting noticed if they offer novel solutions to familiar problems. As McIntosh and Cates (1997) have illustrated, some judges are policy entrepreneurs, pushing for the adoption of favorite legal rules or methodologies. Some neglected legal rules may represent failed attempts at entrepreneurship. Especially if an issue is fairly well settled across the circuits, it simply may not occur to lawyers and judges that there is a new rule to consider.

My impressions of the cases in the different fields lead me to think there is something to this explanation. The environmental cases are con-

---

[12] I had hoped to examine the briefs to see if the precedents were cited there. Unfortunately, the briefs from the years covered here are not readily available to researchers, as they are stored in boxes in a number of different National Archives warehouses around the country.

cerned almost entirely with the interpretation of statutes of fairly recent origin.[13] Search and seizure law goes back much further, as it is primarily constitutional, but it exploded in importance in the 1960s, after the Supreme Court extended the reach of the Fourth Amendment to the states. This means that during the time period of my analysis, judges in environmental and search and seizure cases were still being exposed to new situations, so that they could not help but make new rules. The antitrust cases are different. The statutes involved are old and familiar, as are most case fact patterns. Consequently, many new legal rules in antitrust embody novel approaches to old questions. Judges were sometimes forced to create them in order to interpret new Supreme Court rulings. But this accounts only for some rules. It appears to me that more of the new rules in antitrust than in either of the other fields were products of judicial entrepreneurship.[14]

A final possibility to consider is that judges choose to ignore some rules that they are aware of but disagree with. They might do this to avoid drawing attention to a conflict or simply because they do not wish to expend the effort necessary to explain their disagreement. The cases analyzed here contain clear evidence that judges knowingly disregard new rules at least occasionally, although there is no way of guessing their precise motivations. Without searching systematically, I found two cases where relevant rules were not cited in majority opinions but were mentioned in dissents. Because dissents are circulated, we know that the judges in the majority were aware of the rules. Because judges should be more comfortable ignoring other courts' work when there is no colleague prepared to point it out, it is likely that such behavior occurred in some of the cases without dissents, as well.

Adoption

The last two explanations – that entrepreneurial rules may be missed and disliked rules may be ignored – suggest a connection between the citation and adoption of rules or, more precisely, between failure to cite and

---

[13] Of the seven key environmental statutes identified by O'Leary (1993), all were passed in the 1970s, except for the Clean Air Act, first passed in 1965, and CERCLA, enacted in 1980.

[14] According to Kovacic (1991), federal judges began reshaping antitrust law in a conservative direction in the late 1970s. The appointment of conservative antitrust scholars like Richard Posner, Robert Bork, Frank Easterbrook, and Ralph Winter was expected (and surely meant) to continue this trend.

TABLE 3.6. *Frequency of adoption and rejection of rules by later courts, by field*

Field	Adopt	Reject	N
Antitrust	61.3%	38.8%	80
Search and Seizure	70.9	29.1	110
Environmental	80.0	20.0	110
Total	71.7	28.3	300

rejection. (For entrepreneurial rules, this is because judges who are unaware of them may adhere to preexisting rules that conflict with the new ones, resulting in negative treatments of the new ones.) Further investigation shows this supposition to be well founded. Out of 46 cases with no citation connection to the rule, the rule was adopted in only 23 (50 percent). The adoption rate in cases with a citation connection was 75.6 percent (192 out of 254). Because the two actions are related, we might expect the pattern of citation rates across fields to be repeated for adoption rates. As Table 3.6 shows, this is indeed the case. New rules were treated favorably least often in antitrust and most often in environmental law.

Turning to a broader overview, the new rule was followed by a later court in just under 72 percent of the cases. In the other 28 percent, the rule was implicitly or explicitly rejected.

It is conceivable that this measure exaggerates the amount of conflict in the circuits. Perhaps a few unlucky rules account for most of the negative treatments, while a great majority of the rules were universally accepted. Alternatively, the measure could understate the degree of conflict, if disagreements were spread thinly across many series. The truth lies slightly closer to the second scenario. The initial rule was rejected at least once in twenty-six of the eighty-one series, or 32 percent.

The simple adoption rate might be misleading for another reason, too: It is based on all decisions, including those made by judges whose circuits had already addressed the issue. As noted earlier, judges are expected to follow circuit precedent. Especially if the judges deciding are from the same circuit as those who conceived the new rule, counting their reactions could inflate our estimate of interjudge agreement. This turns out to be the case, though the overestimate is not drastic. If I include only the first decision for each circuit, the adoption rate falls to 67.4 percent ($n = 236$).

Even if an exact number is elusive, we can comfortably state that new rules are treated favorably a little more than two-thirds of the time. In the previous chapter I hypothesized that adoptions should outnumber rejections. The results bear out the hypothesis, but how compellingly? Certainly, a reasonable person could be impressed by the level of cohesion. After all, the circuits are under no obligation to follow one another's leads. Yet, as noted earlier, in most instances judges face only two realistic alternatives. Even if they were to choose positions randomly, the resulting agreement rate should not be much below 50 percent. When we consider as well that they receive similar training and socialization, the amount of conflict might appear the more notable finding. It is also important to recall the selection bias discussed earlier in the chapter. Although it operates in both directions, it seems likely – especially in light of the relationship between noncitation and rejection – that its net effect is to overstate consensus by omitting some cases and series of cases where rejections occurred.

The picture that emerges from this discussion is a complex one. By no means do the circuits form an entirely cohesive unit, constantly aware of one another's actions and moving in tandem to develop the federal law. When new rules are handed down, the federal law frequently comes to mean something different in different states. Still, it more often does not, even though the legal problems involved are rarely simple. These findings suggest the influence of opposing forces. On one side, the goals of making good law and maintaining consistency in the federal system encourage agreement. So do ideological similarities. On the other side, ideological differences lead judges into conflict. The need to conserve time and energy may push in both directions. No one force appears dominant. More than that we cannot say at this point. It may be that all of the forces are strong, that all are weak, or that only one or two have much effect. I attempt to tease out the different effects in the next two chapters.

4

Influences on Circuit Judges' Responses: Case Evidence

In the preceding chapter we examined how judges react to legal rules announced by colleagues. This chapter takes up the question of why they react as they do. Earlier, I identified four goals that appear to be particularly important to circuit judges' decision making. From them I generated eight hypotheses about the treatment of precedents. The hypotheses are listed in Table 4.1, along with the goal or goals from which each was derived. The primary tests of these hypotheses come from an analysis of the 300 cases described in Chapter 3. I present that analysis and a discussion of its implications in this chapter. In Chapter 5, I return to the interviews, to see what insight the judges can provide.

Before the analysis can begin, the variables to be included in it must be introduced. Several of the key concepts presented tricky issues of measurement, and it would be difficult for the reader to evaluate the results without understanding the methodological choices that were made. Accordingly, taking each measure in turn, I describe the reasoning and decisions involved in its construction. However, a simple statement of coding rules is provided early in each discussion so that those less interested in the methodological issues can move quickly to the results.

MEASURES

Measurement of the dependent variable was described in detail in the preceding chapter. Here it is sufficient to note that favorable treatments of rules (adoptions) are coded as one, unfavorable treatments (rejections) as zero.

TABLE 4.1. *Judges' goals and hypotheses derived from them*

GOAL: Promoting policy preferences

(H1) Probability of adopting rule decreases as distance between ideology of rule and ideology of deciding judges increases.

GOAL: Making legally sound decisions

(H2) Probability of adopting increases with prestige of judge promulgating new rule.

(H3) Probability of adopting increases with field-specific expertise of judge promulgating new rule.

(H4) Probability of adopting is lower where there is a dissent from the opinion announcing the rule.

GOAL: Generating coherent, consistent law

(H5) Probability of adopting increases with the strength of support for the rule among circuits already having considered it.

GOAL: Limiting the time spent deciding, in combination with the goal of legal soundness

(H2a) Effect from H2 is greater where judges face more difficulty deciding.

(H3a) Effect from H3 is greater where judges face more difficulty deciding.

(H5a) Effect from H5 is greater where judges face more difficulty deciding.

Ideological Distance

According to the first hypothesis, the probability that a rule will be adopted should vary inversely with the distance between the ideological tendency of the rule and the ideology of the judges now considering it. Judges' ideologies are coded on a traditional five-point scale, from one (very liberal) to five (very conservative). Rule ideology is measured as explained in Chapter 3. A liberal rule is coded as one, a conservative rule as five, to match the metric for judge ideology. The measure of ideological distance, DISTANCE, is the absolute value of the difference between the rule ideology and the ideology of the median judge on the panel hearing the case.

Most individual judges' ideologies are coded from information in the Almanac of the Federal Judiciary. Over the past decade or so, the editors of the Almanac have occasionally surveyed local lawyers active in the federal courts to learn their impressions of courts and individual judges. A sample of lawyers' comments (usually about eight to ten) and the editors' summary of all comments are included for almost all active and

senior judges. Ideology scores are derived from these comments.[1] Judges
for whom no Almanac ratings are available are classified by taking the
nearest integer to the mean Almanac ratings of judges appointed by
the same president. In practice, this means that all unrated appointees
of Republican presidents are given a score of four while Democratic
appointees receive a score of two.

This method of assessing judges' ideologies is unusual. It is also imperfect, relying as it does on rather arbitrary samples of impressionistic
judgments. Yet I believe it is superior to traditional alternatives. It incor-
porates more information than measures based on political party,
whether the judge's or the appointing president's, since the lawyers can
draw on what they have actually observed of a judge's behavior. At the
same time, it is less susceptible to charges of circularity than measures
based directly on judges' voting records. Voting records probably do play
a part in lawyers' evaluations, but so, apparently, do judges' questions
and comments in oral argument and the language they use in opinions.
It seems likely that personal encounters and information acquired from
clerks enter into them as well. The face validity of the measure is reinforced by high correlations between it and judge's party and party of
appointing president – $r = .74$ and $.76$, respectively – and by the fact
that, as shown below, its impact on the ideological direction of circuit
court decisions is quite strong.[2]

The measure of rule ideology has limitations as well, the chief one
being that it is dichotomous. In reality, a rule can fall anywhere along
the liberal/conservative continuum, not just at an endpoint. Yet such
simplification is standard practice in the research on judicial decision
making, and it is unavoidable in this case. Scaling techniques are not
available, because the set of judges deciding varies from case to case. Less
formal coding schemes based on the language or context of the rules
would seem hopelessly subjective and imprecise.

---

[1] Each comment and general summary is scored on the 1–5 scale. The highest and lowest
scores are dropped and the mean of the remaining scores is calculated. If the mean falls
between two categories, the more moderate category is selected. A colleague kindly
agreed to perform a reliability check on a sample of sixty-one judges from the Fifth
through Eleventh Circuits. In no case did our scores for a judge differ by more than one
point on the five-point scale, and they agreed exactly for forty-three (70.5 percent) of
the judges. The resulting correlation was quite high, at $r = .92$.

[2] For another alternative to traditional measures of ideology, see Giles, Hettinger, and
Peppers (1998).

Prestige

Testing H2 requires measuring judicial prestige, a formidable task. Scholars interested in prestige have typically adopted one of two approaches for assessing it, relying on ratings of judges by academics or other judges (Mott 1936; Caldeira 1988; Abraham 1999) or counting citations of a particular judge's or court's decisions by other judges or courts (Merryman 1977; Caldeira 1983; Posner 1990a). I employ a different method, developed in collaboration with Darby Morrisroe.

The ratings method is obviously unsuitable for this kind of study. There are simply too many circuit judges. Counting citations seems more practical, but it suffers from one important limitation: It is not clear what citations measure. Citations of a judge's opinions might reflect not appraisals of the judge but reactions to the opinions themselves (perhaps they are particularly clear or persuasive) or the importance of the issues addressed in them. That some scholars have treated citations as a measure of influence, rather than prestige (Kosma 1998; Landes, Lessig, and Solimine 1998), is further cause for uneasiness.

Nevertheless, one particular form of citation may have much to tell us about judicial prestige. Occasionally when citing an opinion, a judge refers to the opinion author by name. Instances of this practice are rather striking, for they are rare and typically unnecessary. Standard practice requires only that the publication title, volume and page numbers, and deciding court (if not obvious from the publication title) be identified. Custom does require that the authors of concurring or dissenting opinions be mentioned by name. But this convention is not strictly followed, nor is it truly necessary in the typical case, where there is only one dissent or concurrence.

Because name citation is neither obligatory nor common, its occurrence likely reflects something about the name being cited. Two possibilities seem most plausible: Judges cite others by name as a mark of respect or they do so in order to enhance the credibility of their own opinions. Either way, name citations should more often go to judges highly regarded by their peers.

We constructed our measure of prestige in the following way. Using LEXIS, we searched all Court of Appeals opinions written between 1989 and 1991 for references to the names of the judges who wrote the rules included in this study. We restricted the search to circuits other than the judge's own, since citation of circuit colleagues' names appears to be common courtesy, at least in some circuits.[3] We counted the number of cases in which each judge was named in connection with an opinion he or she wrote between 1987 and 1990. The case was counted only once, no matter how many times the judge was named. If the case cited an opinion of the court by the judge, it was counted as a full citation; if it cited only a concurrence or dissent, it was counted as .27 of a citation. Next, we divided each judge's reference score by the sum of the number of majority opinions written by that judge between 1987 and 1990 plus .27 times the number of concurring and dissenting opinions by the same judge in the same period. To make these very small numbers more interpretable, we multiplied each by 128, the sum of the median number of majority opinions and the median number of concurring and dissenting opinions written by our judges between 1987 and 1990. In other words, we calculated the reference score a judge would have received had he or she continued to be cited at the same rate but published as many opinions as the average judge. Finally, we transformed each score by calculating its natural log (after adding 1 to the score). The resulting number is our final measure of prestige.

This may seem like a somewhat complicated scoring system, but each step is a necessary one. I will provide a brief summary of our reasoning here. A full explanation and justification of the method, along with tests of validity, can be found in Klein and Morrisroe (1999).

Let us turn first to the decision to count a citation of a separate (concurring or dissenting) opinion as less than a citation to an opinion of the court. As mentioned above, judges are typically expected to cite the authors of separate opinions by name. Because of this convention, references to concurring or dissenting writers may constitute a less valid indicator of prestige than citations of majority opinion authors. Thus, they should not be weighted as heavily in the construction of the measure. They should not be entirely discounted either, though. Because judges citing a concurrence or dissent know they are expected to name the author, they may choose those opinions carefully, inclining toward the opinions of more prestigious judges. And while they might feel free to ignore a separate opinion that they disagreed with if it was written by a less respected judge, they might feel compelled to confront one written by a more eminent judge, since that opinion is more likely to draw the attention of other judges. In fact, references to majority opinion

---

[3] For example, for Judge Wisdom, we typed in the following search request: "(judge wisdom or wisdom, j.) and date >1988 and date <1992 and not court (fifth circuit)."

and separate opinion authors are correlated at a moderately high level: $r = .52$. Because r-squared $= .27$, we can say that prestige as measured by majority references accounts for 27 percent of the variance in separate references in our sample. Hence the choice – reasonable, though not unassailable – to treat each separate opinion citation as .27 of a majority opinion citation.

A second problem we confronted was how to avoid biases in favor of judges who had been on the bench longer or simply wrote more opinions. For both types of judge, colleagues have more opportunities to cite their work. Their names might come up in opinions more often than others' simply because their cases do. We took two steps to overcome these biases. One was to count only citations to opinions written between 1987 and 1990. The other was to divide each judge's score by the number of opinions he or she had written in that period. Both steps were necessary. Simply dividing by the number of opinions written would have eliminated the numerical disparity in opportunities, but more senior judges would now have been disadvantaged. On average, older opinions are less often cited than more recent ones (Landes and Posner 1976), and older opinions would form a larger proportion for judges who had been on the bench longer.

The log transformation of the scores was a response to the difficulty judges face in garnering citations. Low numbers dominated the distribution of untransformed scores. The modal score was zero, and even though they ranged as high as twelve, more than half of the scores were under one. This distribution suggests that the difference between a score of zero and two is considerably greater than, say, the difference between ten and twelve. The transformed scores reflect this fact.

Expertise

The indicator of judicial expertise used here (for H3) is simpler but less satisfactory. My first inclination was to focus on prior authorship of law review articles among the judges who produced new rules, on the supposition that a judge (or future judge) publishing an article on an area of law knew more about it than other judges. However, too few of the judges wrote articles (just four) for the variable to provide a fair test of the hypothesis.

Instead I have chosen to examine judges' past opinion writing, employing experience as a proxy for expertise. The two concepts are not the same, of course. A judge can write an opinion on a subject without developing a deep understanding of it, especially if the subject is just one of several involved in a case. A judge who arrives at the bench with substantial expertise may enjoy few opportunities to demonstrate it once there. Yet, it is surely reasonable to suppose that experience and expertise will be closely related. Not only does experience build expertise (Unah 1998:94–5), but the causal arrow may run in the other direction as well, with more expert judges more often taking opinion-writing duties upon themselves (or having these duties thrust upon them by relieved colleagues). Logically, then, opinion writing would seem a useful measure of expertise. Additional support comes from the interviews. When I queried judges about other judges' and circuits' expertise, they almost invariably responded in terms of experience.

For each judge announcing a new rule in either antitrust or environmental law, I searched LEXIS for all majority opinions previously written by that judge in that field. To control for the relative frequency of the two types of cases, I standardize scores within each field by taking the difference between the judge's experience score and the mean score for all judges in that field and then dividing the difference by the standard deviation of those scores. All search and seizure expertise scores are set to zero (the mean for all standardized scores).

To understand why search and seizure cases have to be treated specially, consider the following statements from the interviews.

> In antitrust I don't have enough to feel command of it. Search and seizure we have too much – I wish I would never see it again.

> I almost never look at other circuits for search and seizure because we get so much here, so why spend time reading others? If, on the other hand, I want to understand section 71525(A) subsection I of the Clean Air Act as amended as amended as amended as amended as amended, there's almost certainly no law in [my circuit] on this. I look around for who has grappled with it – other circuits, legal scholars.

> Every circuit is involved with [search and seizure]. Forty percent of our cases, if not more, are criminal; almost every one has some element involving a Fourth Amendment issue.

Finally, from a relatively recent appointee:

> Just flat-footed, the thing that strikes terror in my heart is antitrust – when I hit one of those cases I will have to learn a lot. I'd need to do almost as much for an environment case. I know much more about search and seizure.

What becomes apparent from these comments, along with others not included here, is that judges do not perceive the same differences between themselves in the field of search and seizure that they do in antitrust or environmental law. As one judge said about expertise, "I think this depends altogether on the types of cases you get. What you get, you learn a lot about." Because all judges encounter a great deal of search and seizure, they do not view one another as more or less expert. Hence, expertise scores should not be allowed to vary in search and seizure cases. As to where to set them relative to scores in the other fields, the best choice seems to be at their mean, zero. Any other choice would falsely suggest that authors of search and seizure rules are seen as uniformly above or below average in expertise.

Dissent

Hypothesis Four posits that initial dissents make later adoption less likely. This variable is refreshingly easy to measure. DISSENT is coded one if, in the initial case, any judge wrote a separate opinion rejecting the new rule being announced, zero otherwise. It is important to note that the mere presence of a dissenting opinion is not sufficient to make DISSENT equal one; the opinion must express disagreement with the rule, rather than some other part of the majority opinion, to do so.

Existing Support for the Rule

Testing the influence of existing support for a rule (H5) presents only slightly greater difficulty. Two measures come quickly to mind: (1) the difference between the number of circuits adopting and the number rejecting the rule, and (2) the proportion of adoptions among all circuits having considered the rule. Neither works on its own. The first would treat a three-to-zero circuit lineup as identical to a six-to-three split. Under the logic laid out in Chapter 2, the unanimous lineup should carry considerably more weight. The second measure would overcome this problem but fail to take into account the number of circuits supporting a rule. Unanimity would count the same, whether resulting from the decision of just one circuit or eleven.

My solution is simply to combine the two measures. Looking backward from the perspective of the court considering a rule, I count the number of circuits already having adopted the rule – including the one announcing it in the first place – and the number having rejected the rule. I subtract the latter from the former and, if adoptions outnumber

TABLE 4.2. *Descriptive statistics, key variables*

Variable	Min.	Max.	Median	Mean	St. Dev.
ADOPT	0	1	1	.72	.45
DISTANCE	0	4	2	2.06	1.09
PRESTIGE	0	2.60	.67	.89	.75
EXPERTISE	−1.18	2.92	0	−.22	.66
DISSENT	0	1	0	.09	.29
CIRCUITS	−5.73	7	1	1.48	1.87

$N = 300$.

rejections, multiply the difference by the proportion adopting. If rejections outnumber adoptions, the difference is multiplied by the proportion rejecting. Naturally, if adoptions and rejections are equal in number, the score is zero. This coding scheme results in intuitively plausible scores. For instance, a two-to-zero lineup (2.0) is scored as more supportive than a one-to-zero lineup (1.0) or a three-to-one split (1.5); a one-to-three split (−1.5) is treated as less supportive than a two-to-four split (−1.33). Summary statistics for this measure, the four preceding independent variables, and the dependent variable are displayed in Table 4.2.

Decisional Difficulty

The remaining three hypotheses suggest that the influence of other factors should vary with the difficulty judges face in promptly deciding the cases before them. Difficulty is a function of the factual and legal issues in a case and the judges deciding it. I have not been able to construct a credible measure of issue difficulty, but an indicator of judges' characteristics is more manageable. One reasonable choice would be to extend the field-specific expertise measure to all judges. I reject this approach for two reasons. The first is the problem with search and seizure already described. Second, it seems too narrow. Unfamiliarity with a specific issue may handicap judges, but it is not the only thing that can do so. Overwork, difficulty writing opinions quickly, and inexperience working with clerks are hindrances too. All of these, including unfamiliarity, are more likely to be suffered by judges with less experience on bench. Thus, I created the variable SENIORITY by subtracting the year of a judge's initial appointment to the federal bench from the year in which he or she decided the case being analyzed.[4] The measure applies only to opinion authors, as they bear most of the burden of reaching a decision. Hypotheses H2a, H3a, and H5a are tested with three interaction terms constructed by separately multiplying SENIORITY by the measures of prestige, expertise, and previous circuits' actions.

Control Variables

All that remains is to set out control variables. One factor that should have a powerful effect on adoption is the prior behavior of one's own circuit. As noted in Chapter 3, circuit rules generally require panels – though not the court sitting en banc – to follow existing circuit precedent. OWN CIRCUIT is coded 1 if the court's own circuit has previously adopted the rule and –1 if it has previously rejected it. It is coded 0 if (1) the circuit has not yet addressed the issue, (2) two panels of the circuit have reached conflicting decisions, or (3) the court is sitting en banc.

Finally, I include dummy variables for antitrust and search and seizure cases. (Environmental law is the baseline category.) This is done to control for unobserved factors that might cause variation in adoption across fields. The necessity for this is indicated by Chapter 3's findings of substantial variation.

THE MODEL

To summarize, I expect the decision to adopt or reject an existing legal rule to be influenced by the following variables:

- DISTANCE: Ideological distance between the rule and the median judge on the panel deciding the case. Expected sign = –.
- PRESTIGE: Prestige of the judge who created the new rule. Expected sign = +.
- EXPERTISE: Expertise of the judge who created the new rule in antitrust or environmental law. Expected sign = +.
- DISSENT: Whether disagreement with the rule is expressed in the case announcing the rule. Expected sign = –.

---

[4] Although the task of judging differs between district courts and circuit courts, the legal issues encountered are the same. This is far less true of state and federal courts, so the measure of experience counts only years on the federal bench.

- **CIRCUITS**: Strength of support for or opposition to the rule among other circuits. Expected sign = +.
- **SENIORITY**: Years on the federal bench of the current opinion writer. No influence expected.
- **SENPRES**: SENIORITY × PRESTIGE. Expected sign = −.
- **SENEXP**: SENIORITY × EXPERTISE. Expected sign = −.
- **SENCIRC**: SENIORITY × CIRCUITS. Expected sign = −.
- **OWN CIRCUIT**: Previous support for or opposition to the rule by the deciding judges' circuit. Expected sign = +.
- **ANT**: Antitrust case (as opposed to environmental case). No expected sign.
- **SS**: Search and seizure case (as opposed to environmental case). No expected sign.

One final matter must be disposed of before the model can be properly estimated. The analysis is complicated by the relationship between CIRCUITS and several other independent variables. For the second court in each series of cases – the first to consider adopting another court's new rule – CIRCUITS is always equal to one. But in all other instances, CIRCUITS is a function of the dependent variable from earlier cases in the series. If, as hypothesized, variables like PRESTIGE, EXPERTISE, and DISSENT that remain constant through a series of cases do indeed have an effect on adoption, then they must also have an effect on CIRCUITS. For example, if prestige increases the probability of adoption, then it also increases the value of CIRCUITS for later cases, because that variable is based on previous adoptions and rejections in the line of cases. On the other hand, CIRCUITS can have no effect on any of the variables defined by the initial case, since it can never come before them in time.

Another way of putting all this is that CIRCUITS is an intervening variable between those (antecedent) variables and the dependent variable. Not only can the antecedent variables affect adoption directly, but they can do so indirectly by causing changes in CIRCUITS that in turn cause changes in the probability of adoption. The problem with the straightforward model is that it would allow us to estimate only the direct effects of the antecedent variables. In the statistical analysis, the coefficient for each variable would represent its effect with other variables held constant. With CIRCUITS held constant, its effect on adoption – and thus the other variables' indirect effects through CIRCUITS – would be removed.

My solution is to purge CIRCUITS of the influence of these other variables before including it in the model. This can be done by first regress-

TABLE 4.3. OLS *regression of* CIRCUITS *on logically prior variables*

Variable	Coefficient	Standard Error	*p*
PRESTIGE	1.141	.197	<.001
EXPERTISE	.539	.245	.029
DISSENT	−.377	.485	.437
ANT	−1.811	.399	<.001
SS	−1.491	.343	<.001

$N = 219$. R-squared $= .216$.

ing CIRCUITS (using ordinary least squares) on the five variables in the model that come before it in time, PRESTIGE, EXPERTISE, DISSENT, ANT, and SS, and then calculating the residuals from this equation. It would be wrong to do this for all cases. As was just noted, CIRCUITS is always equal to one for the first court to consider adopting another's new rule. The other variables can have no effect on the value of CIRCUITS in these cases, and therefore there is nothing to be purged. Accordingly, these are excluded from the regression.

As Table 4.3 reveals, CIRCUITS is indeed influenced by these other variables, quite strongly in the case of PRESTIGE. Only DISSENT has an insignificant effect. The residuals from this equation, which represent the variation in CIRCUITS not attributable to differences in the other independent variables, are labeled CIRCUITS-R and included in the model in place of the original CIRCUITS variable for all cases in a series aside from the one first faced with the new rule. For this case, CIRCUITS-R is set to one, since, by definition, the court announcing the new rule supported it.[5] As a result of these transformations, the coefficients for variables like PRESTIGE and EXPERTISE are allowed to reflect both their direct effects on the current court's choice and their indirect effects through their influence on earlier judges' choices.

ANALYSIS AND RESULTS

The statistical method used here is probit, a maximum likelihood method of estimation.[6] Ordinary least squares (OLS) regression is generally

[5] Descriptive statistics for CIRCUITS-R are as follows. Median: .826; mean: .27; st. dev.: 1.698; minimum: −6.807; maximum: 4.599.

[6] Different panels' decisions whether to adopt the same rule may be correlated with one another because of some unobserved characteristic of the rule or the opinion

considered inappropriate where, as here, the dependent variable is dichotomous. The OLS assumptions of homoscedasticity and normally distributed errors are unlikely to hold. Perhaps more important, the assumption of linearity is suspect. Consider an independent variable's effect on the probability that the dependent variable will equal one. Under OLS, that effect is assumed to be constant. For example, the effect of a given increase in judicial expertise on the probability of a rule's being adopted would have to be the same whether the prior probability were .5 or .98. This seems clearly wrong. It is easier to imagine expertise having a substantial impact on judges who are wavering than on ones with their minds essentially made up. In fact, it is impossible for the effect to be substantial if the prior probability is .98, because a probability can never go above 1. Probit, unlike OLS, allows the independent variable's impact to vary – specifically, to increase as the probability approaches .5 (Aldrich and Nelson 1984; Long 1997).

For this very reason, probit coefficients are not directly interpretable. They indicate the effect of a unit change in the independent variable not on the dependent variable itself but on the hypothetical distribution underlying the dependent variable, measured in terms of Z-scores. For instance, if the coefficient for DISTANCE were equal to −.2, this would indicate that a one-unit increase in DISTANCE drops the Z-score for the probability of adoption by .2. Obviously this means that it lowers the probability that ADOPT will equal 1. But because the probability change associated with any particular change in Z-score is dependent on the original Z-score, we cannot say how much it lowers the probability without first adopting a starting point.

To interpret the results, I rely on a very helpful program devised by Tomz, Wittenberg, and King (1998). As described in King, Tomz, and Wittenberg (2000), the program uses simulation to generate expected or predicted values for the dependent variable – or increases or decreases in those values – from given scores of the independent variables. It also provides a gauge of the uncertainty of those value estimates. There are two kinds of uncertainty at work, arising from errors in esti-

announcing it. For this reason, robust standard errors provide a better measure of the uncertainty of coefficient estimates than do traditional standard errors (Giles and Zorn 2000). All of the analyses from this point on in the book are shown with robust standard errors, generated through the "cluster" function in STATA 6.0, where the new rule is the clustering variable. There are no important differences between these results and those obtained with traditional standard errors.

mates of coefficients and chance effects on the dependent variable not captured in the model. Failure to note this uncertainty would result in inappropriate and exaggerated claims for the model because, as with anything in statistics, we can draw inferences with only some finite level of confidence.

Simple Model

To minimize complexity, I begin by examining only main effects, leaving aside for the moment the more complicated interactions with SENIOR-ITY. Results are shown in Table 4.4. Significance levels are one-tailed where a sign was predicted, two-tailed otherwise. For all five of the key theoretical variables, the effect is in the predicted direction and statistically significant. Based on these criteria, all of the hypotheses appear to be strongly supported.

What really matters, though, is what the numbers reveal about the effects of the variables on judges' actions. For each of the variables of interest, Table 4.5 lists the estimated change(s) in the probability of adoption caused by the specified change(s) in that one variable. I have tried to ensure that the estimates are informative and realistic. First, results are presented for all three fields. Second, aside from the variable being investigated at the moment, all independent variables are set at their medians. Third, the estimates are based on plausible values for the variable of interest, showing the effects of moving from the tenth percentile

TABLE 4.4. *Simple probit model of rule adoption*

Variable	Coefficient	Standard Error	p (*one-tailed)
DISTANCE	−.223	.073	.001*
PRESTIGE	.431	.137	.001*
EXPERTISE	.533	.208	.005*
DISSENT	−.512	.297	.042*
CIRCUITS-R	.280	.054	<.001*
OWN CIRCUIT	1.005	.218	<.001*
ANT	−.925	.269	.001
SS	−.742	.260	.004
Constant	1.322	.238	
	Wald Chi-sq	63.7	
	$P <$	.0001	
	$N =$	300	

TABLE 4.5. *Estimated changes in probability of adoption*

Variable	Value Change	Mean Change in Probability	Std. Dev.	95% Confidence Interval
Antitrust				
DISTANCE	1.00 → 2.00	−.07	.02	−.03/−.12
	2.00 → 3.00	−.08	.03	−.03/−.14
PRESTIGE	0.00 → .67	.11	.04	.04/.18
	.67 → 1.94	.16	.05	.06/.27
EXPERTISE	−1.04 → −.85	.04	.02	.01/.07
	−.85 → .31	.22	.08	.06/.38
DISSENT	0.00 → 1.00	−.19	.11	.02/−.40
CIRCUITS-R	−2.19 → .83	.32	.06	.20/.43
	.83 → 2.05	.11	.02	.07/.15
Search and seizure				
DISTANCE	1.00 → 2.00	−.07	.02	−.02/−.10
	2.00 → 3.00	−.08	.03	−.03/−.13
PRESTIGE	0.00 → .67	.10	.04	.04/.18
	.67 → 1.94	.14	.04	.06/.23
DISSENT	0.00 → 1.00	−.19	.11	.03/−.41
CIRCUITS-R	−2.19 → .83	.32	.06	.20/.43
	.83 → 2.05	.09	.02	.07/.12
Environmental				
DISTANCE	1.00 → 2.00	−.03	.01	−.01/−.06
	2.00 → 3.00	−.04	.02	−.01/−.08
PRESTIGE	0.00 → .67	.05	.02	.02/.10
	.67 → 1.94	.05	.02	.02/.10
EXPERTISE	−.84 → −.15	.08	.04	.02/.16
	−.15 → .53	.05	.02	.01/.08
DISSENT	0.00 → 1.00	−.12	.09	.01/−.32
CIRCUITS-R	−2.19 → .83	.21	.06	.11/.33
	.83 → 2.05	.04	.01	.02/.07

Note: Probability changes are estimated for changes in specified independent variable from tenth percentile score to median score (first row) and median score to ninetieth percentile score (second row), with other variables held at their medians.

score on that variable to its median score and from the median to the ninetieth percentile score. (For EXPERTISE, the scores used are those within the relevant field, because typical levels of expertise may be different in antitrust and environmental law. Of course, DISSENT has only two possible scores, so just one comparison can be made for it.) Finally, estimates are accompanied by standard deviations and 95 percent confidence intervals.[7]

Two examples should assist in the interpretation of the table. In search and seizure, if the ideological distance between the panel and a rule increases from 1 (tenth percentile score) to 2 (median score), holding other variables at their medians, the probability of adoption should decrease by about .07. Further increasing the distance to 3 (ninetieth percentile score) should reduce the probability by another .08 or so. The results for prestige tell us the following: Presented with two typical search and seizure cases, different only in that the rule being considered was announced by a judge with a .67 (median) prestige score in one case and by a judge with a score of 1.94 (ninetieth percentile) in the other, we can be quite confident that the probability of the rule's being adopted is between .06 and .23 higher in the second case.

The effects in antitrust are slightly larger; in environmental law they are smaller. The difference is attributable to the stronger tendency toward consensus in environmental law. In that field, each case begins with such a high probability of adoption that judges are hard to budge. They are more open to influence in search and seizure and antitrust, where opposing forces are otherwise more balanced.

I believe these results are rather impressive. CIRCUITS-R excepted, no one of the independent variables of interest is capable of shifting judges from strong support for a rule to strong opposition (or vice-versa), but almost all have the power to change the minds of judges who are not firmly committed to one side. To put it another way, only the position of the judges' own circuit[8] and the level of support for a rule among other circuits have the potential to affect the outcome of most cases on their own, yet all of the hypothesized factors can affect outcomes at least fairly often. And when more than one pushes in the same direction, their influence can be quite dramatic. For instance, consider two search and seizure cases: In one, there is a dissent in the initial case, the ideological distance variable is at its ninetieth percentile value, and the other variables are at their median values; in the other, there is no dissent in the initial case, the prestige of the rule's author is equal to the ninetieth

---

[7] Predicted probabilities are based on 10,000 simulations for each analysis. Repeated runs show that results rarely differ by more than .002.

[8] As expected, the influence of OWN CIRCUIT is quite powerful. For example, in search and seizure, the estimated probability of adoption is .37 lower (standard error = .08) where the panel's circuit has already rejected the rule than where it has not yet taken a position.

percentile value, and the ideological distance and the remaining variables are at their medians. The estimated increase in the probability of adoption caused by this moderate variation in just three variables is a whopping .41 (standard deviation = .12).

Moderating Effects of Judicial Experience

In short, the hypotheses have done very well so far. H2a, H3a, and H5a have still to be tested, however. If these hypotheses are correct, the effects of prestige, expertise, and prior circuit support should be weaker for more experienced judges. To see if this is so, I begin by adding to the equation the measure of years on the federal bench (SENIORITY) for each deciding author. Then, I separately add the variables formed by multiplying SENIORTY by PRESTIGE, EXPERTISE, and CIRCUITS-R. Each interaction term should have a negative coefficient.

The results are mixed. The coefficient for the expertise interaction term is small and in the wrong direction. The coefficient for the circuit support interaction term is correctly signed but clearly insignificant (p = .352, one-tailed). Apparently, either expertise and prior circuit activity do not serve as cues, or junior judges are no more likely to rely on them than senior colleagues. On the other hand, prestige does have a greater impact on less experienced judges. The coefficient is correctly signed, and p = .023 (one-tailed), indicating that this term probably belongs in the model. The final model with the interaction included is shown in Table 4.6.

Not surprisingly, most of the other variables' coefficients change very little. For the most part, the probability calculations do not change at all. The only exception is that the impact of dissent increases slightly. For instance, in the full model the effect of moving from zero to one on DISSENT with other variables held at their median is −.14 (standard error = .09) in environmental law, −.21 (.11) in search and seizure.

Calculating the effects of prestige now becomes more complicated. It is necessary to set a value for SENIORITY first and then vary PRESTIGE and FRSTPRES together. Here are some illustrative results. When SENIORITY is set at its median (the middle level of federal bench experience for deciding judges), the impact of prestige is about the same as before. A change in PRESTIGE from its median value to its ninetieth percentile value, with SENPRES moving accordingly, increases the probability of adoption by .06 (.02) in environmental cases, .15 (.05) in search and seizure, and .17 (.05) in antitrust. Among especially experienced judges, the effect is

TABLE 4.6. *Full probit model of rule adoption*

Variable	ADOPT		
	Coefficient	Standard Error	p (*one-tailed)
DISTANCE	−.234	.074	.001*
PRESTIGE	.809	.277	.002*
EXPERTISE	.536	.216	.007*
DISSENT	−.584	.304	.027*
CIRCUITS	.275	.056	<.001*
OWNCIRC	1.017	.219	<.001*
ANT	−.928	.267	.001
SS	−.757	.260	.004
SENIORITY	.021	.018	.261
SENPRES	−.029	.015	.023*
Constant	1.094	.332	
	Wald Chi-sq	62.49	
	P <	.0001	
	N =	300	

considerably smaller and less certain. If SENIORITY is set at its ninetieth percentile score, the same increase in prestige enhances the likelihood of adoption by only .02 (.03), .05 (.06), and .06 (.07). On the other hand, for judges at the tenth percentile of seniority, the effects are .07 (.03), .19 (.06), and .22 (.07).

ALTERNATIVE SPECIFICATIONS

As explained earlier, the analysis required some difficult choices of measurement and specification. Two in particular stand out – the measurement of ideological distance and the replacement of the original CIRCUITS variable with the regression residuals. Although I am convinced that these choices were justified on logical grounds, an examination of their consequences would add another basis for evaluating them. With this in mind, I have rerun the model several times with different variables included. The results strongly affirm the wisdom of the choices. I will briefly describe them here.

Instead of correcting for the effects of prestige and other variables on circuit reactions in the probit model itself, I could have run the probit with the original CIRCUITS variable and later incorporated information about the relationship between CIRCUITS and the other variables when calculating estimated probabilities. This could have been done by going back to the regression of CIRCUITS on the other variables and generating predicted scores for CIRCUITS. Then, for instance, when the value of PRESTIGE was varied to calculate probability changes, the score for CIRCUITS could have been varied along with it to reflect its reaction to PRESTIGE.

If I adopt this course, the results are quite similar to those from the actual model. The predicted values from the two equations are very highly correlated ($r = .98$). To the extent the results differ, the substitute model seems inferior. The probability estimates it generates for the effects of prestige, field experience, and prior circuit reactions are all slightly higher than in the actual model. Thus the latter offers more conservative tests of the hypotheses.

For the measure of ideological distance, there are several plausible alternatives. In the past, scholars have frequently employed the judge's political party or party of the appointing president as indicators of ideology. Tate and Handberg (1991) offer a version of the latter measure that takes into account how much each president cared about the ideology of potential nominees. To test whether different measures of ideological distance would generate different results, I have constructed four new variables – three to parallel the indicators listed above plus one variant of the Tate and Handberg measure. For the first, Democratic judges are given scores of one, Republican judges a five. The second is scored the same way, except according to the party of the appointing president, rather than the party of the judge. The third measure assigns a three to judges appointed by the least ideologically minded presidents, Dwight Eisenhower, Gerald Ford, and Bill Clinton.[9] The last weights both the president's party and the intensity of his preferences by assigning ones or fives to the appointees of the most ideologically committed presidents, Lyndon Johnson, Richard Nixon, Ronald Reagan, and George H.W. Bush, and twos and fours to appointees of the other Democratic and Republican presidents, respectively. For each approach, the actual measure of ideological distance is constructed in the same way as is the original ideological distance variable, as described earlier.

---

[9] The coding choices for this variable and the next follow or are based on descriptions from Tate and Handberg (1991); Songer, Segal, and Cameron (1994); Goldman (1997); and Goldman and Slotnick (1999).

Whichever of these alternate measures is chosen, there is little change from the original model. For most of the variables, the predicted probability changes are always within .02 of those in the original. There are two exceptions. Prestige has a slightly greater effect in three of the four substitute models. More important, the impact of ideological distance is substantially smaller in all of the substitute models. The coefficients for ideological distance range from −.03 (standard error = .04) in the judges' party model to −.07 (.05) in the modified version of the Tate/Handberg scores. The small coefficients are reflected in the probability calculations. To illustrate, whereas moving from the tenth percentile value to the ninetieth percentile value of ideological distance (in search and seizure cases, with other variables held at their medians) decreases the probability of adoption by .14 (st. dev. = .05) in the original model, it does so by only .09 (.07) in the best-performing alternative model, and by no more than .07 in the other three.

These results suggest two things. First, the measure of ideological distance developed here appears to be superior to more traditional ones based on a judge's political party or appointing president. This issue is not central to my research, and I will not offer any more rigorous tests, but the possibility would seem worthy of future study. The second, more significant conclusion is that the consequences of my methodological choices were modest. Most important, they did not slant the analyses in favor of my more controversial hypotheses.

DISCUSSION

Interpretation of Results

The key lesson of the ideology effects is quite clear: Judges prefer to adopt policies they agree with. This preference is strong enough to have a substantial effect on their behavior. The only complicating factor here is that ideological distance is imperfectly measured. As discussed earlier, there is error in the measurement of both rule ideology and judge ideology. The coding for the former is oversimplified. Rules are not simply liberal or conservative; they can be moderate, moderately liberal, extremely conservative, and so on. The measure of judge ideology is based on a somewhat arbitrary sample of subjective judgments. And, although the recognition that ideology can have multiple dimensions goes at least back to Schubert (1962; see also Rohde and Spaeth 1976;

Ducat and Dudley 1987; Epstein and Mershon 1996), in both measures it is treated as unidimensional. In reality, a judge might be a conservative in most respects but liberal in environmental cases, but my measures cannot reflect this.

For the most part, the resulting measurement error should be nonsystematic. Problems with dimensionality and Almanac information should be no more or less likely to lead to overestimates of ideological distance than to underestimates. Only the dichotomizing of rule ideology should have systematic effects, producing more overestimates than underestimates. (For example, if a rule that would ideally be coded as a three on the ideology scale is actually coded as a five, ideological distance will be underestimated for judges with a score of five, correctly estimated for judges with a score of four, and overestimated for all judges with lower scores.) As King, Keohane, and Verba (1994:163–8) illustrate, nonsystematic error in the measurement of an independent variable causes underestimates of that variable's effect. The effects of the error in measuring rule ideology are a bit harder to gauge but should be similar. If ideological distance is overestimated equally for all cases, the calculation of its impact should be unaffected. If only some scores are overestimated, ideological distance will seem to vary more than it really does and thus appear to have a smaller effect on adoption than it really does. The upshot of all this is that the influence of ideology is almost certainly greater than the results show.

The results for PRESTIGE indicate that judges who are more often cited by name by other judges are also more likely to have their rules adopted. This effect is strongest when a relatively junior judge has the responsibility for writing an opinion. I am confident that PRESTIGE validly measures the esteem in which judges are held by colleagues. But why exactly does respect for a judge translate into more favorable treatment of his or her precedents? The results cannot give us a sure answer. It may be that other judges consciously defer to the prestigious ones; they figure that their decisions are right, and so they decide the same way. Or they might unconsciously accord greater weight to arguments from respected judges. Or it might be that more prestigious judges simply write more persuasive opinions or develop more convincing rules. In this last case, a judge's reputation has less impact than the characteristics that reputation was built on.

My guess is that each of these explanations is partly right. The very practice the prestige measure is constructed from suggests that judges pay attention to the names on opinions. The importance of those names also comes across in the interviews, as I will detail in the next chapter. Furthermore, the fact that prestige has a greater effect on more junior judges implies that names count. (Presumably, less experienced judges should not be any more responsive than their senior colleagues to compelling logic or clear, forceful prose, but they certainly might place more reliance on cues.) Nevertheless, it seems equally likely that the measure is capturing something about the judges' products as well as the judges themselves. As in any field, judicial reputations can be inflated, but it would be surprising if they lacked any substantive basis at all. And if judges gain reputations by producing superior work in the first place, the quality of their work probably contributes to its impact.

The same possibilities apply to the effect of experience in a particular field of law, as measured by published opinions: More experienced judges may be more influential because of who they are or because of what they do. Here, though, I suspect that the product is more important than the name. One sign that this is true is the failure to find that junior and senior judges reacted differently to experience. The suspicion is strengthened when we consider what the EXPERTISE variable does and does not measure. It is an indicator of experience in writing opinions, not recognition of one's expertise by colleagues. One could gain considerable experience in a field without attracting much attention. At the same time, a judge could acquire a reputation for expertise through academic writings or association with an important case, without writing more than an average number of opinions on the subject. In short, while reputations may play some part in the expertise effect, expert judges' influence is probably due more to their greater wisdom in the choice of legal rules and their ability to defend those rules convincingly.

The results for DISSENT indicate that when the initial pronouncement of a rule is not unanimous, the rule is less likely to be followed by later courts. Of all the hypotheses, this was the least strongly supported and probably the least compelling on its own terms. It is possible that dissents act as danger signals to later judges. To the extent the results reflect this phenomenon, they are quite interesting, indicating both that judges see and respond to signals and that dissents – Hughes's appeals "to the brooding spirit of the law, to the intelligence of a future day" – can have an impact even in the short term. But it is unclear how much they do reflect it. It may just be that the kinds of rules that occasion dissents – ambitious, suspect as to logic or practicality, etc. – are also more often rejected by later judges. Such a finding is informative, providing evidence of some consistency in the criteria judges use to evaluate rules. But it is not exciting. Unfortunately, lacking a workable measure of a rule's soundness or attractiveness, I am unable to determine which of these two interpretations is more accurate.

The impact of prior circuits' reactions is similarly ambiguous. In fact, it might not even be proper to speak of an impact. An analogy can help show why. Imagine asking a number of experts to predict the outcome of an election. If the first two made different predictions, you would not be able to guess with any confidence what the third would say. But if four of the first five chose the same candidate, you would probably begin to see the one prediction as aberrant and expect the sixth expert to go along with the four. The reason is that the experts begin with similar abilities and knowledge and aim to achieve the same thing, a correct prediction. If the question is a particularly difficult one, they may become badly divided. The easier it is, the more likely it is that a consensus will develop; and the greater the consensus, the higher the probability that the next expert will agree with the dominant position.

The same may be true for judges and legal rules. To the extent it is, prior circuit activity does not actually affect judges' decisions; rather, it serves as a proxy for issue difficulty. Yet even if this possibility accounted entirely for the observed results, the implications would still be quite significant. We would be unlikely to observe a strong relationship between previous and current judges' decisions if those decisions were based entirely on policy preferences (just as we would be unlikely to see such a relationship if we asked election experts which candidate they preferred). A strong relationship can exist only when the members of a group have common grounds for evaluating alternatives. Judges range quite widely in their ideologies, and, as one can see in Appendix A, few of the rules are ideologically easy, in the sense that one alternative or the other is clearly outside the ideological mainstream. Moreover, even if one believed ideology could play some part in the CIRCUITS-R effect, the fact that ideology is controlled for through the inclusion of the ideological distance variables largely nullifies this possibility. We are left with one credible conclusion: If the relationship between previous and current judges' decisions is not a causal one, it most likely results from a common search for legally sound solutions to legal problems.

Thus, even if previous circuit activity has no effect on current judges' behavior, the relationship between the two is theoretically important. But there is no good reason to dismiss the possibility of a causal relationship. The impact of CIRCUITS-R is large enough to flow from multiple sources. Three perfectly plausible ones involve causation. First, because each decision for or against a rule is explained in an opinion, the dominant side has more opportunities to persuade, to hit on the key argument that will convince later judges that its position is correct. The more dominant it is – and so, the fewer the opinions supporting the other side – the less likely it is that later judges will be exposed to a persuasive counterargument. Second, the numbers themselves might serve as an indicator of a position's strength. For instance, if a judge saw that four circuits had adopted a rule while only one had rejected it, she might see that as evidence that the rule was a good one and begin with a presumption in its favor. Finally, a judge might go along with an emerging consensus not because he thought it more likely to be correct but because he wished to minimize conflict and confusion in the federal law.

In the end, some of the results speak clearly enough; others are open to multiple interpretations. For the latter group, additional information would be helpful. The interviews can provide some of that information. I will discuss what help they can give us in the next chapter.

The Model's Utility

I am far more interested in testing specific hypotheses about judges' reactions to one anothers' rulings than in constructing a general model to predict their reactions. I make no claim to have identified and measured all possible influences on adoption. Nevertheless, it is not unreasonable to ask how well the model as a whole performs. Doing so can give us a sense of how important any unobserved influences are.

The easiest way of evaluating the model is to ask how many outcomes it predicts correctly. (Of course, it would be more meaningful to test the model against cases other than those it was built from, but, as is usually the case, that is not possible here.) Predicted values for ADOPT can fall anywhere between 0 and 1. If values above .5 are treated as predicting adoption and values below .5 as predicting rejection, 235 (78.3 percent) of the cases are predicted correctly. Had we guessed in advance that rules would be adopted in every case, we would have been right 215 (71.7 percent) times. The model gets it right 9.3 percent more often or, to put it another way, makes 23.5 percent fewer errors.

Of course, this comparison is neither perfectly fair nor entirely sensible. A priori, there was no justification for guessing that rules would always be adopted. It would have been just as reasonable to predict adoption in every other decision, in which case only about half the predictions would have been right. More important, the model is far more

informative than the comparison suggests. The model allows us to estimate the probability of adoption, not just guess outcomes. When it generates a predicted value of .54, say, it is telling us that in cases like this
the rule is more likely to be followed than not, but only slightly; rejections will be common, too. On the other hand, a probability estimate of
.97 is a strong prediction. What we can ask of a model is that it differ-
entiate between cases in its probability estimates and that the probabilities and outcomes correspond best where the probabilities are highest
or lowest. The model here passes this test rather convincingly, as we can
see by splitting estimated probabilities into thirds: 0–.333, .334–.666,
and .667–1.0. While the probability and outcome correspond in only 50
percent of the cases ($n = 78$) in the middle group, they match 89.7 percent
of the time ($n = 29$) in the first group and 87.7 percent ($n = 195$) in the
last group. Of course, a weak model might lump most cases in the middle
group because it has trouble telling them apart. But the opposite is true
here: Only a little over a quarter of the cases fall in the middle third of
the probability range. In short, the model is able to generate firm predictions, and they are correct almost 90 percent of the time.

The model thus appears to provide a powerful tool for understanding judges' reactions to colleagues' new legal rules. Yet there is clearly
room for improvement. It does not capture all influences on judges' decisions. Undoubtedly some influences are isolated or idiosyncratic, but
there may be other, more systematic ones at work as well. If we could
identify them and devise ways to measure them, we could hope to
produce firmer and more accurate predictions. Information from the
interviews may bring us closer to that goal. I turn to them in the next
chapter.

5

Influences on Circuit Judges' Responses: Interview Evidence

This chapter builds on the preceding one, returning to the interviews to see what light they can shed on circuit judges' decisions to follow or reject new legal rules created by their colleagues. The case analysis provided strong support for the hypotheses, but it could not establish anything with certainty. As already discussed at length, the measures were imperfect. Furthermore, in a statistical analysis, there is always the chance that the relationships uncovered hold only for the cases included, not for the entire population from which they were drawn. The interviews allow us to probe the hypotheses using different methods from a different set of observations. If the results agree, our confidence in them will be enhanced.

Unfortunately, not all of the hypotheses were adequately covered in the interviews. This was partly because of limitations inherent in the method and partly because the interviews took place early in the life of the project, before the full set of hypotheses was developed. As compensation, the interviews go beyond the cases in important ways, contributing additional detail and answering questions the quantitative analysis could not address. In this way they point to other possible influences on rule adoption and aid in the interpretation of ambiguous results from the quantitative analysis. In the interest of narrative flow, I will present all connected ideas together, rather than discuss separately those comments pertaining directly to the hypotheses.

I did not ask the judges any direct question about the impact of policy preferences (H1). It was difficult to see how the question could be framed without offending some judges, but, more important, it would have been superfluous. Of all the hypotheses, this one is the most directly and obviously tied to a specific goal. If policy preferences do play a part in judges' decision making, it must be by leading them to adopt rules that accord with their preferences and reject the rest. As discussed in Chapter 2, the interviews contain abundant evidence that judges care not only about the legal quality of their decisions but also about the consequences of those decisions for justice and fairness. This finding reinforces the results for ideological distance in the case analysis.

Nor was any question about the importance of dissents (H4) included. The reason for this was that I had not yet formulated the hypothesis. Aside from the judge quoted in Chapter 2, who volunteered that he scrutinized an opinion especially closely when he saw a dissent, no other judge mentioned dissents in this context.

ACTIONS OF OTHER CIRCUITS

Fortunately, the interviews have a good deal to tell us about the importance of other judges' characteristics (Hypotheses 2 and 3) and behavior (Hypothesis 5). The discussion of the latter is a bit simpler, so let us turn to it first.

In the portion of each interview covering judges' treatments of new rules devised by their peers, I asked if it mattered to them how other circuits had reacted to a rule. Their answers reveal a remarkable range of opinions. Some judges claimed not to care how the rule had been treated in other circuits. Here is a sample of their remarks:

> If it's factually related and there are three courts on one side and none on the other, I may follow if it makes sense. If it doesn't – I don't give a damn if there are six cases out there if they don't make sense. If I can make a plausible argument on the other side, I'll do it, although I have to convince the other judges on the panel.

> I try not to be influenced by the number of courts. I don't look to the scales, see how they are tipping. I look instead at the reasoning, whether it's compatible with my own approach to the law.

> There are no rules; I pick what I like.

The judges who did pay attention to developments in other circuits gave different reasons for doing so. Some judges mentioned that they took notice when they saw a consensus developing. For instance:

> I don't care what any other circuit decides if . . . [the judge did not finish]. There are several ways to regard law from another circuit. For example, "That's

a very prestigious circuit so we should follow it." I've never subscribed to that view. When I start to care is about when three or four circuits have all agreed it means X and none have said it means Y. If they're on both sides, the numbers do weigh some, but generally very little.

If [my] circuit hasn't spoken and I see seven circuits have taken a position with a pretty logical argument, I'd probably go along. If there's only one other circuit, and I think its opinion doesn't make sense, then I will look a lot farther, at other cases not directly on point but having similar or analogous issues.

I think if there's a generally accepted doctrine I would certainly follow it – if it makes sense. If it doesn't make sense and I see a text that does, I'll follow the text.
[DK: Would it make a difference whether the circuits were 3–0 or 2–1?]
It would make some difference. I would be a little inclined to go with the two, but if the one made more sense I might follow it. If they were 3–0, I would have to be damn sure that I was right before I didn't follow them.

[DK: Does it matter how the circuits divide?] Yes, it certainly does matter. If they're evenly split, I have to make two choices: adopt one rule or the other, or fashion a new one. If they're unanimous – say six all came to the same conclusion – certainly that's pretty convincing evidence that the rule is right.

I had a recent case where only two other circuits had addressed the issue: the First and the D.C. They came out diametrically opposed. I followed the First because I thought its reasoning was better. I will confess that if five, six, or seven circuits have gone one way I find it very difficult – although not impossible – to say we should go the other way.

[DK: Does it make a difference how many circuits line up the same way?] Yeah, it makes a difference, but there was one case where all the circuits were in one direction and I went along, and the Supreme Court reversed all of us. I'm not sure the Supreme Court was wrong – it could have gone either way. [DK: Did you go along just because of the numbers?] I felt my reasoning was correct because all the other circuits had gone the same way.

For these judges, circuit agreement is a sign that a position is sound. To reject a consensus position, they must be particularly confident that it is wrong. Aside from what it tells them about the rule, however, the consensus is unimportant. Other judges focused on the consensus as a good in itself. They reported a reluctance (on their own part or that of colleagues) to cause a circuit conflict. Their comments varied some in intensity of feeling. The following remarks show a moderately strong sentiment:

I think there's a *sotto voce* presumption that unless you have really good reasons, you don't depart from a consensus – for consistency reasons. But there's a coequal duty if you think it's wrong to depart from it and explain why.

If in doubt, I tend to go with [other circuits]. I'm reluctant to create a circuit split, but I will do that if I think the other circuit is wrong.

[DK, later: Does the number of circuits matter?] Three or four on the same side would certainly have more weight than one, but I would pay close attention to the one if that's the only decision on the issue. I think most judges would. There's some value to uniformity.

If there's a previous decision from another circuit, there's a natural tendency to go along unless you have serious reservations – say, the opinion's not well reasoned and persuasive. Judges like to avoid conflict.

The next three comments reveal stronger views:

Sometimes you know a case will go to the Supreme Court. There was this one we knew would, because our decision created a circuit split. A number of judges on the court were horrified by this and wanted to en banc. They thought we should go with the [other circuit].

If there's nothing from the Supreme Court or [my own circuit], what other circuits have done is of extreme importance, I think, in that it influences us. Unless I think what the other panel has done is off the wall I give great weight to it. As [another judge] says, someone has already looked at it and made a rule. Why create a dispute except for a very good reason? So I don't unless, as I say, it's off the wall.

I disagree with the idea that Courts of Appeals should be fully autonomous actors, all going their own way. The idea of disagreeing with others is defended with the percolation idea. I think that's absolutely wrong. Federal law is supposed to mean one thing, not something different in New York, Minnesota, or whatever. . . .

My personal inclination is to join the majority because of my underlying philosophy. If the circuits are split, then I'm on my own, but if they've only gone in one direction, I'll generally go along. It would have to be an off-the-wall position for me to disagree.[1]

Of course, some judges value a consensus both for what it indicates and for itself. Here are the remarks of one such judge:

I often look to other circuits if there's no case from the Supreme Court or my own circuit. Especially if it's a case with lots of application (eight other circuits have seen it, or several state courts). I'm looking for a developing consensus. . . . If the issue is strictly one of federal law, I try for uniformity.

The interviews add in several ways to what we learned from the quantitative analysis in Chapter 4. For one thing, they reveal considerable variation across individual judges, from those who hardly care what

---

[1] This quotation is from the judge referred to in the previous quotation.

other circuits have done to those who are pained by the thought of creating a circuit conflict. There was no way these differences could be uncovered in the quantitative analysis.

More important, when we consider all of the judges' comments together, it is apparent that the strength of existing circuit support for a legal rule has a real impact on the way it is treated in later cases. This is more than we were able to conclude in Chapter 4. Recall that it was impossible to say for sure whether the observed statistical relationship between existing circuit support and current adoption was a causal one. Judges might go along with the dominant position not because it is dominant but because they happen to view the issue in the same light as the judges deciding it before them. The interviews do not allow us to reject this possibility for all cases, but they show that it constitutes, at best, only a partial explanation for the observed relationship; circuit support does have an effect on the decisions of later judges.

Of course, if the quantitative analysis could not establish the presence of an influence, it also could not identify the basis of that influence. Here, again, the interviews help. As already indicated, the judges' comments fall rather neatly into two categories. Those in the first category point to the signaling effect of other circuits' actions: Solid circuit support for a rule marks it as legally sound and makes it more likely that judges who care about legal soundness will adopt it. The comments in the second category all implicate the goal of legal uniformity.

JUDGES' CHARACTERISTICS

To find out about the influence of jurists' characteristics, I asked the judges if, when deciding whether to follow a precedent, they took into account the identity of its author. (Sometimes the wording was slightly different, asking whether they weighted opinions from different judges differently.) The judges rarely distinguished clearly between expertise and general prestige, so it is difficult to draw precise conclusions about H2 and H3. On the plus side, they added interesting detail about their thought processes and the traits that matter to them.

Circuit Reputations

Before turning to their remarks about individual judges, it is interesting to note one characteristic that did not seem to matter much to them. I began the project with the idea that reputations frequently attached to whole courts as well as to individual judges. Certainly there is empirical evidence, both anecdotal and systematic, that this was once true (see Schick 1970; Friedman et al. 1981; Howard 1981; Caldeira 1985). But early in the interview process it became clear that circuit judges today do not usually think in terms of whole courts. In the first several interviews, I asked a variant of this question: "It seems that circuits sometimes gain reputations for general excellence. Are there any circuits today which have a reputation for general excellence or which in your view merit such a reputation?" One judge's answer was not wholly negative. He said,

> Well, I think highly of the Second. I think the Ninth is very fine, but it's so big, it's hard to characterize. These are personal feelings: I know judges on the Second Circuit and that factors into it. I don't know any circuits that are supposed to be head and shoulders above the others. At one time the D.C. Circuit was big on administrative law.

The following reactions were more typical:

> I really don't think so. When I was young, there was the Second Circuit, with Hand, Hand, Frank, and Swan. All the circuits are bigger now with their membership constantly changing. When you get circuits that big, it's not likely that you can have star courts.

> That's a will-o'-the-wisp I wouldn't trust as far as I could throw it. When you back away and look, it's hard to say.

> No. That's a dichotomy between the public and judges. Most federal judges would feel no one circuit is better than the others. The reasons: One, composition changes rapidly. There may be good judges on it now, but bad judges may join, the good may leave. Two, the difference in the size of the circuits. Some are so big they can't have a single reputation.

The judges' general reluctance to express views about other circuits allowed one curious exception. A number of the judges – at either this point or another in the interview – commented on the reputation of the Ninth Circuit. Some spoke for themselves, some reported what they had heard, even though they disagreed, but all suggested a reputation in disrepair. Here are some examples:

> The Ninth Circuit, of course, though it has great individual judges, is so large and its jurisprudence is so diversified over a tremendous area that it doesn't have the same jurisprudential integrity I think we have.

> Some judges on this court would probably tend to derogate Ninth Circuit decisions. . . . Some people say: "Oh, hell, that's just the Ninth Circuit." I

suppose it's because it's so big and all over the ideological spectrum, so people suppose it may be brushed off.

I've seen a tendency on the part of judges to recoil from, reject anything from the Ninth Circuit, because they're way out there, do a lot of experimenting with the law. There are a lot of knee-jerk reactions by other judges; they tend to discount any precedent from the Ninth – consider it too liberal, activist.

I'm thinking of those circuits we tend to look at for precedent. Maybe it's easier to tell where we don't look. [DK: Where?] Well, we don't look to the Ninth; it's off in a category by itself.

The only time I weight [a precedent according to the circuit it came from] is if I hear the Ninth Circuit did something, I usually do the opposite. The sign of the Ninth Circuit is negative.

The last judge quoted was not entirely serious, of course, nor was his view shared by all of the other judges interviewed. (It is worth noting that Ninth Circuit rules fared no worse than others in the case analysis.) Still, these comments show that it is still at least possible for circuits to develop reputations – though perhaps only unfavorable ones. They also give us some insight into the factors that shape other judges' views. In particular, judges appear to take note of the coherence of the law emerging from another circuit as well as its ideological leanings.

On the other hand, I cannot say how and where the judges acquire their information or how reliable it is. Furthermore, these remarks should not obscure the more central finding: Judges typically do not think of whole circuits in evaluative terms and so do not weight precedents according to the circuit they come from.

Prestige and Expertise

Judges do develop opinions about other individual judges, though. Most of those interviewed seemed quite at home with the notion that some of their colleagues were better (or thought to be better) than others. Of course, this is not to say that all of them cared about other judges' skills or reputations. A few stated that the identity of an opinion's author had no effect on their own decisions whether to go along with the precedent. For example:

I don't owe any allegiance to Scalia or Judge Arnold. I don't say I think he's smarter than I am. Hell, he could be having a bad day.

Not really. I know some judges have a national reputation, but usually with that comes bias – ideological and intellectual. There's nothing wrong with that, but you become aware of it – like Posner. I've read some opinions from judges I hadn't heard of that were very good.

These judges were in the minority. Of those who addressed the issue, most felt that the name on the opinion did affect their decision making at times. Where they differed from one another was in their assessments of the effect's size. Following is a series of quotations arranged roughly in ascending order, starting with those from judges who felt the effect was small or infrequent. It is worth noting that not all of the comments were specifically prompted. In some cases judges spontaneously raised the issue.

Once in a great while I feel an initial kick because it's from a great judge – say Friendly or Wisdom. But usually it's the opinion itself, if it's a thoughtful opinion.

I guess it might matter. I wouldn't distinguish by circuit. There are certain judges I know and have a lot of respect for. If I find they said something, I might give it a little more weight. Maybe "weight" is not the right word. I think through the case myself, but if a judge I respect agreed exactly with my position, I'd feel more satisfied, while if that judge were diametrically opposed I would pause.

Sure, the better the judge, the more seriously you take them. Some people you know personally, others just through opinions, but you form a sense of how good they are through their work.

I think so. If it's a judge I know or who is reputed for his scholarship or legal acumen, I will probably give greater deference than if the judge is unknown or has a lesser reputation.

I've been in the business long enough to know many judges. If I know a judge is damn good, well educated, then I would be influenced by an opinion by him.

Sometimes I have my clerks look at the names of colleagues on relevant cases. When I see [a circuit colleague's] name, for example, I know I'm on good ground.

Yeah, you have the greats you always look forward to. Sometimes it's whether you like a judge's general philosophy as indicated in his opinions. Some you care about because their decisions are so carefully reasoned.

And some judges certainly have reputations as being careful, including some on our own court. You can figure they looked at all parts of the problem, didn't just decide off the top of the head. I pay lots of attention to those opinions.

When I see a decision, I want to know who wrote it. There are some people whose judgment I respect and others whose I don't. And you know how philosophically attuned you are to that other person. This is true on the negative side too – if someone is knee-jerk in the other direction, I don't trust them as much.

Oh, yeah. There are some I think I'm more simpatico with. Also, I certainly take note of ones from Posner. I'm impressed by Kearse, Oakes, and some others on the Second Circuit. This is factored in almost unconsciously. Judge Winter is just too conservative. He's supposed to be a fine judge, but I'm not very impressed.

Even if there isn't a definitive body of law in other circuits but there's an opinion by a judge, even a dissent – I respect some judges more than others. . . . For example, Noonan on ethics, Posner on economics. I would want to pick his brain. On the Fourteenth Amendment, Bork.

Yes. It matters very much. I have ratings for judges just like you rate baseball or football players. One of first things I look at is who wrote the opinion. . . . When I see an opinion written by [Judge A, Judge B, or Judge C, all from the judge's own circuit] I give it a good deal of thought before I disagree. The same with judges from other circuits: Campbell, Breyer; I could go down the list. It's a very big factor. Say there was a panel of [A, B, and C] not directly binding on me. It would be very difficult for me – knowing they're consistently fair, learned, researched – I'd be very loath to walk too far away. With other judges, I look and sort of sniff: "This guy's sort of a clown." I don't like to cite them, even if they come out the way I want to go.

It is important not to draw too grand a conclusion from these statements. Some judges claimed to pay no attention to the name on an opinion. Of those who did pay attention, most said they were influenced only occasionally. Yet enough judges said it mattered to them often enough for us to conclude that a legal rule's chances for favorable treatment vary with the respect its author commands. When the judges' comments are combined with the results from Chapter 4, the support for this proposition is truly impressive.

Once again, besides contributing further evidence of a relationship, the interviews allow us to reach additional conclusions about the nature of the relationship. It was impossible to tell from the quantitative analysis whether adoption is influenced by the first judge's reputation or only by the traits, skills, or behaviors on which that reputation is built. The interviews provide an answer. From the comments quoted above, it is clear that the reputation itself has at least some effect. The judges might have said that they treated all opinions equally but that some – especially those from prestigious or expert judges – were better than others. They did not. Instead, they reported paying especially close attention or giving extra weight to opinions simply because they came from colleagues they respected.

This is not to deny that what prestigious and expert judges do, not just who they are, can have a direct impact on other judges' behavior. I will return to this point shortly, in a discussion of the characteristics of rules and opinions. Before that, though, we can consider what the judges' comments reveal about other traits aside from prestige and expertise that can enhance a judge's influence.

Other Attributes

Expertise in a field of law is a rather straightforward concept. Prestige is not. On hearing that prestigious judges are especially influential, our natural reaction is to ask why some judges enjoy more prestige than others. What is it about them that earns their colleagues' respect? Gaining an understanding of judicial prestige is a worthwhile endeavor, but it is outside the scope of this study. The reason the question is relevant here is that the traits that generate prestige may also translate directly into influence. A judge who possesses one of the traits might receive more serious attention from other judges even though he has yet to break into the ranks of the prestigious. Even for esteemed judges, possession of one trait or another might extend their influence beyond what is attributable to prestige.

Furthermore, there is no reason to think that influence flows only from prestige, expertise, or other attributes linked to them. The decision in Chapter 4 to examine only the effects of prestige and expertise was driven by a concern for parsimony in modeling and practical problems of measurement, not a belief that no other characteristics could matter. Taken together, these considerations argue in favor of widening the search for important attributes. The interviews allow us to do so, though only to a limited extent.

In several of the remarks quoted previously, judges touched on specific characteristics that caused them to pay extra attention to another judge's work. Two other judges addressed the point at greater length, in response to follow-up questions:

[DK: What comes to mind when you think of a judge's prestige?] Maturity and breadth of experience. Probity. They have to have had broad life experiences. This is the most generalist job in the world. You have to be a generalist, able to tie everything together.

I might give more weight to individual judges, but not to a court, probably. [DK: What is it about individual judges that would matter to you?] How do you measure soundness? Some are better than others: It's intelligence in part; what we think of their judgment; literary skill in part – some judges' opinions have a particular cachet because they're particularly well written. But there are also occasions where I disagree with the very best and act accordingly.

Taking all of the comments together, it seems that judges may earn respect by displaying expertise, fairness, thoroughness, breadth, thought-fulness, and skill in writing, among other things. These ideas are not star-tling, and the evidence for them is only scattered. Not much more can be said about them at this point other than that they would make good candidates for future research. I do, however, call attention to one intriguing trio of references from the long series of quotations presented earlier: to a "judge's general philosophy" in the seventh quotation, to being "philosophically attuned" and to "knee-jerk" judges in the ninth, and to feelings of sympathy with some judges and discomfort with Judge Winter's conservatism in the tenth. It is hard to say exactly what the judges had in mind, but the remarks, especially the last two, carry a strong hint of ideology. They suggest that these judges – and, presum-ably, some others – give more serious consideration to the opinions of colleagues with similar policy views.[2]

Given what we know about other policy makers, this should not seem strange. For instance, Kingdon (1989) has shown that legislators are more likely to take voting cues from ideologically close colleagues. Still, the situations that legislators and judges encounter are not quite the same, and it is a bit harder to see why judges would look to ideological allies. Legislators may be summoned to the floor to vote on a motion or amendment about which they know little or nothing. Unsure about the vote's implications and fearful of undercutting their own policy ends, they may follow the leads of colleagues with similar preferences. Typically, judges have more time to prepare, and the implications of the decisions they are asked to make are less often purposely obscured by others. For these reasons, a judge should seldom need the help of another to determine the ideological effects of a particular ruling.

A more plausible explanation connects the goal of promoting policy preferences to another generally thought to be antithetical. Anyone who has ever greeted a controversial court decision with joy or disgust knows how difficult it is to separate reactions to policy implications from appraisals of legal reasoning. Psychologists have shown that even when people attempt to make accurate decisions, if they have incentives to reach particular conclusions, they are likely to be more selective in their perceptions and may adopt different decisional heuristics, or shortcuts,

---

[2] Interestingly, one judge gave a very different example of the importance of ideology, noting that he would give extra weight to a liberal opinion written by a conservative judge or a conservative one written by a liberal. In his view, such opinions were evidence that a judge had thought hard about a problem.

than they would otherwise (Kunda 1987, 1990). Rowland and Carp
(1996) have extended a similar insight to the legal arena, offering a
sophisticated and persuasive argument that trial court judges' perceptions and evaluations of case facts can be colored by their policy goals.
Factual judgments matter less in a court of appeals, but legal judgments
may also be unconsciously shaped by policy goals. If policy views affect
judges' views of legal soundness, then, other things equal, judges will
come to have more respect for the legal reasoning of ideologically similar
colleagues. If so, the tendency to look to ideological soulmates can be
attributed in part to the goal of making good law.

CHARACTERISTICS OF RULES AND OPINIONS

I have now argued that traits which engender prestige might also send
direct signals to others that a judge is worth paying attention to. What
seems even more likely is that those traits, when brought to bear in the
construction and justification of the judge's rules and opinions, make
them more attractive or persuasive to later judges, even if those judges
know little about the person who wrote them. In other words, judges
who respect certain qualities in a colleague probably respond positively
when the same qualities appear in a rule or opinion. This seems a reasonable enough assumption, but we need not be content with an assumption. I asked the judges – more or less directly – about it.

Rules

Questions specifically about legal rules' attributes did not typically fit
into the natural flow of the interviews. However, one question encouraged some judges to talk about them. In essence, I asked why some rules
were widely adopted, while others were more often rejected or ignored.
The judges' responses fit reasonably well into three groups.

Those in the first group indicate a concern with a rule's breadth or
ambition. Overly broad rules are suspect because they may work poorly
in circumstances different from those in the original case. Here are two
responses from this group.

I once, with [another judge on the circuit], created one, that _____ are a
mandatory component of a jury pool. It's a circuit court decision that was never
followed that I know of and was crudely commented on. Finally, after ten years
I had to eat my words. Probably it was far more complicated and difficult to live

with than we thought at the time. Other courts probably said, "Where will it stop?" looking at other facts, and so on.

If I think an opinion is too preachy, trying to make broad law, I get a bit leery. I like the case-by-case approach. With the broad approach, the rule can fail when you encounter something unforeseen.

It would be strange if judges worried about rules' effects in unforeseen situations only. Presumably, they also ask how effectively the rules deal with the problems they are meant to address and what new difficulties they create. The next three comments indicate as much. Incidentally, it is hard to imagine reaching these kinds of judgments without any reference to one's own policy preferences, and the third judge admits this quite frankly.

I treat precedents like biological mutations. Biological mutations are roughly random. Some are useful adaptations, some are not. If circuit X comes down with one but the others don't think it's useful, the mutation doesn't survive.

Well, I'll tell a story I probably shouldn't tell. My wife is an actuary who deals with [a federal statute]. An old law school classmate of mine on another circuit wrote an opinion in a _____ case. My wife said not only was it all-out wrong, but it would create havoc in the _____ world if it was followed. She wrote an article on it. A few years have passed, and it turned out that nobody followed it. It was unworkable. So a case may be way out there.

The extent to which a rule is followed depends in substantial part on whether it makes good sense. [DK: How could I identify a rule that makes good sense? Look at the analysis?] The analysis might be okay, but the outcome just doesn't make sense – it's bad for society, unfair to the defendant, etc. It's partly your views of what social policy it would tend to promote.

Comments in the last group have a more legalistic tinge. They suggest that rules can differ widely in their legal plausibility and that judges sometimes make choices that are, in a reasonably objective sense, mistaken.

Sometimes it's just that the decision nobody follows is wrong. The judges read a statute as saying something no one else could see. It may be that it's not thoroughly researched – maybe they just took the words of the statute but other judges look at the legislative history or intent and find a difference. Sometimes there will be a problem that doesn't come up again for years and things have changed. Or there are different facts, and you would get a crazy result if you applied the precedent. Just as judges criticize Congress, we often can't anticipate problems that will come up in the future.

Once in a while a circuit will publish an opinion that just for one reason or another is kind of an anomaly. The panel and maybe the rest of the court don't realize it at the time, but as time passes and other cases come, their own and other circuits say it should be limited to its facts, it shouldn't apply to others. This even happens to the Supreme Court. It hands down a rule, it gets distinguished and distinguished and distinguished and never becomes a rule. If a rule is really out to lunch, that sometimes happens. Maybe the real answer why this happens is that judges are human and make mistakes.

Opinions

Even though the details are interesting, the general conclusion that judges are more receptive to some rules than others is not surprising. It is less clear whether we should expect judges to be influenced by the opinions in which those rules are announced.

Following is one of my favorite comments from a judge. It came early in the interview, before I had asked any substantive questions.

Circuits are not bound to follow the precedents of others, but if the other circuit hands down a decision on a novel area, we'll analyze it, and if the reasoning commands respect and it seems well analyzed, we are disposed to adopt that reasoning. But we're not commanded to, and many times we don't. We come to the conclusion based purely on our own reasoning. But we do respect other jurisdictions – courts of appeals and also state high courts of reputation and expertise – and we defer very often to their reasoning and apply it.

Not only does it give a sense of the complex of considerations that enter into judges' decisions; it also shows how hard it can be for them to describe what goes on in their own minds. Still, many of the judges, like this one, seemed to suggest that they knew a good opinion when they saw one. Except when time constraints did not allow, I asked the judges to try to explain what made one opinion better or worse than another. They had no easy time of it, but their efforts were interesting and, at times, illuminating. Here are several examples.

In interstices cases, where we're forced to create a legal norm, we have to look at logic and reasoning, sometimes just plain common sense. We have to look at our own precedent and see how far this [the other court's rule] would take us away from where those precedents seem to be going. We can use rules of statutory interpretation. Sometimes we can use public policy arguments. If it is good common sense, that means it's on the right track.

I think being a judge is like a craft – there are conventions and rules we should follow. So legally correct decisions follow decisions that are binding and the conventions we should follow in interpreting statutes and cases.

It starts with honesty about the factual record. It's correct if it obeys all the legal principles it's supposed to. If the court has jurisdiction. Once in court, it's legally correct to state the issue accurately, not ones not raised. Honest fact reporting.

How persuasive is it? It grappled with issues and came to some conclusions. If there are good reasons for the conclusions, then I will probably tag along. If they're not very good, I'm not going to follow.

I just look at the four corners, the reasoning, articulation, presentation. I've known judges I thought a lot of where I've read their opinions and said, "Whoa, I think they missed something here." All judges are human and make errors.

Some [opinions] don't have any analysis. Others are thoughtful, have logic, an appreciation of history, an appreciation of legislative intent.

The real important thing is whether the opinion is well reasoned. Do they give all the supporting reasons? If it's purely conclusionary, we don't give it weight, because we don't know how they got there.

Quick opinions or ones where the court has very marginal interest in an issue and so it's not treated thoroughly don't count as much.

Sometimes the facts of the specific case and how the court reasoned can be very persuasive. If the opinion is well done and covers all bases, I think more of it. If the opinion is cursory – doesn't get into the problems it's generating – I pay less attention to it.

If the opinion is clear, follows a rather defined process of logic from premise to conclusion, citing facts to reach a reasoned conclusion – if so, I'd be attracted to it. Logic, presentation, clarity, style. I despise opinions with a bunch of opinions cited saying it's the only decision that could be reached but it doesn't match with the facts.

Clerk: When I read different opinions, I'm influenced by which I think is better written and more logical.
Judge: I think that's right.
Clerk: One might just throw in a sentence. Another explains it and you see the point. It seems sometimes the bad rules are not well explained.
Judge: I think that's exactly right.

Compelling logic; the ability to write clearly, simply; the ability to apply the law to the case.

Ideas have to be transmitted. If you can sense something no one else has thought of and put it in a good way, you can get everybody else to come along. [The judge then related his own experience with an influential footnote, calling it "catchy but true."] So it's partly hitting on the truth and partly the ability to make it shine through.

First you have to be able to read it. If it reads like oatmeal, you can only do so much to get through it. If it's full of platitudes and repetitions of old rules, that suggests a cast of mind that won't promise much. Obviously, you're more influenced by opinions that reveal an inquiring mind.

At the risk of oversimplifying, I suggest that the various thoughts expressed in these statements can be grouped into four categories. Interestingly, only one has the kind of technical, insider flavor that one might expect from members of an exclusive profession. This is the idea, appearing primarily in the first few comments, that good opinions follow certain rules of reasoning or interpretation. The others sound little different from what we might hear if we asked people how they would evaluate an essay or a friend's argument. The judges like to see arguments that obey logical principles or seem consistent with common sense. They are more inclined to respect carefully developed opinions than conclusory ones.[3] And even though they might have been expected to deny this, they admit that they can be swayed – or dissuaded – by another judge's writing style.

As always, the remarks of a relatively small group of judges can give only an indefinite sense of the importance of different influences. It would be rash to conclude that opinion characteristics regularly factor into judges' decisions. What we can safely say is that they sometimes do. This is still a significant statement. It offers an image of judicial decision making far different from the one most often presented in the literature, in which judges' responses are determined by the simple interaction of their own views and the facts and issues before them, perhaps moderated by strategic considerations about how others might react. Rather, like some studies of voting fluidity (Howard 1968 generally; Maltzman and Wahlbeck 1996:583), it suggests that judge's decisions are not preordained because their opinions are not fixed. Their views can be shaped by the opinions of judges who precede them, and shaped not only by demonstrations of erudition and technical skill but also by such everyday virtues as common sense, careful analysis, and good writing.

DECISIONAL DIFFICULTY AND STRENGTH OF INFLUENCES

One set of hypotheses has not yet been discussed. According to H2a, H3a, and H5a, the influence of other judges' attributes and actions

---

[3] Of course, an opinion can say too much, to the point that it arouses suspicions. As one judge said, "There are some opinions that are so opaque and convoluted, at a certain point I get the feeling they're straining over a gnat. It has to be simpler than what I'm reading, so I distrust what I'm reading."

should vary across judges and circumstances. These hypotheses follow from the assumption that judges wish to minimize the time spent deciding any one case (if for no other reason than to relieve caseload pressures). Relying on cues from others, rather than thinking everything out for themselves, should often be tempting, but it should be especially so when judges face particularly difficult issues or otherwise have doubts about their ability to handle them.

Concerned as I was with maintaining a natural flow to the interviews, I could not always probe these issues with much precision. In the course of discussing the factors influencing the treatment of precedents, I typically asked in a general way whether the influences were different in different types of cases. As a result, it is not always easy to relate individual statements to specific hypotheses. Note, too, that I did not ask specifically about the importance of a judge's length of experience, so there is no direct parallel to the quantitative analysis. Nevertheless, the judges' responses are useful for probing the basic logic of the hypotheses.

A few judges felt that the effects of colleagues' qualities and actions on their own behavior did not vary with the circumstances in which they found themselves.

[DK: What about fields where you are less comfortable?] These come up, where I don't know anything about the law there, but that does not have an impact on how willing I am to take the Second Circuit's word, I don't think.

The type of case might matter to a very small degree. I wouldn't draw a distinction. Maybe if a case were very arcane and complicated I might defer, but I usually try to think things through myself, no matter what the area.

Some others offered rather lukewarm endorsements of the notion that influences varied with circumstances. Because these came in response to my suggestions, they should not be weighted too heavily. For example:

First, we get far fewer antitrust cases than search and seizure. Yeah, I'd probably pay more attention to an antitrust case from Posner or Easterbrook than a search and seizure case from the Seventh Circuit.

Finally, a number of prompted responses carried greater conviction, and some judges even raised the point on their own. In the next group of quotations, the first three come from responses to unrelated questions (the third, very early in the interview).

There's some tendency to follow other circuits because that's the easy course. Also, sometimes it's the best course. It depends on the importance of the question: If it's minor, it's easier to follow; if it's monumental, you think, more than just follow.

Well, I think one big consideration is the degree to which judges have strong views on the subject involved. In a highly technical area, where judges are not likely to have strong feelings, I think there's a much greater tendency for a snow-ball effect. Once one case has been decided, it's easier for the others to go along than to take another position. I see this a lot. This sometimes makes a big body of bad law. That's where I've said I'll go against a number of other circuits.

I think all judges are products of their backgrounds, experiences, so there may be areas from which they come – where they have comfort, familiarity – that find a judge more willing to be firm in his position or take the lead in attempting to persuade others. In areas where a judge is not comfortable, I think there might be a tendency to let yourself be persuaded, listen to arguments, even be deferential (that may be too strong a word) to those who know more about the subject.

Yeah, I think in an area where I don't have much experience I would give a great deal of deference to a judge with much more experience than I have. Oh, yes.

Sure, I think that's true. As a practitioner and in other capacities, I learned a lot about utility regulation, so I figure I know more than the run of judges, so I give less weight to others' views than to mine.

Certainly where you're more confident in your own knowledge you're less likely to defer. But even in a case where you are confident, you still hesitate to start overruling others.

Judge: If I feel at home in a field I probably can trust my instincts quicker.
Clerk: It's pragmatic. Say you have an antitrust case with a very difficult issue. You would not intentionally defer, but as a matter of practicality if you have no context you're more likely to go along.

Although, as already noted, the remarks do not always speak clearly to a single hypothesis, both H3a (differential deference to expertise) and H5a (differential deference to circuit support) appear to be confirmed in more than one statement. More important, the remarks provide substantial support for the hypotheses as a group, demonstrating that judges' reliance on cues from colleagues varies with their own levels of comfort and confidence as they confront a legal question.

This is more evidence than we found in the quantitative analysis, and it is worth asking why. The most likely reason is that the quantitative analysis examined only one element of decisional difficulty, experience on the bench. Had it incorporated information about the nature of particular issues and judges' comfort with them, the results might have been clearer. However, it is also possible that, while real, the moderating effects of difficulty are too small or isolated to be detected in an analysis of just 300 cases.

DISCUSSION

The interviews have contributed to the investigation begun in Chapter 4 in four ways, providing a second set of hurdles for most of the hypotheses to clear, additional information about the relationships uncovered in the earlier chapter, evidence of relationships not found there, and a fuller picture of variation across judges. I will discuss each of these in turn.

The interviews had the potential either to undermine or reaffirm most of the findings of Chapter 4. For instance, it was quite conceivable that the judges would universally deny paying attention to, let alone being influenced by, the identity of an opinion's author. Had they done so, the results of the quantitative analysis would have been called into question. But they did not. As with all of the hypotheses tested through the interviews, supportive responses outnumbered negative ones by a wide margin.

In addition to reinforcing the statistical results, the judges' responses have also provided interpretations for the ambiguous results. One of the most elementary of statistical truths is that correlation does not imply causation. There were good theoretical reasons to believe that the statistical relationships found in Chapter 4 were at least partly causal in nature. Yet, for independent evidence of causality we had to look to the interviews, where, indeed, we found it.

Taking the findings from the interviews together with those from Chapter 4, we have very strong evidence that judges' reactions to colleagues' precedents are influenced by certain attributes of those colleagues and by the responses of other circuits to their rulings. There is somewhat less, though still solid, evidence that these effects are more important where the judges charged with a decision face greater difficulty in making it.

The interviews have also identified other influences on judges' behavior, suggesting that they can be moved by the qualities of the rules and opinions they consider and by other attributes of their colleagues aside from prestige and expertise. It is unclear how large a part such things play in judges' decisions, but they at least have the potential to affect outcomes in some cases.

Finally, just as the interviews have painted a more intricate picture of the influences at work, they direct our attention to another kind of complexity – differences among judges. Of course, it is well known that the specific *content* of goals and influences varies across judges. Proponents of attitudinal models of decision making have always operated on the assumption that judges differ with respect to basic values or policy preferences, while other scholars have shown how political environments can lead otherwise similar judges to act differently (e.g., Peltason 1961; Kuklinski and Stanga 1979; Hall 1992). Yet scholars have less often investigated variation in the *types* of goals motivating judges or the *kinds* of influences acting on them. This study joins those examining such issues as judges' role conceptions (e.g., Gibson 1978; Howard 1981; Scheb, Ungs, and Hayes 1989) and the institutional arrangements of court systems (e.g., Brace and Hall 1990) in doing so. One of the clearest lessons of the interviews is that not all judges place the same value on the same goals, nor are they all equally susceptible to the same influences.

I do not wish to make too much of this point. There are strong arguments in favor of parsimony, and more streamlined approaches to judicial decision making can easily be defended. Nevertheless, judges are idiosyncratic human beings, and it may be useful to keep this in mind, especially in the context of works like this one, where commonalities receive so much emphasis.

Complex creatures that they are, it is difficult to guess how judges might balance opportunities to make new law against their fealty toward or apprehensions about the Supreme Court. This issue is the subject of the next chapter.

6

Anticipating the Supreme Court

The evidence from Chapters 4 and 5 indicates that, when facing unsettled legal questions, circuit judges pay serious attention to and are often influenced by the decisions of other circuit judges. That being so, it might seem obvious that Supreme Court decisions would play a major role in their thinking. Circuit judges are expected to respect Supreme Court precedent, after all, and the Court, unlike their peers, has the power to reverse their decisions. Furthermore, as discussed in Chapter 1, researchers typically have found that higher court decisions have a substantial impact on the behavior of lower court judges. And while I noted in Chapter 1 that, strictly speaking, we cannot conclude that lower courts' respect for higher court precedents holds when they consider unsettled issues, there is not much reason to doubt that it does.

In the end, though, this line of reasoning yields little fruit, for the question I wish to answer is not whether circuit judges think carefully about Supreme Court precedents when deciding cases but whether they try to decide cases as they think the current Supreme Court would in their place. The distinction is important for two reasons. First, the Supreme Court's preferences may conflict with its precedents. Because nothing compels the Court to obey the logic of the precedents, the decision that it would be predicted to make may differ from the decision implied by the precedents. More important, by definition, Supreme Court precedents will rarely offer clear guidance to judges debating new legal rules. When they do not, circuit judges might attempt to anticipate the Supreme

Court, but they also might not, choosing instead to rely on their own judgment.[1]

As explained in Chapter 2, neither logic nor the existing research on lower court compliance enables us to say with confidence whether circuit judges attempt to anticipate the Supreme Court or, if they do, whether it is because they fear having their decisions reversed. Unfortunately, the interviews do not either, because I was not actively contemplating the questions when they were conducted. Nonetheless, the interviews did offer judges opportunities to raise the subject. Two queries in particular might have brought it to their minds: "How important would you say other judges' decisions are to you when you're deciding a case? Here I mean the Supreme Court, other panels of your own circuit, or other circuits, so if you feel we should distinguish between them on this and the next few questions, please do"; and "When you're writing an opinion, do you have any particular audience in mind?" Almost all of the judges noted that existing Supreme Court doctrine was binding on them, but interestingly, only six made any kind of reference to the Supreme Court's future behavior, at these or at any other points in the interview.

Two judges indicated that they sometimes practiced anticipatory decision making. Here are their comments.

One thing I have done that's very useful: If I have a real gray-area case, I go to history – look at the Supreme Court cases from the beginning. I watch the issue develop and try to decide what the Supreme Court would do in this case. It clears the cobwebs when you do that.

Of course, we're bound by the Supreme Court, but sometimes there's a question of whether to adhere rigidly to the Supreme Court case or find elbow room to go, not contrary to what the Supreme Court has said, but in a way the Court might disagree with if it heard the same case. [DK: Do you feel you should try to anticipate what the Supreme Court would do?] I like to try. Not all judges think that's proper.

Note the second judge's indication that some colleagues disagree with him.

Another judge offered a somewhat ambiguous statement:

---

[1] For an illustration of the distinction between following precedent and anticipating a higher court, see Romans's (1974) discussion of state supreme court reactions to the U.S. Supreme Court's *Escobedo* and *Miranda* decisions. He argues that the state courts obeyed the Court's precedents when they were clear and directly on point but refused to extend them in the direction the liberal Court clearly seemed to be going.

Obviously, if there's a Supreme Court case on point, we're bound by it. I have, on occasion, if it's an old Supreme Court case that's been chipped away at subsequently, decided in a way that keeps the law moving in that direction. More commonly, we face other circuit decisions. I think it's imperative that we discuss all relevant cases, especially ones from which we're departing. If we can bring fresh thought to the issue, this gives the Supreme Court help, and it needs all the help it can get – that's the percolation theory. Writing to the specific facts in our own case is sometimes very helpful to the Supreme Court in making a general rule.

His second sentence carries a hint of anticipatory behavior, but the rest of the comment suggests a greater desire to help the Supreme Court reach a sound decision than to predict which side it will eventually take.

Another judge also expressed the view that Supreme Court action could be influenced by what the court of appeals did. Here the judge's unwillingness to decide purely on the basis of what the higher court might do was made more explicit.

Once in a while you write for the Supreme Court, and sometimes you win. I had a recent case that was affirmed by the SC. I was absolutely convinced we decided it correctly but was by no means certain it would be affirmed. We wrote it with one justice in mind because we knew that one would see the issue this way. (We hoped others might too.)

Finally, two judges' observations imply that the Supreme Court's reaction is not uppermost in their minds.

The question of precedents is terribly complicated. If the Supreme Court has done something, then you go do it. If the Supreme Court just said something – it's not a rule, just reasoning – you give it what weight it's worth.

Of course, if there's a Supreme Court case, you go over it with a magnifying glass and don't always expand it – sometimes you hold the Court to its statement. We had a case recently where the question was whether our own precedent was still good law after the Supreme Court acted in another case. We took the position that the Supreme Court would have to be pretty clear and direct to overrule it.

That even two judges profess to decide some cases as they think the Supreme Court would is evidence that anticipatory decision making occurs in the courts of appeals. Yet it remains unclear whether enough judges engage in the practice often enough for it to have a significant impact on circuit court law making. As for the possibility that anticipatory behavior is driven by the fear of being reversed by the Supreme Court, very little information is available from the surveys. With the minor exception of the judge who wrote an opinion with one justice in mind, none of the two dozen judges said anything about how the Supreme Court's potential reactions affected their own decisions. In a sense, their omissions count as evidence – if fear of reversal were important to judges, we might have expected more of them to bring it up spontaneously, but not too much should be made of this point.

RESEARCH STRATEGY

The methodological approach of this chapter is a bit unusual. Traditionally, as in Chapter 4, the burden of proof lies with the researcher; hypotheses can be considered supported only if the evidence in their favor is highly convincing. The traditional approach helps to counteract the researcher's presumed bias and allows the accumulation of knowledge to proceed in a more coherent way. New findings – especially those challenging existing understandings – are not accepted easily, only to be discarded a few studies later. But these considerations do not apply to the present investigation. For one thing, I have not taken sides. More important, no answer clearly represents the conventional wisdom. Hence, there is no reason to give one side or the other an advantage. Instead, I will present a more balanced analysis, bringing to bear as much evidence as I can accumulate and then simply observing which side is favored by the weight of the evidence. I will conduct multiple tests of each possibility, using several different measures of key concepts. When an initially interesting result is uncovered, I will gather enough information about it to permit a considered judgment of its significance.

The rest of the chapter is divided into two main sections. The first focuses on circuit judges' attempts to decide a case as the Supreme Court would. I begin by setting out the basic logic of the approach, continue with a description of the dependent variable and control variables, and end with a series of analyses, each with a somewhat different version of the critical independent variable. The second section takes up the issue of judges' fear of reversal. In a single analysis with multiple indicators, I test whether the presence of factors increasing the probability of Supreme Court review influences the judges' decisions. This analysis simultaneously provides an additional test of anticipatory behavior.

MEASURES

We can imagine that judges wishing to predict how the Supreme Court would decide an issue might look for signs in the language and logic of

Court opinions on similar subjects. A researcher attempting to measure anticipatory behavior might begin with the same signs and determine whether circuit judges make decisions in accordance with those signs. However, clear signs probably appear only infrequently, and the task of identifying them would be too labor intensive to allow for analysis of more than just a few issues. For this study, I adopt a broader approach. Rather than focus on individual legal questions, I compare the ideological direction of circuit court decisions with indicators of ideological leanings in the Supreme Court.

As noted in Chapter 2, the evidence that ideology plays a role in Supreme Court decisions is overwhelming. Circuit judges are doubtless aware of this and could be expected to take the Court's ideological position into account when trying to predict its responses. Even if they do not and instead focus on issue-specific indicators of the Court's views, over a number of cases those indicators should reflect the Court's ideology. Either way, if circuit judges are engaging in anticipatory decision making, we should see a correspondence between ideological tendencies in the Supreme Court and the ideological direction of their own decisions.

The key independent variable – the Supreme Court's ideological position – is difficult to measure with precision. To ensure a thorough and fair search for evidence of anticipatory decision making, I will generate several different measures and test them in turn. The discussion of these measures will wait until the dependent variable and control variables have been introduced, so that confusion can be kept to a minimum.

The dependent variable, CONSERVATIVE, is the ideological direction of the circuit court decision: 0 = liberal; 1 = conservative. For the cases examined in Chapter 4, constructing it requires only a simple modification of ADOPT, the dependent variable from that chapter. A liberal decision is either an adoption of a liberal rule or rejection of a conservative one; a conservative decision is an adoption of a conservative rule or rejection of a liberal one. But there is no reason to restrict the analysis to the Chapter 4 cases. The potential response of the Supreme Court could influence the first judges to announce a rule, not just those who confront it later. Therefore, the initial case in each series is also included in the analysis of anticipatory decisions. For these cases, CONSERVATIVE equals 1 if the announced rule is conservative, 0 if it is liberal.

Because the dependent variable is directly related to adoption, the same independent variables that affect adoption should be included in the present analysis, again slightly modified. Thus, now the simple measure of judges' ideology suffices, where before it had to be combined with an indicator of rule ideology to create a measure of ideological distance. IDEOLOGY is the median ideology score of the judges on the panel; it ranges from 1 (liberal) to 5 (conservative).

Some of the other transformations are a bit more complicated. For instance, the measure of the prestige of the rule's creator now becomes PRESTIGE-C. For all cases except initial (rule-announcing) ones, PRESTIGE-C is equal to PRESTIGE if the rule being considered is conservative. (Because, by definition, adoption of a conservative rule is a conservative decision, for conservative rules the effect of the first judge's prestige on CONSERVATIVE is the same as its effect on ADOPT.) PRESTIGE-C is equal to −1 times PRESTIGE when a liberal rule is at issue, because here the force of prestige works against a conservative decision. For initial cases, PRESTIGE-C equals 0, since the judge's own prestige should not affect her decision.

The variables for the first judge's expertise, the presence of dissent in the initial case, the previous rulings of one's own circuit, and the interaction term for seniority and prestige are transformed into EXPERTS-C, DISSENT-C, OWNCIRC-C, and SENPRES-C in precisely the same way. The calculation of CIRCUITS-RC, which measures support for the conservative position among the circuits already addressing the issue, follows the procedure outlined in Chapter 4 for the CIRCUITS residuals. ANT, SS, and SENIORITY are unaltered, because they can affect the ideological direction of decisions directly, not just through adoption decisions. With the exception of SENIORITY, DISSENT-C, and SENPRES-C, each variable is expected to have a positive effect on the probability of a conservative decision. The predicted signs for DISSENT-C and SENPRES-C are negative; no sign is predicted for SENIORITY.

ANALYSIS OF ANTICIPATORY DECISION MAKING

Membership Replacement

The first measure of the focal independent variable, the Supreme Court's ideological leanings, is based on the Court's membership. As departing justices are replaced by appointees thought to be more liberal or conservative, expectations about the Court's future decisions should change accordingly. One way of measuring membership change is to establish a baseline measure that changes with each new appointment to the Court, typically according to the party of the appointee or appointing president (see, e.g., Segal 1984; George and Epstein 1992). However, in the period studied here, the likely consequences of membership change were typically not clear. In only two cases were justices replaced by others thought to be ideologically distant from them. William Brennan and Thurgood Marshall were both succeeded by men who seemed to be substantially more conservative than they – David Souter and Clarence Thomas, respectively. While it is difficult to say how circuit court judges should have reacted to the other appointments, if they attempted to anticipate the reaction of the Supreme Court and based their predictions of its response on the Court's membership, conservative decisions should have become more common after 1990 and 1991, other things being equal.

To test for these effects, I create two dummy variables. The first, SOUTER, takes the value 0 before 1990 (the year of Souter's appointment) and 1 from 1990 on; the other, THOMAS, is scored as 0 before 1991 (the year Thomas was appointed) and 1 from 1991 on. Both should have positive effects. Because the dependent variable is dichotomous, I again employ probit. Probability and confidence estimates are again obtained through the program created by Tomz, Wittenberg, and King.

Table 6.1 contains the results from the first probit, which includes the control variables and the first Supreme Court membership variable, SOUTER. While the other substantive variables perform about as expected, the coefficient for SOUTER is quite small and incorrectly signed. There is no evidence that circuit judges responded to Brennan's retirement and Souter's appointment by making more conservative decisions. Nor did the replacement of Marshall with Thomas appear to affect their behavior as expected. In fact, when the variable THOMAS is substituted for SOUTER, the coefficient is again negative and now considerably larger (−.206; standard error = .198).

Supreme Court Decisions, All Cases

Any conclusions at this point would be premature. The results may have been distorted by the heavy concentration of environmental cases (typically decided in a liberal direction) in the last several years of the period, although the inclusion of the field dummies in the equation makes this explanation less plausible. More important, as measures of ideological tendencies on the Supreme Court, the variables may be too simplistic.

TABLE 6.1. *Probit of conservative decision on* SOUTER *and control variables*

	CONSERVATIVE		
	Coefficient	Standard Error	p (*one-tailed)
SOUTER	−.026	.186	N/A
IDEOLOGY	.245	.064	<.001*
PRESTIGE-C	.682	.183	<.001*
EXPERTS-C	.390	.164	.009*
DISSENT-C	−.647	.336	.027*
CIRCUITS-C	.305	.065	<.001*
OWNCIRC-C	1.037	.204	<.001*
ANT	.668	.234	.004
SS	.955	.208	<.001
SENIORITY	.011	.013	.408
SENPRES-C	−.017	.010	.052*
Constant	−1.418	.326	
	Wald Chi-sq.	85.67	
	$P <$	.0001	
	$N =$	381	

Note: SOUTER = 0 before 1990 and 1 from 1990 on.

Changes in the Supreme Court's membership are easy to track, but we can certainly imagine circuit judges' expending greater effort to read trends in Supreme Court thinking. In particular, they might pay attention to the ideological direction of the Court's recent decisions. To test for this possibility, I employ Spaeth's U.S. Supreme Court Database to generate a measure of the percentage of full-opinion cases decided in a conservative direction by the Court.

Changes in this percentage from one term to another reflect more than just turnover in personnel. Ideological trends could also be shaped by changes in justices' attitudes, differences in the way individual justices' votes combine to produce a decision for the Court, and, most important, the types of cases the Court decides.

The last two factors might require some explanation. Each Supreme Court decision is reached through an aggregation of individual justices' votes. If some decisions are supported by only narrow majorities, small changes in the distribution of liberal and conservative votes across cases could produce very different sets of outcomes. For that reason, individual conservatism rates do not translate directly into a conservatism rate for the Court. Even if each justice cast the same percentage of liberal votes for two consecutive terms, the percentage of liberal decisions by the Court could rise or fall from one to the next.[2]

Leaving aggregation effects aside, the same judicial preferences could yield different court liberalism scores as the issues before the Court change. For instance, suppose the claims reaching the Court became generally more conservative while the preferences of the Court's members stayed the same. A greater number of conservative claims should now be rejected as too extreme; at the same time, "liberal" claims, now more moderate, should be more palatable. The result would be a higher liberalism score for the Court.

In constructing a measure of the Supreme Court's ideological movement, I wish to capture the effects of aggregation, because these represent real changes in the Court's output, but eliminate the merely apparent changes due to shifting issues. (Unlike the former, the latter should not influence circuit judges' thinking.) To accomplish this, I adopt a variant of the technique developed by Baum (1988). The technique operates on the assumption that each justice's ideology is essentially stable, experiencing only small, nonsystematic fluctuations from year to year. Once the assumption is made, common movement in judges' voting scores can be attributed only to issue change. Thus, measuring the common movement generates an indicator of issue change. For example, if all of the justices' voting scores were to become 4 percent more conservative, it would have to be because the parties' claims became 4 percent more liberal. Once this value is used to adjust the Court's conservatism score, any differences that remain from year to year reflect either membership change or aggregation effects.

The assumption of ideological constancy for individual justices is almost certainly not entirely correct. Nevertheless, it is sufficiently realistic, and issue change is sufficiently important, that the adjusted Court scores provide a more accurate gauge of its ideological leanings than unadjusted ones.

---

[2] Imagine a situation in which the Court decides one hundred cases in each of two years. The Court's conservatism rate is the same for the first ninety cases in each year. In the other ten, three justices always vote liberally, three always vote conservatively, and three split their votes evenly between the sides. Only the last three justices need to be considered further. Suppose that in one year Justice A casts a conservative vote in the first five cases and a liberal vote in the last five, Justice B alternates liberal and conservative votes, and Justice C casts a liberal votes in cases 2, 4, 7, 9, and 10, a conservative vote in the rest. The result would be a conservative court decision in seven of the ten cases. Simply reversing the order of Justice B's decisions the next year would produce seven *liberal decisions*, or a four-percentage-point decline in the Court's conservatism rate.

For this study, the adjustment works as follows. Beginning with the October 1983 term, the conservatism score (percent conservative decisions) for each justice who also served in the previous term is subtracted from his or her conservatism score in the previous term. The mean of these differences is calculated and then added to the Court's actual conservatism score for the later term, yielding the adjusted score.[3]

It is impossible to say with certainty how far back in time circuit judges look for trends, but it seems reasonable to assume that they concentrate on recent decisions. I begin by matching courts of appeals decisions in a particular year with those decided by the Supreme Court in the term leading into that year. For example, for 1994 circuit court cases, the variable takes on the value of the Supreme Court's adjusted conservatism score in the October 1993 term, which runs from October 1993 to June 1994. I then test for the effect of this variable on the likelihood of a conservative decision in a circuit court, again including in the equation the (modified) variables from the adoption equation. If circuit judges are anticipating the Supreme Court's response by taking its recent movement into account, the coefficient should be positive. In fact, it is −.004 (standard error = .024). Supreme Court conservatism in the preceding term appears to have no effect on circuit court decisions.

Perhaps the one-year span is too brief to allow circuit judges to see clearly what is happening at the Supreme Court. To be sure, we can replace the one-term Supreme Court conservatism score with one encompassing the previous term as well (so that now the score for 1994 cases is based on Supreme Court decisions in the 1992 and 1993 terms). This measure fares no better (coefficient = −.006, standard error = .028).

Supreme Court Decisions, Field Specific

Measures based on general conservatism scores in the Supreme Court, while more sophisticated than those based on appointments, can still be further refined. As noted in Chapter 4, judicial ideology is probably best understood as multidimensional. To gauge trends in the Supreme Court, circuit judges may look not at general conservatism but at ideological

---

[3] For example, if the mean difference in conservatism scores for the justices serving in both the 1988 and 1989 terms is −5 percent, this indicates that the claims reaching the Court in the 1989 term were more conservative (causing the justices' votes to appear more liberal). The Court's conservatism score for the 1989 term is increased by five percentage points to reflect this change.

TABLE 6.2. *Corrected percent conservative of full-opinion decisions rendered by the Supreme Court in all cases, economic cases, and criminal cases, 1983–94 terms*

Term	All Cases	Economic	Criminal
1983	59.69	56.87	80.17
1984	54.83	56.31	74.66
1984	58.17	58.64	81.26
1986	58.10	64.41	80.13
1987	53.17	46.16	71.78
1988	58.34	51.82	84.95
1989	55.72	45.67	84.76
1990	61.05	57.20	87.39
1991	61.56	55.96	80.68
1992	65.61	59.65	89.93
1993	63.91	59.81	82.80
1994	62.19	55.11	78.39

trends in specific fields. The Supreme Court database classifies issues narrowly enough for us to group antitrust, search and seizure, and environmental decisions separately. However, the Court hears so few cases in each field (seldom as many as five per year; none in some years) that the change in the conservatism rate from year to year is not meaningful. As an alternative, I turn to intermediate classifications available in the database, repeating the scoring process described above, but now separately for economic issues and criminal issues. Instead of the Supreme Court's conservatism score being the same for all cases in a particular year, the score for search and seizure cases in that year is calculated from the Court's criminal cases, while the score for antitrust and environmental cases is derived from the Court's economic cases (see Table 6.2).

If we again begin with scores from the Supreme Court term leading into the year of the circuit case, we finally find a result in the predicted direction. The probit coefficient for the Supreme Court measure is .012, with a standard error of .012 ($p = .174$, one-tailed). Such a lonely and rather feeble success does little to bolster the proposition that circuit judges engage in anticipatory decision making. Still, in the interest of full and fair testing, we can explore this result in greater depth by returning to the probability estimation procedure described in Chapter 4. First, all variables are set to their median values and, to save space, the field is set to search and seizure (there is very little difference across fields). Then the Supreme Court variable is changed from its tenth percentile value to its median and from its median to its ninetieth percentile value. For each change, the resulting difference in the probability of a conservative decision is calculated. The first change results in an estimated .03 increase in the probability (standard deviation = .03; 95 percent confidence interval = −.03 to .08). For the change from the median to the ninetieth percentile value, the results are .02 (.03), −.03 to .07. To put these in perspective, consider the results for the same transformations in the circuit panel's ideology: .11 (.04), .04 to .19 and .05 (.02), .02 to .08. The estimated effects of the Supreme Court's conservatism are quite a bit smaller and less precise. Our best guess is that they are slightly positive, but there is almost as much chance that they are null or negative.

When a two-year measure of field-specific Court scores is substituted, the results are weaker. In fact, the coefficient is incorrectly signed (−.002, standard error = .019). Incidentally, the poor results cannot be attributed to my transformations of the Supreme Court's conservatism scores. If I substitute the Court's unadjusted conservatism scores, they perform much worse; for example, the coefficient for the one-year field-specific measure is less than .001, with a standard error of .012.

CONSERVATIVE DECISIONS AND THE FEAR OF REVERSAL

To this point, the evidence seems to run heavily against anticipatory decision making. However, one could argue that the set of variables included in the equation is masking an important effect. There is more variation in the measure of Supreme Court conservatism between search and seizure, antitrust, and environmental cases than within the fields. But with fields of law controlled for through dummy variables, this variation is effectively removed from the analysis. The coefficient for Supreme Court liberalism reflects only the effects of changes within a field, not differences across fields. To illustrate, when the field dummies are removed from the equation, the effect of field-specific Supreme Court conservatism is far greater: coefficient = .023; standard error = .006. With other variables held at their medians, moving from the tenth percentile value to the ninetieth percentile value of Supreme Court conservatism results in about a .34 increase in the probability of a conservative circuit court decision (standard deviation = .09). These numbers suggest that greater Supreme Court conservatism in antitrust and criminal cases is reflected in greater conservatism in those types of cases in the courts of appeals.

As dramatic as they are, though, the numbers cannot tell us whether the circuit courts' conservatism in search and seizure and antitrust cases results from judges' conscious choices to decide cases as they think the Supreme Court would. They could just as easily arise from faithful adherence to existing Supreme Court precedent. Or they might simply reflect litigants' costs and benefits. Antitrust plaintiffs and, even more, criminal defendants usually have less to lose and more to gain from appeals than their opponents do and so may bring weaker cases to the circuit courts. In fact, it was for these very reasons that the field dummies were originally included in the equation as control variables. Nevertheless, because this is the first evidence we have encountered that gives even tenuous support to the anticipation argument, it warrants further consideration.

While there is no way to determine for sure whether conservatism in search and seizure and antitrust comes from anticipatory decision making, we can look for additional evidence with a test slightly different from those already used. This test focuses on search and seizure and antitrust cases and asks whether circuit judges are more likely to make conservative decisions when the threat of reversal by the Supreme Court is greater. If the judges were reaching conservative decisions for some reason other than a desire to decide as the Court would, there would be no reason for their behavior to vary with the Court's likely response. Therefore, were we to observe such a relationship, it would count as persuasive evidence of anticipatory behavior. A finding that the threat of reversal had no effect would not allow us to dismiss outright the possibility that we are seeing anticipatory behavior, since such behavior could arise from other causes, but it would certainly weigh against it. Naturally, either finding would also help answer the second key question motivating this part of the research – to what extent the fear of reversal drives circuit judges' decisions.

Operationalizing the Threat of Reversal

The investigation proceeds from an elementary observation: Even if a circuit court decision is appealed, it can be reversed only if the Supreme Court – which enjoys almost complete discretion – agrees to review it. Therefore, if fear of reversal plays a part in circuit judges' decision making, its influence should be stronger in cases that the High Court is more likely to select for review. Following this logic, I draw on the literature on certiorari to identify factors increasing the probability of Court review and then ask whether the presence of those factors affects circuit court decisions.

The task of operationalizing those factors is complicated by temporal perspectives. In deciding whether to hear a case, the Supreme Court can consider circumstances appearing before, after, or at the time of the circuit court's decision. For obvious reasons, certiorari researchers adopt the same point of view. As a consequence, the literature points to some factors that simply cannot be known to circuit judges before they hand down their decision. For example, researchers have repeatedly shown that the Supreme Court is more likely to grant certiorari if the federal government, through the solicitor general, asks it to (e.g., Tanenhaus et al. 1963; Caldeira and Wright 1988; Perry 1991). Circuit judges cannot react to this signal, because it does not occur until after they have decided their case. Thus, some possible influences on the Supreme Court must be excluded from an analysis of circuit court decisions. Others can be included, but only with modifications.

One of the most important influences on Supreme Court certiorari decisions is the presence of intercircuit conflict. Not only do the Supreme Court's own rules state that disagreement among lower courts makes an issue more certworthy; empirical evidence shows that the Court takes this rule seriously (Ulmer 1984; Caldeira and Wright 1988; Perry 1991). From the perspective of the circuit judges about to decide a case, there are four possibilities: Either (1) all previous circuits have decided the issue in a conservative direction; (2) all have decided it liberally; (3) the circuits are in conflict; or (4) no other circuit has yet addressed the issue. If the circuits are in conflict, the probability of Supreme Court review is already heightened. In the situations where previous circuits are in unanimous agreement, the deciding court has the potential to create a conflict – in the first scenario through a liberal decision, in the second, through a conservative one. Assuming, as we are, that the Supreme Court is likely to decide in a conservative way, the circuit judges should be reluctant to create conflict through a liberal decision; doing so would increase the probability of both review and reversal. Breaking with a liberal consensus should increase the probability of review but not the danger of reversal, so the consensus should not have much of an effect on judges' thinking.

Thus, compared with the situation where it is the first to address an issue, the presence of situations (1) or (3) should make a conservative decision significantly more attractive to a panel of judges attempting to avoid reversal by a conservative Supreme Court. Situation (2) might make a conservative decision less attractive, but its effect should be quite small. To see if this is true, I create three dummy variables, CONFLICT, UNANCON, and UNANLIB, corresponding to situations (3), (1), and (2), respectively. The omitted category serving as a baseline for comparison is situation (4).

The Supreme Court is also more favorably disposed to hear cases presenting issues of real consequence – those affecting more than just the immediate parties. One very important way an outsider can signal interest in a case is through participation as an amicus curiae, or friend of the court. Caldeira and Wright (1988) found that when amici participated at the certiorari stage, either in support of or in opposition to a petition, the Supreme Court was more likely to grant the petition. This finding can be interpreted in different ways: It may be, as Caldeira and Wright suspect, that amicus briefs alert the justices to a case's significance; alternatively, since outsiders are generally highly selective in their participation, amicus participation may simply serve as a proxy for case importance without telling the Court anything it did not already know. Either way, the logic can be extended to the circuit courts. Of course, the judges could not be sure how potential amici would react to a decision not yet rendered. However, because amicus participation in the courts of appeals is uncommon, they could reasonably assume that amici appearing before them would continue to participate if the case were appealed. Even if they did not assume this, amicus participation, as already noted, may be an indicator of case significance.

The simplest way to measure amicus curiae participation is through a dummy variable coded 1 if one or more amicus briefs is submitted to the court of appeals, 0 otherwise. However, such filings are so rare – occurring in only 22 of the 240 cases analyzed here – that the test might be too stringent. Accordingly, I construct a second dummy variable scored as 1 if there is amicus participation in the case itself or any of the other cases involving the same legal issue. The second variable is labeled AMICUS-I (for "issue") to distinguish it from the first, AMICUS-C (for "case").

Finally, even if some of the criteria the Supreme Court employs remain constant, the number (O'Brien 1997) and subject matter (Pacelle 1991) of the cases heard at the Court vary greatly over time. The number of cases the Court hears in an area could be read as an indicator of its interest in that area. If circuit judges aim to avoid reversal, they should feel safer making decisions in areas where the Court has been hearing few cases, more constrained in those areas where it has been more active. To measure Supreme Court attention to different fields, I return to the Supreme Court Database and separately count the Court's decisions in antitrust and search and seizure cases. For each circuit court case, the variable CERT takes on the value of the number of cases in the relevant field of law decided by the Supreme Court in the term leading into the current year and the term before that (two terms being chosen in order to provide large enough numbers for meaningful comparison).

Results

The most straightforward way to investigate the impact of these variables is to return to the basic equation from this chapter, but this time analyzing only search and seizure and antitrust cases, omitting the measures of Supreme Court ideology, and including the new variables. If circuit court conservatism is caused at least in part by the desire to avoid reversal, conservative decisions should be particularly likely when the factors increasing the likelihood of Supreme Court review are present; that is, the certiorari-related variables should have positive effects on the probability of conservative decisions.

Results are presented in Tables 6.3 (model coefficients) and 6.4 (predicted probabilities). They provide no support for the conclusion that circuit judges are moved by the fear of reversal. Signs that the Supreme Court is interested in a particular field of law, as measured by its activity in that area (CERT), have no effect at all on the likelihood that circuit judges will decide cases in that field in a conservative direction. The negative sign for CONFLICT, if taken seriously, would indicate that when other circuits have split on the proper resolution of an issue, the court now deciding it and facing an increased probability of review by a conservative Supreme Court is more likely to issue a liberal decision. The presence of an amicus brief somewhere in the line of cases at least operates in the right direction, but its effect is negligible. (If, instead, the case-specific amicus variable, AMICUS-C, is substituted for AMICUS-I, its coefficient is incorrectly signed.)

Only the presence of a unanimous line of conservative decisions (UNANCON) has anything like a significant effect on circuit judges' decisions. But this one finding cannot save the proposition that circuit judges are acting to avoid reversal. As the results for UNANLIB show, the presence of a unanimous line of *liberal* decisions has a far greater impact.

TABLE 6.3. *Probit of conservative decision on factors making Supreme Court review more likely and control variables*

	CONSERVATIVE		
	Coefficient	Standard Error	p (*one-tailed)
AMICUS-I	.109	.207	.300*
CERT	.002	.023	.467*
CONFLICT	−.120	.304	N/A
UNANCON	.452	.301	.067*
UNANLIB	−.905	.445	.021*
IDEOLOGY	.219	.075	.002*
PRESTIGE-C	.534	.191	.003*
EXPERTS-C	.403	.264	.063*
DISSENT-C	−.707	.333	.017*
CIRCUITS-C	−.003	.104	N/A
OWNCIRC-C	.964	.202	<.001*
SENIORITY	.016	.017	.337
SENPRES-C	−.028	.010	.004*
ANT	−.225	.226	.319
Constant	−.437	.540	
	Wald Chi-sq	82.68	
	$P<$	.0001	
	$N=$	240	

Note: AMICUS-I = 1 if an amicus curiae brief is filed in any of the cases involving the issue being decided, 0 otherwise. CERT is equal to the number of cases in that area of law heard by the Supreme Court in the previous two terms. CONFLICT = 1 if a circuit conflict already exists at the time a court confronts an issue, 0 otherwise. UNANCON = 1 if all preceding circuits have decided the issue in a conservative direction, 0 otherwise.

The Supreme Court's predilections were clearly conservative, and judges fearing reversal should have been much more reluctant to break with a conservative consensus than with a liberal one. The results suggest the opposite.

LANGUAGE IN THE OPINIONS

The results to this point have told a consistent story. Nevertheless, before conclusions are drawn it may be wise to consider one last source of evidence. If judges do try to decide cases as they think the Supreme Court would, we might find evidence of this in their written opinions. To search for this evidence, I have closely examined the relevant discussion in each of the cases where one of this study's new rules was first announced.

TABLE 6.4. *Estimated changes in probability of conservative decision, antitrust and search and seizure cases*

Variable	Value Change	Mean Change in Probability	Standard Deviation	95% Confidence Interval
Antitrust				
CERT	3 → 16	.01	.11	−.19/.22
AMICUS-I	0 → 1	.03	.07	−.11/.16
CONFLICT	0 → 1	−.05	.11	−.27/.17
UNANCON	0 → 1	.14	.09	−.05/.31
UNANLIB	0 → 1	−.33	.15	−.01/−.60
Search and seizure				
CERT	3 → 16	.01	.10	−.16/.21
AMICUS-I	0 → 1	.03	.06	−.10/.15
CONFLICT	0 → 1	−.04	.10	−.23/.16
UNANCON	0 → 1	.12	.08	−.04/.29
UNANLIB	0 → 1	−.33	.16	−.01/−.62

Note: For CERT, probability changes are estimated for changes from its tenth percentile score to its ninetieth percentile score. For all calculations, all other variables are held at their medians.

(The choice to concentrate on the initial cases was based on the supposition that anticipatory decision making is most likely to be found in those cases, where there is no persuasive precedent from another circuit to be considered.)

Counterevidence is scarce. In forty of the eighty-one discussions, references to the Supreme Court are cursory at best, with the Court not cited at all in eighteen of them. More than half the discussions (forty-two) contain no references to Supreme Court cases decided in the preceding five years; in only twenty-five of the remaining thirty-nine are the Court's decisions addressed in more than a line or two of text. Because cursory analyses of Supreme Court precedents and analyses in which recent cases are not cited cannot support inferences of anticipatory decision making, only a quarter to a third of the cases are left as credible candidates.

Among these cases, there is little in the judges' language to suggest attempts to predict what the Supreme Court would do. When judges engage in serious discussions of Supreme Court cases, they usually couch those discussions in terms of the applicability of precedents or the principles that can be derived from them. The case of *Business Electronics Corp. v. Sharp Electronics Corp.*, 780 F.2d 1212 (5th Cir. 1986), provides an example of a typical discussion. A recent Supreme Court decision is addressed at some length, but only after an extensive consideration of logic and circuit court cases. Moreover, it is introduced in this way: "The Supreme Court's recent decision in *Monsanto Co. v. Spray-Rite Service Corp.* further confirms that this circuit's divergence from the *Cernuto* rationale is correct" (1217, citations omitted). The circuit judges do not cite *Monsanto* as evidence of where the Supreme Court is moving. In fact, they do not even seem to rely on it to reach their conclusion; rather, they invoke it to buttress a conclusion already reached.

In only three cases (involving four rules) have I found language indicating that circuit judges were attempting to predict the Supreme Court's behavior or, at least, were paying close attention to trends in its thinking. Of these cases, one – *Jack Walters and Sons Corp. v. Morton Building*, 737 F.2d 698 (7th Cir. 1984) – cannot be taken seriously as an instance of anticipatory decision making. The opinion in this antitrust case devotes some space to pro-defendant trends in Supreme Court decisions before announcing a rule that favors defendants. But the opinion was written by Judge Posner, whose strongly held and forcefully asserted positions on antitrust policy were developed prior to the Supreme Court decisions cited in his opinion. It is reasonable to suppose that Posner saw the trend in the Supreme Court as justifying his ruling, but it is very hard to believe that he decided as he did because he thought the Supreme Court would have decided that way in his place.

There is less reason to doubt that Supreme Court trends influenced circuit judges' thinking in a second case, *U.S. v. Torres*, 926 F.2d 321 (3rd Cir. 1991). In its analysis of the exclusionary rule's application to sentencing decisions under the federal sentencing guidelines, the court wrote, "The Supreme Court, therefore, has veered from an absolutist approach and instead has restricted the rule's application 'to those areas where its remedial objectives are thought most efficaciously served'" (323, citations omitted). But the cases cited begin back in the 1970s and run only until 1984, several years before the circuit court decision. Thus, here, too, there is no adequate basis to conclude that the judges attempted to anticipate the Supreme Court.

One case provides clear evidence of anticipatory decision making. In *Smith Steel Casting Co. v. Brock*, 800 F.2d 1329 (1986), judges of the Fifth Circuit wrote the following:

Although the Supreme Court has never ruled upon the applicability of the exclusionary rule to proceedings before OSHRC, we are placed by *Lopez-Mendoza* in the position of trying to determine what the Supreme Court would hold if confronted with the issue. Based on Justice O'Connor's reasoning ... we hold pursuant to *Lopez-Mendoza* that the exclusionary rule does not extend to OSHA enforcement actions for purposes of correcting violations of occupational safety and health standards. Further, again under Justice O'Connor's reasoning in *Lopez-Mendoza*, we hold that the exclusionary rule applies where the object is to assess penalties against the employer for past violations of OSHA regulations, unless, under the reasoning announced in *Leon*, the good faith exception can be applied to the Secretary's actions in obtaining the tainted evidence. (1334)

In the end, this analysis of the judges' opinions suggests that the Supreme Court's potential actions may sometimes enter into circuit judges' thinking but are not a major influence on their decisions. In this it is consistent with the findings from the rest of this chapter.

DISCUSSION

Vertical Dynamics

As noted at the beginning of the chapter, scholars have amassed compelling evidence that lower court judges frequently subordinate their own views to those of higher courts. Sometimes their own views win out, however. The temptation to decide freely must be especially great when they are presented with issues not yet decided by the higher court. Not only can they see a chance to shape policy in a meaningful way, but they cannot tell with certainty how the higher court would decide the issue, even if they wished to know. Judges who feel duty bound to follow clear directives from above may be more comfortable following their own judgment where the higher court has not ruled, even if they suspect that it would not share their judgment.

In this chapter, I have tried to determine whether circuit court deference to the Supreme Court carries over into these types of cases and, if so, whether this happens because circuit judges wish to avoid reversal. Employing a variety of measures and approaches, and interpreting the results generously, I have still found only a little evidence that anticipatory decision making occurs and essentially no evidence that it results from fear of reversal.

Of course, the results should not be taken as conclusive. First, they cover only three fields of law over a twelve-year period. Signals from the

Supreme Court might be clearer or circuit judges might be more attuned to them in other fields and other times. Second, the measures of Supreme Court trends are somewhat crude. This strikes me as appropriate. I think the measures accurately reflect the only cues available to circuit judges in many cases. Furthermore, as already noted, cues coming from the Supreme Court should reflect its ideological leanings. So even if circuit judges were following cues researchers could not observe, we would still find a relationship between the ideological direction of their decisions and the ideology of the Supreme Court. Still, in some cases, specific language or doctrinal trends in Supreme Court opinions might point clearly toward particular answers, and scholars able to identify such cases might find more evidence of anticipatory behavior in them.

Third, I was able to include only indirect indicators of the likelihood of reversal, leaving open the possibility that the threat of reversal mattered in cases where I could not identify it. Finally, the behavioral alternatives considered here are limited to adoption or rejection of a particular legal rule. A more nuanced approach – perhaps considering things like the specific language of the rules or a court's treatment of additional substantive or procedural issues in a case – might have revealed other forms of anticipatory behavior.

Nevertheless, because the tests are at least reasonably fair and the results obtained from them are clear and highly consistent, we are justified in taking the results and their implications seriously. The results speak most directly to the question of how circuit judges approach their opportunities to shape the federal law. They do not allow us to conclude that anticipatory decision making is nonexistent – especially in light of Reddick and Benesh's (2000) findings – but they strongly suggest that it is rare. Circuit judges seem to welcome and take advantage of chances to exercise their own judgment. They may very well take the Supreme Court's precedents seriously, but their decisions on unsettled issues appear to be made with little regard for what the Court might do in their place or how it might react to their decisions.

This point will be developed at greater length in the next chapter. For now, though, it is important to note that this conclusion is not necessarily inconsistent with other scholars' findings of circuit court responsiveness to ideological change in the Supreme Court. Those studies covered the whole range of cases, not just those involving unsettled issues of law. My findings suggest that had routine and nonroutine cases been examined separately, substantial responsiveness might have been observed only among the former.

This point links to one first raised in Chapter 1. As I noted there, evidence of responsiveness can result from attempts to decide cases as a higher court would, but it also can result from nothing more than adherence to precedent across a large number of cases and legal issues. The findings here imply that the latter explanation is closer to the truth.

Judges' Motivations

The apparent difference between unsettled and routine circuit court cases – much stronger Supreme Court influence in the latter than in the former – is still more interesting for what it suggests about circuit judges' motivations. If we ask why judges might generally shade their decisions in favor of the Supreme Court's views, two answers seem most plausible. First, they might do so because they think it right – perhaps they define legal soundness to include deference to the higher court. Second, they might do so because they wish to avoid having their decisions reversed on appeal.

If the second answer is correct, the next question is why judges would fear reversal. There are a number of possibilities, but one is particularly important here: Reversal interferes with judges' pursuit of their policy preferences. This possibility has received serious attention, especially in recent years, as seen in the work of Cameron (1993) and colleagues (Songer, Segal, and Cameron 1994; Cameron, Segal, and Songer 2000) and McNollgast (1995).

Determining whether fear of reversal, a concern for legally sound decision making, or some other consideration best explains lower court deference would tell us a good deal about the relative influence of the Supreme Court and lower courts on legal policy. The Supreme Court's ability to control the development and application of the law across the country is substantially more limited and less certain to the extent that compliance arises from fear of reversal rather than from the urge to perform one's job well. The latter motivation should hold with roughly equal force at different times and in different legal areas. But the former is strong only when and where the Supreme Court maintains active supervision or at least a credible threat of reversal. The Supreme Court's control must be even weaker if judges care about reversal only insofar as it affects their favored policies, rather than their self-esteem, professional reputations, chances for advancement, and the like. This is because deference will make sense only where the expected policy benefits of deferring are greater than the expected policy benefits of going one's own way.

Taken together with existing evidence, the results of the present study give us some reason to doubt that lower court compliance and responsiveness result from fear of reversal. Cases involving unsettled issues of law would seem to be more deserving of the Supreme Court's attention and, thus, more likely to be reviewed. As reported in Chapter 3, the certiorari grant rate for the cases in this analysis was over 10 percent, several times as high as the typical rate for all cases. If judges were acting so as to avoid reversal, we should not find less evidence of constraint in cases that are more likely to find their way to the High Court.

This reasoning is not conclusive, however. While routine cases are less likely to be reviewed, noncompliant decisions in such cases may be especially likely to be reversed. Furthermore, the incentives to break with the Supreme Court may be substantially weaker where rules are already settled, since there is no realistic chance of having much impact on the law. In the end, we cannot draw firm inferences about the relative importance of fear of reversal or the desire to do the right thing, judicially speaking.

The results have something more definite to say about why judges might strive to avoid being reversed. When judges decide cases involving settled issues of law, the consequences of reversal are typically limited to the judges' own jurisdictions.[4] In contrast, reversals of rulings on live issues can change policy for the worse (from the lower court's perspective) across the country. If deference to the Supreme Court were driven by strategic calculations of likely policy outcomes, evidence of these calculations would appear most clearly where policy and strategy matter most – that is, in cases involving unsettled issues. But this study focused on unsettled issues, and the evidence failed to appear.

This is not to say that circuit judges do not act strategically, for the findings do not justify such a stark conclusion. After all, given the very low probability of Supreme Court review and the even lower probability of reversal (the Court might agree with the lower court), risking reversal for the chance of setting policy at one's desired point may be a sound general strategy. It is also possible that circuit judges act strategically, but

---

[4] The assumption here is that most or all other circuits continue to adhere to Supreme Court precedent. Of course, this may not always be the case. Some Supreme Court decisions may be met with widespread evasion or defiance. Aged precedents might be viewed as obsolete and disregarded. Such instances are exceptional, however.

in more subtle ways, such as in how they choose which issues to decide or how they frame arguments in favor of their conclusions. What the results do suggest is that consistency between the decisions of the courts of appeals and the preferences of the Supreme Court is probably best explained by something other than the strategic pursuit of policy preferences.

7

Implications and Future Directions

This book began with a story of law making in the courts of appeals, depicting the creation of and reaction to a new legal rule in the area of search and seizure. The final chapter begins the same way, but this story is very different from the first.

In 1984, the Seventh Circuit was called on to decide whether judges have the power to authorize video surveillance of private buildings. The question was examined with care and at great length in the court's opinion; the discussion runs to more than 150 lines in LEXIS. The three judges on the panel all agreed that judges do possess the power.[1] Over the next ten years, another six cases in five circuits raised the question. In all six cases, the Seventh Circuit's rule was adopted.[2]

One feature distinguishing this story from the earlier one is the unanimity in the circuits. Another is the absence of the Supreme Court. But the biggest difference is in our ability to uncover hidden elements of the story. The intervening chapters have been devoted to exploring factors that could influence judges' behavior. We are now in a better position to say which of these factors offer more or less plausible explanations for the observed actions. To illustrate this, I will briefly discuss several possible accounts of the electronic surveillance decisions, along the way considering how details from the cases reflect on them.

One credible explanation is that the judges, as conservatives, preferred a conservative rule – one favoring the state over criminal defendants. Ideology may help account for the judges' actions, but it leaves

---

[1] *U.S. v. Torres*, 751 F.2d 875 (7th Cir. 1984).
[2] The citations can be found in Appendix A under search and seizure rule #3.

something to be explained. Five of the opinions were written by judges coded as moderately conservative, but two were written by liberals. The average ideology for the other judges on the panels was just to the conservative side of moderate. We must look a bit further for explanations.

Perhaps the judges decided as they did because they thought it was what the Supreme Court would do. This seems doubtful, after the analysis reported in Chapter 6, and the courts' opinions contain nothing to counter this suspicion. The Supreme Court and its cases receive no more than a line or two of discussion in four of the opinions; much more attention is devoted to other circuit court decisions, statutory language, and legislative history. Even in the three cases where the Supreme Court is more prominently featured, the discussions are couched purely in terms of existing precedent. There are no references to how the current Supreme Court might decide nor any special emphases on more recent precedents.

What about judges' attributes? Maybe the prestige of the rule's author was sufficient to sway later judges in its favor. This is a plausible notion. The Seventh Circuit's opinion was written by Richard Posner, one of the most respected of federal judges. His opinion is cited in all of the subsequent cases, often repeatedly or at length. Were Posner mentioned by name in some of the discussions, the case would appear to be clinched; however, he is not.

Perhaps it was Posner's abilities, as manifested in the opinion, that influenced other judges, rather than or in addition to his name. I have already mentioned that his written analysis was fairly thorough. It, or the presentation of it, might also have been particularly persuasive. Or it might just be that the rule itself makes considerably more legal or policy sense than the alternative. Some support for these explanations can be found in the other courts' opinions. For instance, the second court to hear the issue, after citing the Seventh Circuit opinion several times, concluded, "Finding the reasoning in *Torres* to be compelling, we join the Seventh Circuit..." (*Biasucci*, 509). The fourth panel to hear it wrote, "We are in agreement with the Seventh Circuit's statement that 'we cannot think of any basis on which the rule might be thought sufficiently flexible to authorize a pen register, bug, or wiretap, but not a camera'" (*Mesa-Rincon*, 1436).

At no point in this line of cases did conflict develop. With each additional panel that decided the issue the same way, the consensus in favor of the rule became stronger. According to the evidence from Chapters 4 and 5, the courts' unanimity should have encouraged other judges to adopt the rule, especially in the later cases. Here, too, the judges' own words mesh with expectations. Each of the last three opinions notes the unanimity among previous decisions. This emphasis is particularly strong in the final case:

> Additionally, several of our sister circuits have addressed the issue before us. ... [T]hese circuits have unanimously held that Rule 41(b) is flexible enough to encompass silent video surveillance and that such surveillance is regulated by the requirements of the Fourth Amendment. We are persuaded by their reasoning and have found no authority to the contrary. Accordingly, we hold. ... (*Falls*, 679)

At the end of this discussion, we still possess only an incomplete account of the judges' behavior. Still, I believe the account is fuller and more satisfying than it would have been without the benefit of this study. The purpose of this chapter is to highlight the study's contributions and implications more directly. I will begin with a brief review of key findings before discussing what they suggest about circuit court policy making, specifically, and judicial decision making, more broadly. The chapter ends with some thoughts about how future research could improve on and extend the study.

SUMMARY OF FINDINGS

The primary goal of this work has been to better understand the influences at play in circuit judges' decisions on unsettled issues of law. Its guiding questions have centered on two types of interactions – among circuit judges and between circuit judges and the Supreme Court. For the first type, I asked about the factors affecting circuit judges' treatments of one another's new legal rules and the resulting levels of conflict and agreement. For the second, I asked how closely the Supreme Court supervised circuit court law making and how much of a constraint its presence imposed.

The evidence reported here suggests that circuit judges agree about new rules considerably more often than they disagree. This is not to say that conflict is rare, however; a third of the new rules were rejected by other courts at one time or another. The balance of conflict and consensus indicates the presence of competing forces, as do the findings from the case analysis and interviews.

As most scholars would surely have supposed, one of the important forces is ideology. Liberal judges prefer liberal rules to conservative ones, and conservative judges do the opposite.

Other influences come from outside the judges' own minds. The probability that a rule will be favorably treated in a given case is in part a function of how previous courts have reacted to it. Its chances are affected as well by the qualities of its author, particularly his or her prestige and expertise. And although the evidence for this comes only from the interviews, there is reason to believe that the opinion in which a rule is announced can also play a part in how it is received. These outside influences appear to be greatest in those cases where, for one reason or another, a decision is most difficult to reach – although here, too, the evidence is a bit thin.

The remaining factors present greater interpretive problems. A dissent from the announcement of a rule is associated with a lower probability of adoption by other courts. It seems likely that the dissent itself has an impact on later judges' thinking, but we cannot be sure of this. It may be nothing more than an indicator of a troublesome legal question, useful to the researcher but not to other judges. The finding that the probability of adoption varies quite substantially across fields of law was not even predicted. I believe, as argued in Chapter 3, that it can be traced to differences in the legal contexts and the types of rules developed, but here, too, some uncertainty must remain.

The findings as to circuit court–Supreme Court interactions can be more succinctly summarized. On one side, the Supreme Court is anything but a hands-on supervisor. True, its rate of review was unusually high in the cases studied here, but even so the great majority of cases ended at the courts of appeals. Even when the Court did step in to resolve a question, it was often only after several years had passed.

For their part, circuit judges seemed to act with little regard for what the Supreme Court might think. The Supreme Court's past views, as expressed in precedents, counted for a good deal in both the interviews and the written opinions; its current or future views mattered far less. The quantitative analysis revealed no evidence of circuit judges' reacting to ideological trends in the Supreme Court or exercising more caution when the chances of Supreme Court review were greater. In the interviews, the judges made almost no mention of the Court's potential reactions.

INTERCOURT DYNAMICS IN LAW MAKING

At this point, it may be useful to step back from the specific findings and consider their broader implications. What do they suggest about the policymaking role of circuit judges in a system where hundreds of other judges have authority equal to theirs and nine have far more? It would be possible to give some very general answers to this question, but here, too, it makes more sense to treat vertical and horizontal dynamics separately.

Vertical Dynamics

At the most fundamental level, the results of this investigation suggest that Howard's (1981) phrase "mini–Supreme Courts" is appropriate in more than just its narrow sense (i.e., that they usually have the final say in a case). Circuit judges are given numerous chances to make law unimpeded by the Supreme Court, and they seem to take advantage of these opportunities. The result, if these inferences are correct, is that much of the federal law in any circuit looks as it does because court of appeals judges think it should look that way. Viewed from the perspective of the Supreme Court, the chief lesson seems to be that it cannot maintain anything like complete control over the evolution of federal legal policy. Outside of the relatively few areas each year in which it can actively intervene, its power to shape developments is tightly circumscribed.

The picture painted here should not seem particularly foreign to political scientists, who have frequently observed the difficulties supervisors face in directing the behavior of subordinates. Although the analogy should not be forced, at a general level there are considerable similarities between the federal court system and typical government bureaucracies. Most important, they both involve superiors with limited capacities to oversee compliance and few sanctions with which to coerce it, along with subordinates who possess strong preferences of their own and must answer in their day-to-day work to colleagues and the people they serve. This being so, it may be instructive to consider the conclusions Brehm and Gates (1997) drew from their extensive theoretical and empirical study of American bureaucracy. In brief, they found that while supervisors can have some impact on the behavior of subordinates, their influence is far less than that of the subordinates' own preferences and colleagues. At the same time, bureaucrats tend to perform their jobs faithfully, rather than shirking or undercutting their superiors' policies.

If the analogy between judges and bureaucrats is a fair one, we might expect to find the same near-paradox in circuit court decision making, with judges gladly seizing opportunities to make law but making law that, in the end, is not dramatically different from what would have emerged from the Supreme Court. While I have no systematic analysis to present, I think that this description rings true. Certainly it is hard to detect evidence of wild law making among the rules listed in Appendix A. And, as already discussed, other research typically shows strong links between Supreme Court and circuit court outputs.

To the extent that policy divergence between these courts is limited, the Brehm and Gates argument suggests that two forces deserve the most credit. First, people at different levels of an organization tend to share many of the same values. In the courts, the shared values may sometimes be policy preferences or more general views of justice. More commonly, I suspect, what judges share is a concern for legal soundness and common standards for evaluating it. Second, even when values conflict, subordinates' desire to perform their jobs well encourages them to respect existing policies. For circuit judges, this means giving serious attention to Supreme Court precedents even when they are not directly applicable.

Much of the foregoing is speculation, of course. It should not obscure the clearer and more important point to emerge from this study: The constraints circuit judges operate under appear to be largely self-imposed. At least when deciding live issues, most of what they do is done, it seems, because they think it right. If this inference is correct, we cannot hope to understand the development of federal law without continued intensive study of decision making in the courts of appeals.

Horizontal Dynamics

If circuit court decision making were entirely controlled by a higher force, there would be no horizontal dynamics to consider. But Supreme Court control appears far from perfect. Hence, interactions among circuit judges merit serious attention.

To put the findings of this study in context, it might help to begin by considering the extremes of logical possibilities. At one end, judges could act with absolute independence, utterly ignoring the previous efforts of other judges to address the issues now before them. In a slightly different version of this scenario, the judges might adhere to precedents from their own circuits while disregarding all others. At the other extreme, they could subordinate their own views entirely, simply falling into step with the judges who reached the issue before them. We would not expect real behavior to fall precisely at either extreme, so it is not surprising to find indications of both independence and cooperation. The data show clearly that judges are influenced by their deeply held individual attitudes. Furthermore, they tend to stick with judges of their own circuit, regardless of what others do. On the other hand, the circuits do not act in anything like perfect isolation. The evidence is equally strong that judges respond to the actions and attributes of judges from other circuits.

What may be surprising is how distant the reality seems to be from the extreme of perfect independence. It may well fall closer to this extreme than the other – it is hard to judge precisely – but in the conception of judicial decision making developed here, individualism is certainly not an overwhelming force. In this respect, I think the present conception differs markedly from more traditional ones. A striking thing about the traditional image in the judicial decision-making literature is how little the views of others seem to figure in judges' thinking. This is true even of strategic accounts, where the potential reaction of others is taken into consideration only insofar as it can affect the accomplishment of one's own already chosen ends.

I do not wish to overstate this point. Judges' capacity to persuade colleagues, through the force of logic, erudition, personality, or whatever else, received serious attention in such classic works as Murphy's *Elements of Judicial Strategy* (1964), Danelski's (1968) study of chief justices' leadership powers, and Howard's (1968) exploration of fluidity in justices' voting. Researchers examining intercourt citation patterns (Merryman 1954, 1977; Friedman et al. 1981; Caldeira 1985) have at least noted the possibility that judges are influenced by colleagues on other courts. Other scholars have offered more forceful claims (e.g., Shapiro 1965; Marvell 1978). Yet, I think it is fair to say that such studies are vastly outnumbered by those portraying judges – implicitly or explicitly – as isolated and self-sufficient. The present study, in both its theoretical underpinnings and empirical findings, falls squarely in the smaller camp.

GOALS AND DECISION MAKING

When the hypotheses about interjudge influence were constructed back in Chapter 2, they were based on assumptions about what judges hope to accomplish in their decision making. The interviews provided a good deal of direct evidence supporting the assumptions. But judges' claims about their motivations are entitled to only so much credence. Judges cannot be expected to understand their own motivations perfectly or to report them with undiluted candor. If they could, scholarly debates about judges' goals would have ended long ago. As Baum (1997) has shown in his masterly examination of the subject, these debates are not only very much alive, they occupy a central place in the decision-making literature.

Like any tests of hypotheses, the results of this study reflect back on the underlying assumptions. Thus, they contribute new evidence to the debates about judges' goals. Baum identifies three questions at the heart of these debates: How much is judicial behavior driven by goals related to the content of legal policy as opposed to other kinds of goals? Do judges care only how well the content reflects their views of good public policy, or do they appraise it according to more legalistic criteria as well? In pursuit of their public policy goals, to what extent do they act strategically? This study has the most to say about the second question, although it touches on the others as well.

Legal vs. Policy Goals

The first point to note is that the study does nothing to undermine the widely held position that policy preferences matter a good deal to judges. It is true that I was not able to ask about policy preferences directly in the interviews, and the impact of ideology in the statistical analysis was not quite as strong as I had anticipated. But the judges' frank admissions that they cared about the outcomes of the cases they decided point to the influence of personal values, and as already explained, the impact of ideology was almost surely underestimated as a result of measurement error.

A far more interesting implication of the study is that legal goals, too, have a real effect on judges' decisions. This implication flows from several different findings. Perhaps the most compelling of these are the results for prestige and expertise. It is hard to think of any reason, apart from a desire to reach legally sound decisions, why judges would respond to such attributes when debating whether to follow a colleague's lead. They would have no reason to assume that experienced or highly regarded judges were more likely to share their ideological leanings or would otherwise have a greater tendency to choose policies compatible with their own preferences. Standing alone, the goal of saving time might lead judges to follow others, but they would follow blindly, not discriminating between leaders. Similarly, judges wishing to maintain good relations with colleagues or enhance the prospects of their own future rulings should dispense courtesy widely, not selectively. Judges might hope to improve their own reputations through association with an esteemed name; however, the way to do this is by mentioning the prestigious judge's name, not simply adopting his or her rule. And if the idea is to strengthen one's reputation by adopting wise rules, then we are back to the original goal of making legally sound decisions.

The finding that initial dissents are associated with subsequent rejections of a rule points clearly in the same direction. I have noted the difficulty of ascertaining the precise nature of this association; it may or may not be causal. But regardless of whether it is, it probably cannot be explained adequately without reference to the goal of making good law. For instance, dissents might influence later decisions by directing attention to some weakness in the rule. Because, in the typical law-making case, it is considerably easier for judges to identify where their sympathies lie than to weigh the legal arguments, ideological caution flags must have far less utility for them than legal ones. To put this another way, while it is easy to imagine dissents alerting judges to legal problems they might not have seen otherwise, it is harder to picture judges realizing that a rule conflicts with their personal values only after reading a dissent.

If the relationship is not causal, it is still easier to explain it with legal goals than with policy goals. Dissents might be associated with rules that are *legally* problematic (because of faulty logic, questionable textual or historical interpretations, etc.) and thus more likely than others to be rejected later. But this proposition does not translate easily into *ideological* terms. Although judges may disagree somewhat about methods of legal reasoning or interpretation, presumably they tend to evaluate positions under similar legal standards. On average, the more compelling a legal argument is thought to be by one judge, the more compelling it should appear to others. This is not true of policy positions. Because ideology varies so widely, policies that are particularly attractive to one group of judges are likely to seem deplorable to others. So while a legally based dissent suggests something about the rule, an ideologically based dissent is far more likely to reflect the composition of the panel. For instance, ideologically extreme rules may be more likely than others to occasion dissents, but it takes two judges with ideologically extreme positions to adopt an extreme rule; it takes only one to dissent from a mainstream rule. To take a different kind of example, it is easy to imagine a scenario in which one rule is adopted unanimously by three moderate to conservative judges, while an equally conservative rule is announced over a dissent because one of the panel members has more liberal preferences. We would not expect the second rule to be rejected more often than the first by later judges. The point is that dissent is simply not a useful indicator of ideological difficulties.

To this point I have not even considered the fact that ideology was controlled for in the statistical analysis. When we recall this, it seems evident that policy preferences do little to account for the relationship between dissent and rejection. A large share of the burden must fall to other goals. We have seen that the goal of legal soundness provides a plausible explanation, and it is difficult to think of any other goal that could do as well.

Much the same line of argument applies to the relationship between other circuits' support for a rule and the present judges' decision whether to adopt or reject. Rather than try the reader's patience by repeating the arguments made in Chapter 4, I will simply highlight the key points. First, judges should rarely need help in determining their own policy preferences. Even if they did, simply observing the level of support for a rule would be of little use; they would need to know the preferences of the earlier judges as well. (Conservative judges should not look more favorably on a rule because it has been adopted by two liberal panels, for instance.) In contrast, judges could quite sensibly view existing support as a gauge of a rule's legal soundness. Thus, if existing support influences later judges' choices, it probably does so by way of legal goals, rather than policy preferences.

On the other hand, unlike with dissents, if the relationship here is not a causal one, policy preferences may help explain it. A consensus in favor of a rule could arise because the alternative is too ideologically extreme for most judges. In such instances, later judges should also favor the rule. This is a reasonable suggestion, but an examination of the rules in Appendix A shows that it has limited value. For almost all of the rules, it is relatively easy to think of an alternative comfortably in the ideological mainstream. Again, the pursuit of legally sound decisions seems a more plausible explanation.

In this case, though, other factors may also be at play. By far the most likely is the desire to maintain clarity and consistency in the law. This goal naturally connects the behavior of judges across time. If one cares about this goal and earlier judges are unanimous – or nearly so – in support of a rule, one's inclination should be to go along. Because, in addition, several judges reported thinking this way, the evidence for this goal is quite solid.

There are some other credible possibilities. For instance, the goal of deciding quickly might encourage judges to adopt the dominant position. Even if they chose simply to follow the first precedent they found, the probability of that precedent's coming from the majority side would be a function of the strength of the consensus. Still, neither this account nor any other I have been able to think of is as compelling as those based on legal goals.

In short, while this study reaffirms the view that policy preferences matter, it also provides substantial evidence of the importance of legal goals. As just described, the goal of making legally sound decisions offers the best explanation of the findings concerning judicial prestige and expertise and initial dissents. It is also the most plausible basis for the effects of opinion and rule characteristics identified by the judges in Chapter 5. It and the goal of maintaining consistency in the law best explain the impact of existing circuit support.

Before turning to Baum's other questions, I wish to clarify the claim being made here. Even the strongest proponents of the attitudinal model at the Supreme Court level concede that legal considerations may sometimes factor into lower court judges' decisions. If this were all I meant to say, the length of the preceding discussion would be hard to justify. In fact, my claim differs in two significant ways.

First, I believe the study establishes the importance not just of legal considerations, generally, but of legal *goals*, specifically. As I noted in Chapter 2, in research on judicial decision making the law is quite frequently viewed as a constraint, something that interferes – more or less often, depending on circumstances – with what judges really want to do, make good policy. In this conception, judges do not actively pursue legally satisfying answers to questions; they simply refrain (perhaps) from giving answers that strike them as legally wrong. This conception is not consistent with the evidence uncovered here. When we see that rules from prestigious and expert judges fare better than others, that they do so in part because other judges give these rules more respectful attention, and that the other judges also take into account the existing support for a rule, the quality of the opinion in which it is presented, and the character of the rule itself, the impression created is very much one of active pursuit of solutions, not reluctant submission to constraints.

The distinction between legal soundness as a goal and law as a constraint is meaningful and important. One reason, as the preceding discussion shows, is that legal goals bring additional influences into play. (This point has implications not just for judges' behavior but also for how scholars study it. If we begin by assuming away the possibility that legal goals matter to judges, we deny ourselves the chance of discovering some interesting relationships.) Another reason is that it implies different kinds of balancing of law and policy. If law is simply a constraint, policy preferences should dominate judges' decision making when legal answers are hard to discern. But if making good law is a goal, this will not necessarily be the case; judges might choose to exert the extra effort needed to arrive at a legally sound ruling.

This last point is closely related to the second key element of my claim: Legal goals matter in all kinds of cases, not just in routine ones involving well-settled issues or frivolous claims. To see why this is important, consider again Segal and Spaeth's (1993:69–72) list of reasons why legal goals might be expected to carry little weight at the Supreme Court. First and second, the justices "lack electoral or political accountability [and] ambition for higher office." Third, they control their own jurisdiction. And fourth, their decisions cannot be reversed by a higher court. It is striking how well these conditions describe the situation facing circuit court judges, especially in cases of the sort I have examined here. To start with, circuit judges are no more accountable than Supreme Court justices. Additionally, while they might desire higher office, the prospects for achieving it are so slim and the chance that any one decision will affect those prospects is so small that it is hard to conceive of ambition having more than an occasional influence on their decisions. Their decisions are subject to reversal by the Supreme Court, but given the Court's extremely low rate of review and the findings reported in Chapter 6 of this book, it seems unlikely that the threat of reversal has substantial effects. Thus, mandatory jurisdiction – with the consequent surfeit of legally easy cases – is by far the most important feature distinguishing the courts of appeals from the Supreme Court. Yet, because of this study's focus on unsettled issues, the vast majority of easy cases have been eliminated from its analysis. Open questions are not always difficult, but they typically admit of more than one credible answer.

The upshot of all this is that legal goals appear to matter even where they would seem particularly unlikely to do so. There are two important implications. First, legal goals may be important even in the Supreme Court or other courts like it. Second, and more broadly, the influence of legal goals may be more pervasive in all courts than is suggested by much of the decision-making literature.

Other Questions About Goals

The study does not speak as forcefully to Baum's other questions, but it does offer some additional insights. Most important, it suggests that judges' concerns extend beyond the content of the legal policies they make. In particular, it points to the potential importance of judges' desire to minimize the time they spend on any one case. As I noted previously, this motivation could help account for the relationship between existing support for a rule and the present judges' decision. It could do so even more persuasively in combination with the goal of making legally sound decisions. The notion that judges would go along with a majority simply to save time might be hard to swallow, but it is easy enough to imagine them doing so because they lack time *and* wish to make the right decision. The same can be said about the effects of rule creators' prestige and expertise. These traits, like circuit support, may act as cues for judges searching for legally sound answers, and cue taking should be made more attractive by the desire to find those answers quickly.

Given this logic, I predicted that the effects of prestige, expertise, and circuit support would be especially strong for less experienced judges or in other situations where judges faced particular difficulty reaching a decision. There was some evidence to this effect in both the cases and the interviews, but it was mixed. The failure to find stronger results might reflect the fact that all circuit judges, regardless of experience, are now subject to serious time pressures. Nevertheless, more consistent results would have allowed greater confidence in the conclusion that the goal of deciding cases promptly plays an important part in judges' decisions.

As to Baum's third question – whether or not judges act strategically in pursuit of their policy preferences – I cannot offer firm conclusions. The analyses in Chapter 6 revealed very little evidence that circuit judges attempt to anticipate the Supreme Court or are especially cautious in deciding cases that are more likely to be reviewed. But this does not mean that judges do not think strategically. Strategic calculations involve estimates of costs, benefits, and the probabilities that certain events will occur. Judges appear to derive great satisfaction from setting policy where they think it belongs. It is questionable whether the costs of being reversed would often outweigh this satisfaction, and it is certain that the probability of reversal is generally low. Thus, it may be that in the great majority of cases the strategically wise course is to decide as one thinks right.

As I argued in Chapter 6, what the findings of that chapter do imply is that circuit court congruence with and responsiveness to Supreme Court doctrine is probably not driven by strategic calculations. In other words, the study gives us no reason to doubt that circuit court judges think strategically, but it does suggest limits to what strategic accounts of decision making can explain.

FUTURE DIRECTIONS

My choice to discuss the implications of this study rather boldly and lengthily reflects my belief that they are interesting, not a delusion that the study establishes anything conclusively. The research reported here covers just three fields of law in a single twelve-year period, and its measures, while carefully constructed, are necessarily imperfect. I do not have any particular reason to think that research into other times or fields would produce very different conclusions, but it is always possible, and we could draw more confident inferences if the results were replicated. Perhaps more important, future researchers might be able to better some of the measures used here. The measures of ideology might be improved, for instance, although the fact that scholars have struggled with this problem for decades does not inspire optimism. Efforts to measure judges' expertise or decisional difficulty would likely be more fruitful.

The study was also limited in that it covered only U.S. Courts of Appeals. Because institutional context and legal culture vary across court systems, the mix of goals and strength of influences at play most likely vary, too. Still, I suspect that the broad conclusions of this study – especially that judges act on a combination of goals and that they give respectful attention to their peers – would hold for other court systems as well, even for courts that have no, or at best tenuous, official connections. This belief is bolstered by Shapiro's (1970) essay on the development of tort law in the U.S. states. Shapiro identified an intriguing puzzle: Although constructed in fifty-two separate jurisdictions (including the U.S. Supreme Court and British courts), tort law in the United States and England came to share "a remarkably uniform core" (50). He attributed this in part to "a common professional discipline" and "shared channels of communication and incentives to use them" (51). His language and ideas are somewhat different from mine, but the key point is the same: Judges from different legal jurisdictions can influence one another's decisions. Indeed, his argument goes further, suggesting that influence can cross political boundaries, even national borders.

As valuable as it would be to subject this study's findings to additional tests and to see how well they apply in other contexts, I hope that future research investigates other possibilities, too. After all, I have focused on only some important aspects of law making. As noted at various stages, but primarily in Chapter 5, there are a number of potential influences on judges' behavior that I could identify but was not able to examine systematically. Examples are certain characteristics of legal rules, the judges who produce them, and the opinions that announce them. It is doubtful that many of these have truly important effects on judges' decisions, but some may. Even among the less significant ones, the potential for influence is always there. They might hold particular interest for scholars investigating developments in a specific area of law.

Just as important, it might be wise to consider outside influences on judges' decisions aside from the products and attributes of fellow jurists. Although the goals of maintaining consistency and deciding promptly may encourage attention only to other judges, the goal of making good law should lead judges to consider ideas from additional sources. And if they can be swayed by the reputations or quality of arguments of other judges, they might also respond to the lawyers arguing before them, to academics writing in law journals, or to others in the legal arena. Even if judges did not take such actors' own ideas entirely seriously – and even though judges have clerks and ready access to electronic databases – these other actors still have an important part to play in bringing ideas to judges' attention, and their assessments of those ideas may count for something in judges' thinking. In the end, these considerations lead to a conclusion previously suggested by scholars like Shapiro (1970), Marvell (1978), and Epstein and Kobylka (1992): Understanding how judges make law probably requires looking beyond the judges themselves.

Appendix A
Rules and Cases

Note: **Liberal/Conservative** indicates the ideological implications of the rule. **Adopt/Reject** refers to the later court's treatment of the rule.

Search and seizure
1. A reasonable suspicion is sufficient to justify an X-ray search of a suspect at the border. **Conservative.**
   U.S. v. Vega-Barvo, 729 F.2d 1341 (11th Cir., 1984)
   U.S. v. Saldarriaga-Marin, 734 F.2d 1425 (11th Cir., 1984) – **Adopt.**
   U.S. v. Oyekan, 786 F.2d 832 (8th Cir., 1986) – **Adopt.**
2. The inevitable discovery exception to the exclusionary rule does not apply to a search unless the government was actively pursuing the alternative line of investigation at the time of the violation. **Liberal.**
   U.S. v. Satterfield, 743 F.2d 827 (11th Cir., 1984)
   U.S. v. Cherry, 759 F.2d 1196 (5th Cir., 1985) – **Adopt.**
   U.S. v. Owens, 782 F.2d 146 (10th Cir., 1986) – **Adopt.**
   U.S. v. Silvestri, 787 F.2d 736 (1st Cir., 1986) – **Reject.**
   U.S. v. Drosten, 819 F.2d 1067 (11th Cir., 1987) – **Adopt.**
   U.S. v. Boatwright, 822 F.2d 862 (9th Cir., 1987) – **Reject.**
   U.S. v. Evans, 848 F.2d 1352 (5th Cir., 1988) – **Adopt.**
   U.S. v. Ramirez-Sandoval, 872 F.2d 1392 (9th Cir., 1989) – **Reject.**
   U.S. v. Buchanan, 904 F.2d 349 (6th Cir., 1990) – **Adopt.**
   U.S. v. Buchanan, 910 F.2d 1571 (7th Cir., 1990) – **Reject.**
   U.S. v. Thomas, 955 F.2d 207 (4th Cir., 1992) – **Reject.**

U.S. v. Eng, 971 F.2d 854 (2nd Cir., 1992) – **Adopt.**
U.S. v. Kennedy, 61 F.3d 494 (6th Cir., 1995) – **Reject.**

3. Judges have the power to authorize video surveillance of private buildings. **Conservative.**
   U.S. v. Torres, 751 F.2d 875 (7th Cir., 1984)
   U.S. v. Biasucci, 786 F.2d 504 (2nd Cir., 1986) – **Adopt.**
   U.S. v. Cuevas-Sanchez, 821 F.2d 248 (5th Cir., 1987) – **Adopt.**
   U.S. v. Mesa-Rincon, 911 F.2d 1433 (10th Cir., 1990) – **Adopt.**
   U.S. v. Koyomejian (panel), 946 F.2d 1450 (9th Cir., 1991) – **Adopt.**
   U.S. v. Koyomejian (en banc), 970 F.2d 536 (9th Cir., 1992) – **Adopt.**
   U.S. v. Falls, 34 F.3d 674 (8th Cir., 1994) – **Adopt.**

4. An authorization of video surveillance must satisfy the four provisions of Title III of the Omnibus Crime Control and Safe Streets Act of 1968 that implement the Fourth Amendment's requirement of particularity. **Liberal.**
   U.S. v. Torres, 751 F.2d 875 (7th Cir., 1984)
   U.S. v. Biasucci, 786 F.2d 504 (2nd Cir., 1986) – **Adopt.**
   U.S. v. Cuevas-Sanchez, 821 F.2d 248 (5th Cir., 1987) – **Adopt.**
   U.S. v. Mesa-Rincon, 911 F.2d 1433 (10th Cir., 1990) – **Adopt.**
   U.S. v. Koyomejian (panel), 946 F.2d 1450 (9th Cir., 1991) – **Adopt.**
   U.S. v. Koyomejian (en banc), 970 F.2d 536 (9th Cir., 1992) – **Adopt.**
   U.S. v. Falls, 34 F.3d 674 (8th Cir., 1994) – **Adopt.**

5. An authorization of video surveillance need not satisfy any provisions of Title III other than those mentioned in the previous rule. **Conservative.**
   U.S. v. Torres, 751 F.2d 875 (7th Cir., 1984)
   U.S. v. Biasucci, 786 F.2d 504 (2nd Cir., 1986) – **Adopt.**
   U.S. v. Cuevas-Sanchez, 821 F.2d 248 (5th Cir., 1987) – **Adopt.**
   U.S. v. Mesa-Rincon, 911 F.2d 1433 (10th Cir., 1990) – **Adopt.**
   U.S. v. Koyomejian (panel), 946 F.2d 1450 (9th Cir., 1991) – **Reject.**
   U.S. v. Koyomejian (en banc), 970 F.2d 536 (9th Cir., 1992) – **Adopt.**
   U.S. v. Falls, 34 F.3d 674 (8th Cir., 1994) – **Adopt.**

6. A canine sniff at the door of a residence is a search under the Fourth Amendment. **Liberal.**

U.S. v. Thomas, 757 F.2d 1359 (2nd Cir., 1985)

U.S. v. Lingenfelter, 997 F.2d 632 (9th Cir., 1993) – **Reject.**

7. A canine sniff of an automobile from the outside is not a search under the Fourth Amendment. **Conservative.**

U.S. v. Dicesare, 765 F.2d 890 (9th Cir., 1985)

U.S. v. Hardy, 855 F.2d 753 (11th Cir., 1988) – **Adopt.**

U.S. v. Stone, 866 F.2d 359 (10th Cir., 1989) – **Adopt.**

U.S. v. Dovali-Avila, 895 F.2d 206 (5th Cir., 1990) – **Adopt.**

U.S. v. Morales-Zamora, 914 F.2d 200 (10th Cir., 1990) – **Adopt.**

U.S. v. Rodriguez-Morales, 929 F.2d 780 (CA1, 1991) – **Adopt.**

U.S. v. Hernandez, 976 F.2d 929 (5th Cir., 1992) – **Adopt.**

U.S. v. Jeffus, 22 F.3d 554 (4th Cir., 1994) – **Adopt.**

U.S. v. Friend, 50 F.2d 548 (8th Cir., 1995) – **Adopt.**

8. A person is "seized" for purposes of the Fourth Amendment when police officers deliberately place a roadblock in front of a car she is riding in. **Liberal.**

Jamieson v. Shaw, 772 F.2d 1205 (5th Cir., 1985)

Brower v. County of Inyo, 817 F.2d 540 (9th Cir., 1987) – **Reject.**

9. A formal written agreement is not necessary to constitute an arrangement establishing customs waters. (Drug smuggling cases.) **Conservative.**

U.S. v. Gonzalez, 776 F.2d 931 (11th Cir., 1985)

U.S. v. Santa-Lara, 783 F.2d 989 (11th Cir., 1986) – **Adopt.**

U.S. v. Peterson, 812 F.2d 486 (9th Cir., 1987) – **Adopt.**

U.S. v. Alomia-Riascos, 825 F.2d 769 (4th Cir., 1987) – **Adopt.**

U.S. v. Davis, 905 F.2d 245 (9th Cir., 1990) – **Adopt.**

10. Administrative search exception for closely regulated industries extends to warrantless drug testing of voluntary participants in the regulated activity. **Conservative.**

Shoemaker v. Handel, 795 F.2d 1136 (3rd Cir., 1986)

Railway Labor Executives' Assn. v. Burnley, 839 F.2d 575 (9th Cir., 1988) – **Reject.**

Rushton v. Nebraska Public Power Dist., 844 F.2d 562 (8th Cir., 1988) – **Adopt.**

Lovvorn v. City of Chattanooga, 846 F.2d 1539 (6th Cir., 1988) – **Reject.**

PBA, Local 318 v. Township of Washington, 850 F.2d 133 (3rd Cir., 1988) – **Adopt.**

11. Jockeys may constitutionally be subjected to random drug tests. **Conservative.**
    Shoemaker v. Handel, 795 F.2d 1136 (3rd Cir., 1986)
    Dimeo v. Griffin (panel), 924 F.2d 664 (7th Cir., 1991) –
    Reject.
    Dimeo v. Griffin (en banc), 943 F.2d 679 (7th Cir., 1991) –
    Adopt.

12. Test for validity of an allegedly pretextual stop is whether a reasonable officer would have made the seizure in the absence of illegitimate motivation. **Liberal.**
    U.S. v. Smith, 799 F.2d 704 (11th Cir., 1986)
    U.S. v. Johnson, 815 F.2d 309 (5th Cir., 1987) – **Adopt.**
    U.S. v. Causey, 834 F.2d 1179 (5th Cir., 1987) – **Reject.**
    U.S. v. Guzman, 864 F.2d 1512 (10th Cir., 1988) – **Adopt.**
    U.S. v. Trigg, 878 F.2d 1037 (7th Cir., 1989) – **Reject.**
    U.S. v. Cummins, 920 F.2d 498 (8th Cir., 1990) – **Reject.**
    U.S. v. Valdez, 931 F.2d 1448 (11th Cir., 1991) – **Adopt.**
    U.S. v. French, 974 F.2d 687 (6th Cir., 1992) – **Reject.**
    U.S. v. Ferguson (panel), 989 F.2d 202 (6th Cir., 1992) –
    Adopt.
    U.S. v. Hassan El, 5 F.3d 726 (4th Cir., 1993) – **Reject.**
    U.S. v. Ferguson (en banc), 8 F.3d 385 (6th Cir., 1993) –
    Reject.
    U.S. v. Scopo, 19 F.3d 777 (2nd Cir., 1994) – **Reject.**
    U.S. v. Cannon, 29 F.3d 472 (9th Cir., 1994) – **Adopt.**
    U.S. v. Dirden, 38 F.3d 1131 (10th Cir., 1994) – **Adopt.**
    U.S. v. Whren, 53 F.3d 371 (DC Cir., 1995) – **Reject.**
    U.S. v. Hernandez, 55 F.3d 443 (9th Cir., 1995) – **Adopt.**
    U.S. v. Johnson, 63 F.3d 342 (3rd Cir., 1995) – **Reject.**
    U.S. v. Botero-Ospina, 71 F.3d 783 (10th Cir., 1995) –
    Reject.
    U.S. v. Parker, 72 F.3d 1444 (10th Cir., 1995) – **Reject.**

13. Exclusionary rule does not apply to OSHA enforcement actions to correct violations. **Conservative.**
    Smith Steel Casting Co. v. Brock, 800 F.2d 1329 (5th Cir., 1996)
    Trinity Industries v. OSHRC, 16 F.3d 1455 (6th Cir., 1994) –
    Adopt.

14. Exclusionary rule does apply when OSHA attempts to impose penalties for violations of OSHA regulations. **Liberal.**

Smith Steel Casting Co. v. Brock, 800 F.2d 1329 (5th Cir., 1996)

Trinity Industries v. OSHRC, 16 F.3d 1455 (6th Cir., 1994) – **Adopt.**

15. For warrant authorizing covert search to be acceptable under Fourth Amendment and Rule 41, it must provide explicitly for notice to occupants within a reasonable, but short, time subsequent – no more than 7 days after – unless strong showing of necessity. **Liberal.**

   U.S. v. Freitas, 800 F.2d 1451 (9th Cir., 1986)

   U.S. v. Johns, 851 F.2d 1131 (9th Cir., 1988) – **Adopt.**

   U.S. v. Villegas, 899 F.2d 1324 (2nd Cir., 1990) – **Adopt.**

   U.S. v. Pangburn, 983 F.2d 449 (2nd Cir., 1993) – **Adopt.**

16. Police chase does not constitute seizure unless there is restraint on individual's freedom to leave accomplished by means of physical force or a show of authority. **Conservative.**

   Galas v. McKee, 801 F.2d 200 (6th Cir., 1986)

   Cameron v. City of Pontiac, 813 F.2d 782 (6th Cir., 1987) – **Adopt.**

   Brower v. County of Inyo, 817 F.2d 540 (9th Cir., 1987) – **Adopt.**

17. Random drug testing of prison inmates is permissible under Fourth Amendment. **Conservative.**

   Spence v. Farrier, 807 F.2d 753 (8th Cir., 1986)

   Carr v. Lewis, 1994 U.S. App. LEXIS 7976 (9th Cir., 1994) – **Adopt.**

   Smith v. Vance, 1994 U.S. App. LEXIS 29289 (6th Cir., 1994) – **Adopt.**

   Lucero v. Gunter, 17 F.3d 1347 (10th Cir., 1994) – **Adopt.**

18. Before turning over requested documents, employer may require OSHA to obtain subpoena. **Liberal.**

   Brock v. Emerson Electric Co., 834 F.2d 994 (11th Cir., 1987)

   McLaughlin v. A.B. Chance Co., 842 F.2d 724 (4th Cir., 1988) – **Reject.**

   McLaughlin v. Kings Island, 849 F.2d 990 (6th Cir., 1988) – **Adopt.**

19. Removal of baggage is not a seizure where passenger had relinquished bag to third party (checked at airport) and removal was brief so as not to interfere with travel. **Conservative.**

U.S. v. Lovell, 849 F.2d 910 (5th Cir., 1988)
U.S. v. Brown, 884 F.2d 1309 (9th Cir., 1989) – **Adopt.**
U.S. v. Harvey, 961 F.2d 1361 (8th Cir., 1992) – **Adopt.**
U.S. v. Johnson, 990 F.2d 1129 (9th Cir., 1993) – **Adopt.**

20. Exceptions to the exclusionary rule apply to Rule 41 (e) requests for return of and suppression of illegally seized evidence. **Conservative.**
U.S. v. Roberts, 852 F.2d 671 (2nd Cir., 1988)
Center Art Galleries-Hawaii v. U.S., 875 F.2d 747 (9th Cir., 1989) – **Adopt.**

21. Fact that the government serves a subpoena is not enough to bring a case under the inevitable discovery doctrine. **Liberal.**
U.S. v. Roberts, 852 F.2d 671 (2nd Cir., 1988)
Center Art Galleries-Hawaii v. U.S., 875 F.2d 747 (9th Cir., 1989) – **Adopt.**

22. For valid Terry search, officer must have actual suspicion that weapons are present (not just objectively reasonable suspicion). **Liberal.**
U.S. v. Lott, 870 F.2d 778 (CA1, 1989)
U.S. v. Cummins, 920 F.2d 498 (8th Cir., 1989) – **Reject.**
U.S. v. Newberry, 1993 U.S. App. LEXIS 4906 (9th Cir., 1993) – **Adopt.**
U.S. v. Baker, 47 F.3d 691 (5th Cir., 1995) – **Reject.**

23. For Fourth Amendment excessive force claim, must show "significant injury." **Conservative.**
Johnson v. Morel, 876 F.2d 477 (5th Cir., 1989)
Titran v. Ackman, 893 F.2d 145 (7th Cir., 1990) – **Reject.**
Hay v. City of Irving, 893 F.2d 796 (5th Cir., 1990) – **Adopt.**
Wilks v. Reyes, 5 F.3d 412 (9th Cir., 1993) – **Reject.**
Burrows v. City of Tulsa, 1994 U.S. App. LEXIS 12662 (10th Cir., 1994) – **Reject.**

24. Interception of cordless phone calls is not prohibited by Wiretap Act or Fourth Amendment. **Conservative.**
Tyler v. Berodt, 877 F.2d 705 (8th Cir., 1989)
U.S. v. Smith 978 F.2d 171 (5th Cir., 1992) – **Adopt.**
In re Askin, 47 F.3d 100 (4th Cir., 1995) – **Adopt.**

25. Secretary of Labor has the authority to review all safety and health records of employer in response to employee complaint. **Conservative.**
Dole v. Trinity Industries, 904 F.2d 867 (3rd Cir., 1990)

Trinity Industries v. OSHRC, 16 F.3d 1455 (6th Cir., 1994) – **Adopt.**

26. Regardless of whether actions are provocative, when law enforcement agents act in entirely lawful manner, they do not impermissibly create exigent circumstances. **Conservative.**
    U.S. v. MacDonald, 916 F.2d 766 (2nd Cir., 1990)
    U.S. v. Lopez, 937 F.2d 716 (2nd Cir., 1991) – **Adopt.**
    U.S. v. Acosta, 965 F.2d 1248 (3rd Cir., 1992) – **Adopt.**
    U.S. v. Richard, 994 F.2d 244 (5th Cir., 1993) – **Reject.**
    U.S. v. Johnson, 12 F.3d 760 (8th Cir., 1993) – **Reject.**

27. Evidence suppressed under the exclusionary rule may be considered in determining the appropriate guidelines range in sentencing. **Conservative.**
    U.S. v. Torres, 926 F.2d 321 (3rd Cir., 1991)
    U.S. v. McCrory, 930 F.2d 63 (DC Cir., 1991) – **Adopt.**
    U.S. v. Lynch, 934 F.2d 1226 (11th Cir., 1991)- **Adopt.**
    U.S. v. Tejada, 956 F.2d 1256 (2nd Cir., 1992) – **Adopt.**
    U.S. v. Jessup, 966 F.2d 1354 (10th Cir., 1992) – **Adopt.**
    U.S. v. Nichols, 979 F.2d 402 (6th Cir., 1992) – **Reject.**
    U.S. v. Jenkins, 4 F.3d 1338 (6th Cir., 1993) – **Adopt.**
    U.S. v. Montoya-Ortiz, 7 F.3d 1171 (5th Cir., 1993) – **Adopt.**
    U.S. v. Wilson, 11 F.3d 346 (2nd Cir., 1993) – **Adopt.**
    U.S. v. Kim, 25 F.3d 1426 (9th Cir., 1994) – **Adopt.**

Environmental law

1. The criminal provisions of the Resource Conservation and Recovery Act (RCRA) do not apply only to owners and operators. **Liberal.**
   U.S. v. Johnson & Towers, 741 F.2d 662 (3rd Cir., 1984)
   U.S. v. NEPACCO, 810 F.2d 726 (8th Cir., 1986) – **Adopt.**
   U.S. v. Dean, 969 F.2d 187 (6th Cir., 1992) – **Adopt.**

2. To violate the criminal provisions of RCRA, defendants must know that the waste they dispose of is hazardous. **Liberal.**
   U.S. v. Johnson & Towers, 741 F.2d 662 (3rd Cir., 1984)
   U.S. v. Hayes International Corp., 786 F.2d 1499 (11th Cir., 1986) – **Reject.**
   U.S. v. Hoflin, 880 F.2d 1033 (9th Cir., 1989) – **Adopt.**
   U.S. v. Dee, 912 F.2d 741 (4th Cir., 1990) – **Adopt.**

3. To violate the criminal provisions of RCRA, defendants must know they are required to have a permit. **Liberal.**

U.S. v. Johnson & Towers, 741 F.2d 662 (3rd Cir., 1984)

U.S. v. Hayes International Corp., 786 F.2d 1499 (11th Cir., 1986) – **Reject.**

U.S. v. Dee, 912 F.2d 741 (4th Cir., 1990) – **Reject.**

U.S. v. Baytank, 934 F.2d 599 (5th Cir., 1991) – **Reject.**

U.S. v. Dean, 969 F.2d 187 (6th Cir., 1992) – **Reject.**

U.S. v. Self, 2 F.3d 1071 (10th Cir., 1993) – **Reject.**

U.S. v. Laughlin, 10 F.3d 961 (2nd Cir., 1993) – **Reject.**

U.S. v. Wagner, 29 F.3d 264 (7th Cir., 1994) – **Reject.**

4. To violate the criminal provisions of RCRA, defendants must be aware that they have no permit. **Liberal.**

   U.S. v. Johnson & Towers, 741 F.2d 662 (3rd Cir., 1984)

   U.S. v. Hayes International Corp., 786 F.2d 1499 (11th Cir., 1986) – **Adopt.**

   U.S. v. Hoflin, 880 F.2d 1033 (9th Cir., 1989) – **Reject.**

   U.S. v. Speach, 968 F.2d 795 (9th Cir., 1992) – **Adopt.**

   U.S. v. Laughlin, 10 F.3d 961 (2nd Cir., 1993) – **Reject.**

5. To have standing under the citizens suit section (section 505) of the Clean Water Act, party must show "injury in fact" as described in *Sierra Club v. Morton*. **Conservative.**

   Sierra Club v. SCM Corp., 747 F.2d 99 (2nd Cir., 1984)

   FOE v. Consolidated Rail Corp., 768 F.2d 57 (2nd Cir., 1985) – **Adopt.**

   Sierra Club v. Simkins Industries, 847 F.2d 1109 (4th Cir., 1988) – **Adopt.**

6. Under Endangered Species Act, before the taking of threatened animal can occur, determination must be made that population pressures within the animal's ecosystem cannot otherwise be relieved. **Liberal.**

   Sierra Club v. Clark, 755 F.2d 608 (8th Cir., 1985)

   Christy v. Hodel, 857 F.2d 1324 (9th Cir., 1988) – **Adopt.**

7. Comprehensive Environmental Response, Compensation, and Liability Act (CERCLA) imposes strict liability on current owners and operators. **Liberal.**

   New York v. Shore Realty, 759 F.2d 1032 (2nd Cir., 1985)

   Levin Metals Corp. v. Parr-Richmond Terminal Co., 799 F.2d 1312 (9th Cir., 1986) – **Adopt.**

   Tanglewood East Homeowners v. Charles-Thomas, 849 F.2d 1568 (5th Cir., 1988) – **Adopt.**

   U.S. v. Monsanto Co., 858 F.2d 160 (4th Cir., 1988) – **Adopt.**

Idaho v. Hanna Mining Co. (9th Cir., 1989) – **Adopt.**

Dedham Water Company v. Cumberland Farms Dairy 889 F.2d 1146 (CA1, 1989) – **Adopt.**

U.S. v. R.W. Meyer, 889 F.2d 1497 (6th Cir., 1989) – **Adopt.**

U.S. v. Kayser-Roth, 910 F.2d 24 (CA1, 1990) – **Adopt.**

Hercules Incorporated v. EPA, 938 F.2d 276 (DC Cir., 1991) – **Adopt.**

B.F. Goodrich Co. v. Murtha, 958 F.2d 1192 (2nd Cir., 1992) – **Adopt.**

U.S. v. Alcan Aluminum Corp., 964 F.2d 252 (3rd Cir., 1992) – **Adopt.**

8. There is no causation requirement in Section 9607 (A) of CERCLA. **Liberal.**

New York v. Shore Realty, 759 F.2d 1032 (2nd Cir., 1985)

U.S. v. Monsanto Co., 858 F.2d 160 (4th Cir., 1988) – **Adopt.**

Ohio v. Department of Interior, 880 F.2d 432 (DC Cir., 1989) – **Adopt.**

U.S. v. Alcan Aluminum Corp., 964 F.2d 252 (3rd Cir., 1992) – **Adopt.**

Nurad v. William E. Hooper and Sons, Corp., 966 F.2d 837 (4th Cir., 1992) – **Adopt.**

Farmland Industries v. Morrison-Quirk Grain Corp., 987 F.2d 1335 (8th Cir., 1993) – **Adopt.**

9. States have no right to injunctive relief under CERCLA. **Conservative.**

New York v. Shore Realty, 759 F.2d 1032 (2nd Cir., 1985)

Cadillac Fairview/California v. Dow Chemical Co., 840 F.2d 691 (9th Cir., 1988) – **Adopt.**

10. Defendant has no right to jury trial in civil action brought by federal government for alleged violations of Clean Water Act. **Conservative.**

U.S. v. Tull, 769 F.2d 182 (4th Cir., 1985)

U.S. v. M.C.C. of Florida, 772 F.2d 1501 (11th Cir., 1985) – **Adopt.**

11. Private party may recover response costs under CERCLA even if its action was not pursuant to governmental authorization. **Liberal.**

Wickland Oil Terminals v. Asarco, 792 F.2d 887 (9th Cir., 1986)

Cadillac Fairview/California v. Dow Chemical Co., 840 F.2d 691 (9th Cir., 1988) – **Adopt.**

Tanglewood East Homeowners v. Charles-Thomas, 849 F.2d
1568 (5th Cir., 1988) – **Adopt.**

Richland-Lexington Airport District v. Atlas Properties, 901
F.2d 1206 (4th Cir., 1990) – **Adopt.**

12. Environmental cleanup response costs are not *property*
damages, for insurance purposes. **Conservative.**

Mraz v. Canadian Universal Insurance Co., 804 F.2d 1325 (4th
Cir., 1986)

Continental Insurance Cos. v. NEPACCO, 811 F.2d 1180 (8th
Cir., 1987) – **Reject.**

Aetna Casualty and Surety Co. v. Pintlar Corp., 948 F.2d 1507
(9th Cir., 1990) – **Reject.**

13. Party seeking to recover CERCLA response costs directly from
responsible party (not Superfund) does not have to comply
with 60 day notice period in sec. 9612 (a). **Liberal.**

Dedham Water Co. v. Cumberland Farms Dairy, 805 F.2d
1074 (CA1, 1986)

Idaho v. Howmet Turbine Component Co., 814 F.2d 1376 (9th
Cir., 1987) – **Adopt.**

Walls v. Waste Resource Corp., 823 F.2d 977 (6th Cir., 1987) –
Adopt.

U.S. v. Carolina Transformer Co., 978 F.2d 832 (4th Cir.,
1992) – **Adopt.**

14. CERCLA applies to pollution occurring before enactment.
Liberal.

U.S. v. NEPACCO, 810 F.2d 726 (8th Cir., 1986)

U.S. v. Monsanto Co., 858 F.2d 160 (4th Cir., 1988) –
Adopt.

U.S. v. R.W. Meyer, 889 F.2d 1497 (6th Cir., 1989) – **Adopt.**

U.S. v. Gurley, 43 F.3d 1188 (8th Cir., 1994) – **Adopt.**

15. CERCLA authorizes recovery of pre-enactment response costs.
Liberal.

U.S. v. NEPACCO, 810 F.2d 726 (8th Cir., 1986)

O'Neil v. Picillo, 883 F.2d 176 (CA1, 1989) – **Adopt.**

16. Party contesting fine under CERCLA has burden of proof to
show costs government sues for are not consistent with NCP.
Liberal.

U.S. v. NEPACCO, 810 F.2d 726 (8th Cir., 1986)

U.S. v. R.W. Meyer, 889 F.2d 1497 (6th Cir., 1989) – **Adopt.**

U.S. v. Hardage, 982 F.2d 1436 (10th Cir., 1992) – **Adopt.**

U.S. v. Alcan Aluminum Corp., 990 F.2d 711 (2nd Cir., 1993)
– Reject.

Washington State DOT v. Washington Natural Gas Co., 59
F.3d 793 (9th Cir., 1995) – Adopt.

17. All costs incurred by government in actions that are not
inconsistent with NCP are presumed reasonable. **Liberal.**

U.S. v. NEPACCO, 810 F.2d 726 (8th Cir., 1986)

U.S. v. Hardage, 982 F.2d 1436 (10th Cir., 1992) – Adopt.

18. Government remedial action under CERCLA is acceptable
unless arbitrary and capricious. **Liberal.**

U.S. v. NEPACCO, 810 F.2d 726 (8th Cir., 1986)

U.S. v. R.W. Meyer, 889 F.2d 1497 (6th Cir., 1989) – Adopt.

U.S. v. Hardage, 982 F.2d 1436 (10th Cir., 1992) – Adopt.

In re Bell Petroleum Services, 3 F.3d 889 (5th Cir., 1993) –
Adopt.

Washington State DOT v. Washington Natural Gas Co., 59
F.3d 793 (9th Cir., 1995) – Adopt.

19. Costs of environmental cleanup are damages under liability
insurance policies. (Note: this line truncated when *Continental*
is vacated for rehearing.) **Liberal.**

Continental Insurance Cos. v. NEPACCO, 811 F.2d 1180 (8th
Cir., 1987)

Maryland Casualty Co. v. Armco, 822 F.2d 1348 (4th Cir.,
1987) – Reject.

20. Costs of environmental cleanup are *not* damages under liability
insurance. **Conservative.**

Maryland Casualty Co. v. Armco, 822 F.2d 1348 (4th Cir.,
1987)

Continental Insurance Co. v. NEPACCO, 842 F.2d 977 (8th
Cir., 1988) – Adopt.

Cincinnati Insurance Co. v. Milliken and Co., 857 F.2d 979
(4th Cir., 1988) – Adopt.

Grisham v. Commercial Union Insurance Co., 927 F.2d 1039
(8th Cir., 1991) – Adopt.

New Castle Cty. v. Hartford Accident and Indemntiy Co., 933
F.2d 1162 (3rd Cir., 1991) – Reject.

Indep. Petrochemical Corp. v. Aetna Casualty & Surety Co.,
944 F.2d 940 (DC Cir., 1991) – Reject.

Aetna Casualty and Surety Co. v. Pintlar Corp., 948 F.2d 1507
(9th Cir., 1990) – Reject.

21. EPA may regulate waters internal to a waste processing system, not just discharge. **Liberal.**
    Texas Municipal Power Agency v. Administrator, 836 F.2d 1482 (5th Cir., 1988)
    Public Service Co. of Colorado v. EPA, 949 F.2d 1063 (8th Cir., 1991) – **Adopt.**

22. CERCLA imposes successor liability on corporations which have merged with or consolidated with corporation that is a responsible party as defined in the Act. **Liberal.**
    Smith Land & Improvement Corp. v. Celotex Corp., 851 F.2d 86 (3rd Cir., 1988)
    Louisiana-Pacific Corp. v. Asarco, 909 F.2d 1260 (9th Cir., 1990) – **Adopt.**
    Anspec Co. v. Johnson Controls, 922 F.2d 1240 (6th Cir., 1991) – **Adopt.**
    U.S. v. Carolina Transformer Co., 978 F.2d 832 (4th Cir., 1992) – **Adopt.**
    U.S. v. Mexico Feed and Seed Co., 980 F.2d 478 (8th Cir., 1992) – **Adopt.**
    John S. Boyd Co. v. Boston Gas Co., 992 F.2d 401 (CA1, 1993) – **Adopt.**
    City Management Corp. v. U.S. Chemical Co., 43 F.3d 244 (6th Cir., 1994) – **Adopt.**

23. CERCLA permits imposition of joint and several liability where harm is indivisible. **Liberal.**
    U.S. v. Monsanto Co., 858 F.2d 160 (4th Cir., 1988)
    O'Neil v. Picillo, 883 F.2d 176 (CA1, 1989) – **Adopt.**
    Amoco Oil Co. v. Borden, 889 F.2d 664 (5th Cir., 1990) – **Adopt.**
    U.S. v. R.W. Meyer, 889 F.2d 1497 (6th Cir., 1989) – **Adopt.**
    U.S. v. Kayser-Roth, 910 F.2d 24 (CA1, 1990) – **Adopt.**
    B.F. Goodrich Co. v. Murtha, 958 F.2d 1192 (2nd Cir., 1992) – **Adopt.**
    U.S. v. Alcan Aluminum Corp., 964 F.2d 252 (3rd Cir., 1992) – **Adopt.**
    U.S. v. Alcan Aluminum Corp., 990 F.2d 711 (2nd Cir., 1993) – **Adopt.**
    In re Bell Petroleum Services, 3 F.3d 889 (5th Cir., 1993) – **Adopt.**

24. CERCLA defendants have burden of proof for establishing a reasonable basis for division of liability. **Liberal.**

U.S. v. Monsanto Co., 858 F.2d 160 (4th Cir., 1988) –
Adopt.

O'Neil v. Picillo, 883 F.2d 176 (CA1, 1989) – **Adopt.**

U.S. v. Alcan Aluminum Corp., 964 F.2d 252 (3rd Cir., 1992)
– **Adopt.**

U.S. v. Alcan Aluminum Corp., 990 F.2d 711 (2nd Cir., 1993)
– **Adopt.**

In re Bell Petroleum Services, 3 F.3d 889 (5th Cir., 1993) –
Adopt.

25. RCRA does not waive the United States' sovereign immunity to civil penalties imposed by states. **Conservative.**

    U.S. v. Washington, 872 F.2d 874 (9th Cir., 1989)

    Mitzelfelt v. Department of Air Force, 903 F.2d 1293 (10th Cir., 1990) – **Adopt.**

    Ohio v. U.S. DOE, 904 F.2d 1058 (6th Cir., 1990) – **Adopt.**

26. CERCLA does not authorize response costs for removal of asbestos from structure of building. **Conservative.**

    First United Methodist Church of Hyattsville v. U.S. Gypsum Co., 882 F.2d 862 (4th Cir., 1989)

    Dayton Indep. Sch. Dist. v. U.S. Mineral Products Co., 906 F.2d 1059 (5th Cir., 1990) – **Adopt.**

    3550 Stevens Creek Assocs. v. Barclays Bank of California, 915 F.2d 1355 (9th Cir., 1990) – **Adopt.**

    California v. Blech, 976 F.2d 525 (9th Cir., 1992) – **Adopt.**

    Kane v. U.S., 15 F.3d 87 (8th Cir., 1994) – **Adopt.**

27. There is no quantitative requirement for defining a hazardous substance under CERCLA. **Liberal.**

    Amoco Oil Co. v. Borden, 889 F.2d 664 (5th Cir., 1990)

    B.F. Goodrich Co. v. Murtha, 958 F.2d 1192 (2nd Cir., 1992) –
    Adopt.

    U.S. v. Alcan Aluminum Corp., 964 F.2d 252 (3rd Cir., 1992)
    – **Adopt.**

    U.S. v. Alcan Aluminum Corp., 990 F.2d 711 (2nd Cir., 1993)
    – **Adopt.**

    Stewman v. Mid-South Wood Products of Mena, 993 F.2d 646 (8th Cir., 1993) – **Adopt.**

28. For parent company to be responsible as operator under CERCLA, it must be actively involved in activities of subsidiary; general authority or ability to control is not sufficient. **Conservative.**

    U.S. v. Kayser-Roth, 910 F.2d 24 (1st Cir., 1990)

John S. Boyd Co. v. Boston Gas Co., 992 F.2d 401 (1st Cir., 1993) – **Adopt.**

Jacksonville Elec. Auth. v. Bernuth Corp., 996 F.2d 1107 (11th Cir., 1993) – **Adopt.**

Lansford-Coaldale Joint Water Auth. v. Tonolli Corp., 4 F.3d 1209 (3rd Cir., 1993) – **Adopt.**

U.S. v. TIC Inv. Corp., 68 F.3d 1082 (8th Cir., 1995) – **Adopt.**

29. Control of decisions about hazardous waste is not necessary for parent company to be responsible as operator under CERCLA. **Liberal.**

U.S. v. Kayser-Roth, 910 F.2d 24 (1st Cir., 1990)

Jacksonville Elec. Auth. v. Bernuth Corp., 996 F.2d 1107 (11th Cir., 1993) – **Adopt.**

Lansford-Coaldale Joint Water Auth. v. Tonolli Corp., 4 F.3d 1209 (3rd Cir., 1993) – **Adopt.**

U.S. v. TIC Inv. Corp., 68 F.3d 1082 (8th Cir., 1995) – **Adopt.**

30. CERCLA authorizes recovery of litigation costs, including attorney's fees, in private response action. **Liberal.**

G.E. v. Litton Indust. Automation Sys., 920 F.2d 1415 (8th Cir., 1990)

Gopher Oil Co. v. Union Oil Co., 955 F.2d 519 (8th Cir., 1992) – **Adopt.**

Stanton Road Assocs. v. Lohrey Enterprises, 984 F.2d 1015 (9th Cir., 1993) – **Reject.**

Donahey v. Bogle, 987 F.2d 1250 (6th Cir., 1993) – **Adopt.**

In re Hemingway Transport, 993 F.2d 915 (1st Cir., 1993) – **Reject.**

FMC Corp. v. Aero Industries, 998 F.2d 842 (10th Cir., 1993) – **Reject.**

31. In determining operator liability for individual in CERCLA suit, court must look to the extent of defendant's personal participation in the alleged wrongful conduct. **Conservative.**

Riverside Mkt. Dev. Corp. v. International Bldg. Prods., 931 F.2d 327 (5th Cir., 1991)

Nurad v. William E. Hooper and Sons Co., 966 F.2d 837 (4th Cir., 1992) – **Reject.**

U.S. v. Carolina Transformer Co., 978 F.2d 832 (4th Cir., 1992) – **Reject.**

Sidney S. Arst Co. v. Pipefitters Welfare Educ. Fund, 25 F.2d 417 (7th Cir., 1994) – **Adopt.**

U.S. v. Gurley, 43 F.3d 1188 (8th Cir., 1994) – **Adopt.**

Control Data Corp. v. S.C.S.C. Corp., 53 F.3d 930 (8th Cir., 1995) – **Adopt.**

Antitrust

1. Prices above average total cost are not necessarily non-predatory. **Liberal.**

   Transamerica Computer Co. v. IBM, 698 F.2d 1377 (9th Cir., 1983)

   Barry Wright Corp. v. ITT Grinnell Corp., 724 F.2d 227 (1st Cir., 1984) – **Reject.**

   Arthur S. Langenderfer v. S.E. Johnson Co., 729 F.2d 1050 (6th Cir., 1984) – **Reject.**

   Drinkwine v. Federated Publications, 780 F.2d 735 (9th Cir., 1985) – **Adopt.**

   Henry v. Chloride, 809 F.2d 1334 (8th Cir., 1987) – **Reject.**

   McGahee v. Northern Propane Gas Co., 858 F.2d 1487 (11th Cir., 1988) – **Reject.**

   Morgan v. Ponder, 892 F.2d 1355 (8th Cir., 1989) – **Reject.**

2. A firm's intent is irrelevant to the question of whether its pricing is predatory. **Conservative.**

   Barry Wright Corp. v. ITT Grinnell Corp., 724 F.2d 227 (1st Cir., 1984)

   Henry v. Chloride, 809 F.2d 1334 (8th Cir., 1987) – **Adopt.**

   McGahee v. Northern Propane Gas Co., 858 F.2d 1487 (11th Cir., 1988) – **Reject.**

   AA Poultry Farms v. Rose Acre Farms, 881 F.2d 1396 (7th Cir., 1989) – **Adopt.**

3. A party need not allege that it suffered a direct anticompetitive effect to challenge a merger or acquisition under the Clayton Act section 7. It is sufficient to show injuries expected to result from the lessening of competition or anticompetitive acts made possible by the acquisition. **Liberal.**

   Arthur S. Langenderfer v. S.E. Johnson Co., 729 F.2d 1050 (6th Cir., 1984)

   G. Heileman Brewing Co. v. Christian Schmidt Brewing Co., 753 F.2d 1354 (6th Cir., 1985) – **Adopt.**

   Monfort of Colorado v. Cargill, 761 F.2d 570 (10th Cir., 1985) – **Adopt.**

4. The fact that a combining group is not drawn from people who compete economically among themselves is a ground for applying rule of reason analysis rather than per se analysis to a Sherman Act section 1 claim. **Conservative.**

   M & H Tire Co. v. Hoosier Racing Tire Corp., 733 F.2d 973 (1st Cir., 1984)

   Cha Car v. Calder Race Course, 752 F.2d 609 (11th Cir., 1985) – **Adopt.**

5. A maximum resale price maintenance scheme is not per se illegal where prices are not predatory. **Conservative.**

   Jack Walters and Sons Corp. v. Morton Building, 737 F.2d 698 (7th Cir., 1984)

   USA Petroleum Co. v. Atlantic Richfield Co., 859 F.2d 687 (9th Cir., 1988) – **Reject.**

   Indiana Grocery v. Super Valu Stores, 864 F.2d 1409 (7th Cir., 1989) – **Adopt.**

6. It is impossible for two companies under common ownership to conspire in violation of the Sherman Act. **Conservative.**

   Century Oil Tool v. Production Specialties, 737 F.2d 1316 (5th Cir., 1984)

   Greenwood Utilities Commission v. Mississippi Power Co., 751 F.2d 1484 (5th Cir., 1985) – **Adopt.**

   Directory Sales Mgmt. Corp. v. Ohio Bell Telephone Co., 833 F.2d 606 (6th Cir., 1987) – **Adopt.**

   Advanced Health-Care Services v. Radford Comm. Hospital, 910 F.2d 139 (4th Cir., 1990) – **Adopt.**

   Guzowski v. Hartman, 969 F.2d 211 (6th Cir., 1992) – **Adopt.**

   Siegel Transfer v. Carrier Express, 54 F.3d 1125 (3rd Cir., 1995) – **Adopt.**

7. For a lawsuit to fall under the sham exception to the Noerr-Pennington doctrine (and thus constitute anti-competitive behavior), the suit must be baseless. **Conservative.**

   Omni Resource Development Corp. v. Conoco, 739 F.2d 1412 (9th Cir., 1984)

   Rickards v. Canine Eye Registration Foundation, 783 F.2d 1329 (9th Cir., 1986) – **Adopt.**

   Westmac v. Smith, 797 F.2d 313 (6th Cir., 1986) – **Reject.**

8. It is legally impossible for a hospital to conspire with its medical staff in violation of the Sherman Act. **Conservative.**

Weiss v. York Hospital, 745 F.2d 786 (3rd Cir., 1984)

Potters Medical Center v. The City Hospital Assn., 800 F.2d 568 (6th Cir., 1986) – **Adopt.**

Nanavati v. Burdette Tomlin Memorial Hospital, 857 F.2d 96 (3rd Cir., 1988) – **Adopt.**

Bolt v. Halifax Hospital Medical Center, 891 F.2d 810 (11th Cir., 1990) – **Reject.**

Oksanen v. Page Memorial Hospital (panel), 912 F.2d 73 (4th Cir., 1990) – **Reject.**

Nurse Midwifery Associates v. Hibbett, 918 F.2d 605 (6th Cir., 1990) – **Adopt.**

Todorov v. DCH Healthcare Authority, 921 F.2d 1438 (11th Cir., 1991) – **Reject.**

Oksanen v. Page Memorial Hospital (en banc), 945 F.2d 696 (4th Cir., 1991) – **Adopt.**

9. The members of a medical staff are capable of conspiring with each other in violation of the Sherman Act. **Liberal.**

    Weiss v. York Hospital, 745 F.2d 786 (3rd Cir., 1984)

    Nanavati v. Burdette Tomlin Memorial Hospital, 857 F.2d 96 (3rd Cir., 1988) – **Adopt.**

    Bolt v. Halifax Hospital Medical Center, 891 F.2d 810 (11th Cir., 1990) – **Adopt.**

    Pinhas v. Summit Health, Ltd., 894 F.2d 1024 (9th Cir., 1989) – **Adopt.**

    Oksanen v. Page Memorial Hospital (panel), 912 F.2d 73 (4th Cir., 1990) – **Adopt.**

    Nurse Midwifery Associates v. Hibbett, 918 F.2d 605 (6th Cir., 1990) – **Adopt.**

    Oksanen v. Page Memorial Hospital (en banc), 945 F.2d 696 (4th Cir., 1991) – **Adopt.**

    Capital Imaging Assoc's v. Mohawk Valley Medical Assoc's, 996 F.2d 537 (2nd Cir., 1993) – **Adopt.**

    Willman v. Heartland Hospital East, 34 F.3d 605 (8th Cir., 1994) – **Adopt.**

10. As a matter of law, any action taken by the medical staff as a group satisfies the "contract, combination, or conspiracy" requirement of section 1 of the Sherman Act. **Liberal.**

    Weiss v. York Hospital, 745 F.2d 786 (3rd Cir., 1984)

    Nanavati v. Burdette Tomlin Memorial Hospital, 857 F.2d 96 (3rd Cir., 1988) – **Adopt.**

Bolt v. Halifax Hospital Medical Center, 891 F.2d 810 (11th Cir., 1990) – **Reject.**

Pinhas v. Summit Health, Ltd., 894 F.2d 1024 (9th Cir., 1989) – **Adopt.**

Oksanen v. Page Memorial Hospital (panel), 912 F.2d 73 (4th Cir., 1990) – **Reject.**

Nurse Midwifery Associates v. Hibbett, 918 F.2d 605 (6th Cir., 1990) – **Reject.**

Oksanen v. Page Memorial Hospital (en banc), 945 F.2d 696 (4th Cir., 1991) – **Reject.**

Capital Imaging Assoc's v. Mohawk Valley Med. Assoc's, 996 F.2d 537 (2nd Cir., 1993) – **Reject.**

Willman v. Heartland Hospital East, 34 F.3d 605 (8th Cir., 1994) – **Reject.**

11. If a suit is successful, it cannot be considered sham under the Noerr-Pennington doctrine. **Conservative.**

    Columbia Pictures Industries v. Redd Horne, 749 F.2d 154 (3rd Cir., 1984)

    In re Burlington Northern, 822 F.2d 518 (5th Cir., 1987) – **Reject.**

    Sessions Tank Liners v. Joor Manufacturing., 827 F.2d 458 (9th Cir., 1987) – **Reject.**

    South Dakota v. Kansas City Southern Industries, 880 F.2d 40 (8th Cir., 1988) – **Reject.**

    Eden Hannon and Co. v. Sumitomo Trust and Banking Co., 914 F.2d 556 (4th Cir., 1990) – **Adopt.**

    Columbia Pictures Industries v. Prof. Real Estate Investors, 944 F.2d 1525 (9th Cir., 1991) – **Adopt.**

    Boulware v. Nevada, 960 F.2d 793 (9th Cir., 1992) – **Reject.**

12. Under either per se or rule of reason analysis of a tying claim, plaintiff must show that there is a substantial danger that the seller will acquire market power in the tied product market. **Conservative.**

    Carl Sandburg Village Condo. Assn. No. 1 v. First Condo. Dev. Co., 758 F.2d 203 (7th Cir., 1984)

    Will v. Comprehensive Accounting Corp., 776 F.2d 665 (7th Cir., 1985) – **Adopt.**

    Hand v. Central Transport, 779 F.2d 8 (6th Cir., 1986) – **Adopt.**

    Gonzales v. St. Margaret's House Housing Dev. Fund Corp., 880 F.2d 1514 (2nd Cir., 1989) – **Reject.**

13. To prove a claim of illegal tying under rule of reason analysis, a plaintiff must show that the defendant has market power in the tying product market. **Conservative.**

    Amey v. Gulf Abstract and Title, 758 F.2d 1486 (11th Cir., 1985)

    Will v. Comprehensive Accounting Corp., 776 F.2d 665 (7th Cir., 1986) – **Adopt.**

    Hand v. Central Transport, 779 F.2d 8 (6th Cir., 1986) – **Adopt.**

    The Great Escape v. Union City Body Company, 791 F.2d 532 (7th Cir., 1986) – **Adopt.**

    Grappone v. Subaru of New England, 858 F.2d 792 (1st Cir., 1988) – **Reject.**

    Town Sound and Custom Tops v. Chrysler Motors Corp., 1991 U.S. App. LEXIS 17956 (3rd Cir., 1991) – **Reject.**

    Virtual Maintenance v. Prime Computer, 957 F.2d 1318 (6th Cir., 1992) – **Reject.**

    Town Sound and Custom Tops v. Chrysler Motors Corp., 959 F.2d 468 (3rd Cir., 1992) – **Reject.**

    Breaux Brothers Farms v. Teche Sugar Co., 21 F.3d 83 (5th Cir., 1994) – **Reject.**

14. Bribery provision of Robinson-Patman Act applies to passing of payments only between sellers and buyers, not to agents. **Conservative.**

    Seaboard Supply Co. v. Congoleum Corp., 770 F.2d 367 (3rd Cir., 1985)

    Feeney v. Chamberlain Mfg. Corp., 831 F.2d 93 (5th Cir., 1987) – **Adopt.**

    Environmental Tectonics v. W.S. Kirkpatrick Inc., 847 F.2d 1052 (3rd Cir., 1988) – **Adopt.**

    Stephen Jay Photography v. Olan Mills, 903 F.2d 988 (4th Cir., 1990) – **Adopt.**

15. Threats against manufacturer by dealers along with termination of other dealer are not sufficient to establish conspiracy against other dealer. **Conservative.**

    National Marine Electronic Distributors v. Raytheon Co., 778 F.2d 190 (4th Cir., 1985)

    Arnold Pontiac-GMC v. General Motors Corp., 786 F.2d 564 (3rd Cir., 1986) – **Reject.**

    The Garment District v. Belk Stores Services, 799 F.2d 905 (4th Cir., 1986) – **Adopt.**

Oltz v. St. Peter's Community Hospitals, 861 F.2d 1440 (9th Cir., 1988) – **Reject.**

Bailey's v. Windsor America, 948 F.2d 1018 (6th Cir., 1991) – **Adopt.**

Robinson-Bock Distributing Co. v. Pioneer/Eclipse Corp., 1993 U.S. App. LEXIS 22029 (7th Cir., 1993) – **Adopt.**

16. For manufacturer's termination of distributor to be illegal per se, must be pursuant to price maintenance agreement with another distributor. **Conservative.**

    Business Electronics Corp. v. Sharp Electronics Corp., 780 F.2d 1212 (5th Cir., 1986)

    Westman Commission Co. v. Hobart International, 796 F.2d 1216 (10th Cir., 1986) – **Adopt.**

    Morrison v. Murray Biscuit Co., 797 F.2d 1430 (7th Cir., 1986) – **Adopt.**

    McCabe's Furniture v. La-Z-Boy Chair Co., 798 F.2d 323 (8th Cir., 1986) – **Adopt.**

17. Dealer cannot claim damages for termination where loss is of profits arising from violations of antitrust laws. **Conservative.**

    Local Beauty Supply v. Lamaur Inc., 787 F.2d 1197 (7th Cir., 1986)

    Todorov v. DCH Healthcare Authority, 921 F.2d 1438 (11th Cir., 1991) – **Adopt.**

18. Showing that plaintiff lowered prices to existing customers and lost potential customers is sufficient proof of antitrust injury under Robinson-Patman Act. **Liberal.**

    Rose Confections v. Ambrosia Chocolate Co., 816 F.2d 381 (8th Cir., 1987)

    J.F. Feeser v. Serv-A-Portion, 909 F.2d 1524 (3rd Cir., 1990) – **Adopt.**

19. Noerr immunity does not apply to lobbying of private model-code association, even where government usually adopts its standards. **Liberal.**

    Indian Head v. Allied Tube and Conduit Corp., 817 F.2d 938 (2nd Cir., 1987)

    Sessions Tank Liners v. Joor Mfg., 827 F.2d 458 (9th Cir., 1987) – **Reject.**

20. A prestigious trademark is not itself persuasive evidence of market power. **Conservative.**

Mozart Co. v. Mercedes-Benz of North America, 833 F.2d 1342 (9th Cir., 1987)

Grappone v. Subaru of New England, 858 F.2d 792 (1st Cir., 1988) – **Adopt.**

Town Sound and Custom Tops v. Chrysler Motors Corp., 959 F.2d 468 (3rd Cir., 1992) – **Adopt.**

21. Predatory hiring (to keep competition from getting an employee) is a Sherman Act. sec. 2 violation. **Liberal.**

    Universal Analytics, Inc. v. MacNeal-Schwendler Corp., 914 F.2d 1256 (9th Cir., 1990)

    Midwest Radio Co. v. Forum Publishing Co., 942 F.2d 1294 (8th Cir., 1991) – **Adopt.**

22. To establish predatory hiring, must show predatory intent or clear nonuse in fact. **Conservative.**

    Universal Analytics, Inc. v. MacNeal-Schwendler Corp., 914 F.2d 1256 (9th Cir., 1990)

    Midwest Radio Co. v. Forum Publishing Co., 942 F.2d 1294 (8th Cir., 1991) – **Adopt.**

23. A price squeeze in a fully regulated industry will not normally constitute exclusionary conduct under Sherman Act sec. 2. **Conservative.**

    Town of Concord v. Boston Edison Co., 915 F.2d 17 (1st Cir., 1990)

    City of Anaheim v. Southern California Edison Co., 955 F.2d 1373 (9th Cir., 1992) – **Reject.**

Appendix B
Interview Questions

This is a copy of the notes I used to conduct the interviews. Most interviews departed from the order and wording given here in some way, but it gives a generally accurate picture of how the interviews were conducted, following introductions.

I'm interested in whether judges tend to specialize, develop expertise in particular areas: Are there any particular fields of law in which you consider yourself expert [prompt: any in which you specialize?]

Does this circuit have special expertise in any areas?

I'm particularly interested in three areas of law: antitrust; search and seizure; and environmental law.

Thinking back over the last 10 or 15 yrs., are there any circuits (or individual judges?) with particular expertise in antitrust (in your own opinion or by general reputation)?

Would it be possible to rank the circuits in some way?

What about search and seizure? Environmental law?

It seems that circuits sometimes gain reputations for general excellence. [If needs cue: An example would be the 2nd Circuit in the 1940s and 50s.] Are there any circuits today which have a reputation for general excellence or which in your view merit such a reputation?

Is it possible to rank the circuits on this dimension (perhaps high, medium, and low)?

Returning for a moment to the three areas of law I mentioned – antitrust, search and seizure, and environmental law – would you say that any of these areas are generally more or less difficult than the others?

I mean, do they generally vary in the amount of mental effort you have to put in to decide cases?

Of the three areas, which do you have the greatest interest in? Which the least?

Now I'd like to ask some questions about how you view different aspects of your work.

First, when you're writing an opinion, do you have any particular audience in mind?

I would imagine that when you are deciding a case, you might have certain general objectives in mind. Let me mention some possible objectives: could you tell me how important, if at all, each one is to you when you're deciding a case?

a) Making sure that the body of law in an area is coherent and consistent.

b) Deciding cases promptly/keeping up with caseload

c) Insuring that the outcome of the specific case is good (just, beneficial to society)

d) Making sure the decision is legally correct, regardless of whether you are happy with the specific outcome.

In your view, what makes a decision legally right or wrong? In other words, how can we distinguish good law from bad, apart from our feelings about outcomes?

Are there other types of objectives which come to mind when you're deciding a case?

How important would you say other judges' decisions are to you when you're deciding a case? Here I mean Supreme Court, other panels of your own circuit, or other circuits, so if you feel we should distinguish between them on this and next few questions please do.

Can you estimate the percentage of cases not covered by Supreme Court or circuit precedent?

How do you usually find out about decisions of other judges? [Prompt: briefs; clerks; own research; contact with other judges.]

How good a job do the briefs usually do of bringing relevant cases to your attention?

We'd expect judges to be more likely to adopt legal rules from other decisions in certain cases than in others. For instance, if the decision is clearly relevant, as opposed to one which is not. I'm wondering if there are other factors that affect this choice too. For example, would you be more inclined to adopt rules from certain courts or judges than others? Why? Anything else about the other courts?

Could there be something about the case itself or the issues involved that would make you more or less likely to adopt the earlier legal rule? [Prompt: field you're expert in; care about issue; difficulty]

What about the earlier decision itself? Are there any characteristics that would make it more or less likely that you'd adopt the rule?

I'd like to end with a question close to the heart of the project. It seems that sometimes a court sets down a legal rule and the rule catches on quickly – lots of courts adopt it. Other times it becomes very controversial. Still other times, it is pretty much ignored and falls by the wayside. I want to ask if from your own experience you have ideas about why some rules get treated differently from others. Maybe why some get attention and others don't? Of those that get attention, why sometimes it's smooth sailing while other times it's rocky?

References

Abraham, Henry J. 1999. *Justices, Presidents, and Senators*. Lanham, Maryland: Rowman & Littlefield Publishers, Inc.

Aldrich, John H., and Forrest D. Nelson. 1984. *Linear Probability, Logit, and Probit Models*. Sage University Paper Series on Quantitative Applications in the Social Sciences. Beverly Hills, California: Sage Publications.

Baum, Lawrence. 1980. "Response of Federal District Judges to Court of Appeals Policies: An Exploration." *Western Political Quarterly* 33:217–24.

———. 1988. "Measuring Policy Change in the U.S. Supreme Court." *American Political Science Review* 82:905–12.

———. 1997. *The Puzzle of Judicial Behavior*. Ann Arbor: University of Michigan Press.

Becker, Theodore L. 1966. "A Survey Study of Hawaiian Judges: The Effect on Decisions of Judicial Role Variation." *American Political Science Review* 60:677–80.

Brace, Paul, and Melinda Gann Hall. 1990. "Neo-Institutionalism and Dissent in State Supreme Courts." *Journal of Politics* 52:54–70.

Brehm, John, and Scott Gates. 1997. *Working, Shirking, and Sabotage*. Ann Arbor: University of Michigan Press.

Brembeck, Winston L., and William S. Howell. 1976. *Persuasion: A Means of Social Influence*. Second Ed. Englewood Cliffs, New Jersey: Prentice-Hall.

Brigham, John. 1978. *Constitutional Language: An Interpretation of Judicial Decision*. Westport, Connecticut: Greenwood Press.

Caldeira, Gregory A. 1983. "On the Reputation of State Supreme Courts." *Political Behavior* 5:83–108.

———. 1985. "The Transmission of Legal Precedent: A Study of State Supreme Courts." *American Political Science Review* 79:178–93.

———. 1988. "In the Mirror of the Justices: Sources of Greatness on the Supreme Court." *Political Behavior* 10:247–66.

Caldeira, Gregory A., and John R. Wright. 1988. "Organized Interests and Agenda-Setting in the U.S. Supreme Court." *American Political Science Review* 82:1109–27.

Cameron, Charles M. 1993. "New Avenues for Modeling Judicial Politics." Paper presented at the Conference on the Political Economy of Public Law, Rochester, New York.

Cameron, Charles M., Jeffrey A. Segal, and Donald Songer. 2000. "Strategic Auditing in a Political Hierarchy: An Informational Model of the Supreme Court's Certiorari Decisions." *American Political Science Review* 94: 101–16.

Caminker, Evan H. 1994. "Precedent and Prediction: The Forward-Looking Aspects of Inferior Court Decisionmaking." *Texas Law Review* 73:1–82.

Canon, Bradley C., and Lawrence Baum. 1981. "Patterns of Adoption of Tort Law Innovations: An Application of Diffusion Theory to Judicial Doctrines." *American Political Science Review* 75:975–87.

Cardozo, Benjamin N. 1921. *The Nature of the Judicial Process*. New Haven, Connecticut: Yale University Press.

Clayton, Cornell W. 1999. "The Supreme Court and Political Jurisprudence: New and Old Institutionalisms." In Cornell W. Clayton and Howard Gillman, eds., *Supreme Court Decision-Making: New Institutionalist Approaches*. Chicago: University of Chicago Press.

Cross, Frank B., and Emerson H. Tiller. 1998. "Judicial Partisanship and Obedience to Legal Doctrine: Whistleblowing on the Federal Courts of Appeals." *Yale Law Journal* 107:2155–76.

Danelski, David. 1968. "The Influence of the Chief Justice in the Decisional Process of the Supreme Court." In Thomas P. Janige and Sheldon Goldman, eds., *The Federal Judicial System: Readings in Process and Behavior*. New York: Holt, Rinehart, and Winston.

Davis, Sue, and Donald R. Songer. 1989. "The Changing Role of the United States Courts of Appeals: The Flow of Litigation Revisited." *Justice System Journal* 13:323.

Ducat, Craig R., and Robert L. Dudley. 1987. "Dimensions Underlying Economic Policymaking in the Early and Later Burger Courts." *Journal of Politics* 49:521–39.

Eagly, Alice H., and Shelly Chaiken. 1993. *The Psychology of Attitudes*. Fort Worth, Texas: Harcourt Brace Jovanovich.

Edwards, Harry T. 1991. "The Judicial Function and the Elusive Goal of Principled Decisionmaking." *Wisconsin Law Review* 1991:837–65.

Epstein, Lee, and Jack Knight. 1998. *The Choices Justices Make*. Washington, D.C.: Congressional Quarterly Press.

Epstein, Lee, and Joseph F. Kobylka. 1992. *The Supreme Court and Legal Change*. Chapel Hill: The University of North Carolina Press.

Epstein, Lee, and Carol Mershon. 1996. "Measuring Political Preferences." *American Journal of Political Science* 40:261–94.

Federal Judicial Center. 1993. "Structural and Other Alternatives for the Federal Courts of Appeals." Report to the United States Congress and the Judicial Conference of the United States.

Fiellin, Alan. 1962. "The Functions of Informal Groups in Legislative Institutions." *Journal of Politics* 24:72–91.

Fisher, William W., III, Morton J. Horwitz, and Thomas A. Reed, eds. 1993. *American Legal Realism*. New York: Oxford University Press.

Fiske, Susan T., and Shelley E. Taylor. 1991. *Social Cognition*. Second Ed. New York: McGraw-Hill, Inc.

Friedman, Lawrence M., Robert A. Kagan, Bliss Cartwright, and Stanton Wheeler. 1981. "State Supreme Courts: A Century of Style and Citation." *Stanford Law Review* 33:773–818.

Friendly, Henry J. 1961. "Reactions of a Lawyer – Newly Become Judge." *Yale Law Journal* 71:218–38.

Gardner, James N. 1975. "The Ninth Circuit's Unpublished Opinions: Denial of Equal Justice?" *American Bar Association Journal* 61:1224.

George, Tracey E., and Lee Epstein. 1992. "On the Nature of Supreme Court Decision Making." *American Political Science Review* 86:323–37.

Gibson, James L. 1978. "Judges' Role Orientations, Attitudes, and Decisions: An Interactive Model." *American Political Science Review* 72:911–24.

—— 1983. "From Simplicity to Complexity: The Development of Theory in the Study of Judicial Behavior." *Political Behavior* 5:7–49.

Giles, Micheal W., Virginia A. Hettinger, and Todd C. Peppers. 1998. "Alternative Measures of Preferences for Judges of the Courts of Appeals." Paper presented at the 1998 Annual Meeting of the Midwest Political Science Association, Chicago.

Giles, Micheal W., and Christopher Zorn. 2000. "Gibson Versus Case-Based Approaches: Concurring in Part, Dissenting in Part." *Law and Courts* 10(Spring):10–16.

Gillman, Howard, and Cornell W. Clayton. 1999. "Beyond Judicial Attitudes: Institutional Approaches to Supreme Court Decision-Making." In Cornell W. Clayton and Howard Gillman, eds., *Supreme Court Decision-Making: New Institutionalist Approaches*. Chicago: University of Chicago Press.

Glick, Henry R. 1992. "Judicial Innovation and Policy Re-invention: State Supreme Courts and the Right to Die." *Western Political Quarterly* 45: 71–92.

Goldman, Sheldon. 1975. "Voting Behavior on the United States Courts of Appeals Revisited." *American Political Science Review* 69:491–506.

—— 1997. *Picking Federal Judges: Lower Court Selection from Roosevelt Through Reagan*. New Haven, Connecticut: Yale University Press.

Goldman, Sheldon, and Elliot Slotnick. 1999. "Clinton's Second Term: Picking Judges Under Fire." *Judicature* 82:264–84.

Gruhl, John. 1980. "The Supreme Court's Impact on the Law of Libel: Compliance by Lower Federal Courts." *Western Political Quarterly* 33: 502–19.

Gulati, Mitu, and C.M.A. McCauliff. 1998. "On Not Making Law." *Law and Contemporary Problems* 61:157–227.

Haire, Susan, and Stefanie Lindquist. 1997. "Social Security Disability Cases in the U.S. Courts of Appeals." *Judicature* 80:230–6.

Hall, Melinda Gann. 1992. "Electoral Politics and Strategic Voting in State Supreme Courts." *Journal of Politics* 54:427–46.

Hellman, Arthur. 1989. "Jumboism and Jurisprudence: The Theory and Practice of Precedent in the Large Appellate Court." *University of Chicago Law Review* 56:541–601.

1995. "By Precedent Unbound: The Nature and Extent of Unresolved Intercircuit Conflicts." *University of Pittsburgh Law Review* 56:693–800.

1998. "Light on a Darkling Plain: Intercircuit Conflicts in the Perspective of Time and Experience." *Supreme Court Review* 1998:247–302.

Howard, J. Woodford, Jr. 1968. "On the Fluidity of Judicial Choice." *American Political Science Review* 62:43–56.

1981. *Courts of Appeals in the Federal Judicial System*. Princeton, New Jersey: Princeton University Press.

Hurwitz, Jon. 1988. "Determinants of Legislative Cue Selection." *Social Science Quarterly* 69:212–23.

Johnson, Charles A. 1979. "Lower Court Reactions to Supreme Court Decisions: A Quantitative Examination." *American Journal of Political Science* 23: 792–803.

1987. "Law, Politics, and Judicial Decision Making: Lower Federal Court Uses of Supreme Court Decisions." *Law and Society Review* 21:325–40.

Johnson, Charles A., and Bradley C. Canon. 1984. *Judicial Policies: Implementation and Impact*. Washington, D.C.: Congressional Quarterly Press.

King, Gary, Robert O. Keohane, and Sidney Verba. 1994. *Designing Social Inquiry: Scientific Inference in Qualitative Research*. Princeton, New Jersey: Princeton University Press.

King, Gary, Michael Tomz, and Jason Wittenberg. 2000. "Making the Most of Statistical Analyses: Improving Interpretation and Presentation." *American Journal of Political Science* 44:341–55.

Kingdon, John W. 1989. *Congressmen's Voting Decisions*. Third Ed. Ann Arbor: University of Michigan Press.

Kitchin, William I. 1978. *Federal District Judges: An Analysis of Judicial Perceptions*. Baltimore, Maryland: Collage Press.

Klein, David, and Darby Morrisroe. 1999. "The Prestige and Influence of Individual Judges on the U.S. Courts of Appeals." *The Journal of Legal Studies* 28:371–91.

Knight, Jack, and Lee Epstein. 1996. "The Norm of *Stare Decisis*." *American Journal of Political Science* 40:1018–35.

Kornhauser, Lewis A. 1995. "Adjudication by a Resource-Constrained Team: Hierarchy and Precedent in a Judicial System." *Southern California Law Review* 68:1605–29.

Kosma, Montgomery N. 1998. "Measuring the Influence of Supreme Court Justices." *The Journal of Legal Studies* 27:333–72.

Kovacic, William E. 1991. "Reagan's Judicial Appointees and Antitrust in the 1990s." *Fordham Law Review* 60:49–123.

Kunda, Ziva. 1987. "Motivated Inference: Self-Serving Generation and Evaluation of Causal Theories." *Journal of Personality and Social Psychology* 53: 636–47.

1990. "The Case for Motivated Reasoning." *Psychological Bulletin* 108: 480–98.

Kuklinski, James, and John Stanga. 1979. "Political Participation and Governmental Responsiveness: The Behavior of California Superior Courts." *American Political Science Review* 73:1090–9.

Landes, William M., Lawrence Lessig, and Michael E. Solimine. 1998. "Judicial Influence: A Citation Analysis of Federal Courts of Appeals Judges." *Journal of Legal Studies* 27:271.

Landes, William M., and Richard A. Posner. 1976. "Legal Precedent: A Theoretical and Empirical Analysis." *Journal of Law and Economics* 19: 249–307.

Lawler, James J., and William M. Parle. 1989. "Expansion of the Public Trust Doctrine in Environmental Law: An Examination of Judicial Policy Making by State Supreme Courts." *Social Science Quarterly* 70:134–48.

Levi, Edward H. 1948. *An Introduction to Legal Reasoning.* Chicago: University of Chicago Press.

Lindquist, Stefanie A. 2000. "The Judiciary as Organized Hierarchy: Intercircuit Conflicts in the Federal Appellate Courts." Paper presented at the Annual Meeting of the Midwest Political Science Association, Chicago, April 26–30.

Llewellyn, Karl. 1951. *The Bramble Bush.* New York: Oceana.

Long, J. Scott. 1997. *Regression Models for Categorical and Limited Dependent Variables.* Thousand Oaks, California: Sage Publications.

Macey, Jonathan R. 1989. "The Internal and External Costs and Benefits of Stare Decisis." *Chicago-Kent Law Review* 65:93–113.

Maltzman, Forrest, and Paul J. Wahlbeck. 1996. "Strategic Policy Considerations and Voting Fluidity on the Burger Court." *American Political Science Review* 90:581–92.

Marvell, Thomas B. 1978. *Appellate Courts and Lawyers: Information Gathering in the Adversary System.* Westport, Connecticut: Greenwood Press.

Mathy, Pamela. 1985. "Experiment in Federal Appellate Case Management and the Prehearing Conference Program of the United States Court of Appeals for the Seventh Circuit." *Chicago-Kent Law Review* 61:431–82.

Matthews, Donald R., and James A. Stimson. 1975. *Yeas and Nays.* New York: Wiley-Interscience.

McIntosh, Wayne V., and Cynthia L. Cates. 1997. *Judicial Entrepreneurship: The Role of the Judge in the Marketplace of Ideas.* Westport, Connecticut: Greenwood Press.

McNollgast. 1995. "Politics and the Courts: A Positive Theory of Judicial Doctrine and the Rule of Law." *Southern California Law Review* 68:1631–89.

Merryman, John Henry. 1954. "The Authority of Authority: What the California Supreme Court Cited in 1950." *Stanford Law Review* 6:613.

———. 1977. "Toward a Theory of Citations: An Empirical Study of the Citation Practice of the California Supreme Court in 1950, 1960, and 1970." *Southern California Law Review* 50:381–428.

Mott, Rodney L. 1936. "Judicial Influence." *American Political Science Review* 30:295.

Murphy, Walter F. 1964. *Elements of Judicial Strategy.* Chicago: University of Chicago Press.

Newman, Jon O. 1984. "Between Legal Realism and Neutral Principles: The Legitimacy of Institutional Values." *California Law Review* 72:200–16.

O'Brien, David M. 1997. "The Rehnquist Court's Shrinking Plenary Docket." *Judicature* 81:58–65.

O'Leary, Rosemary. 1993. *Environmental Change: Federal Courts and the EPA.* Philadelphia: Temple University Press.

Oakes, James L. 1975. "Law Reviews and Judging." *New York University Law Review* 50:2–5.

Pacelle, Richard L., Jr. 1991. *The Transformation of the Supreme Court's Agenda: From the New Deal to the Reagan Administration.* Boulder, Colorado: Westview Press.

Pacelle, Richard L., Jr., and Lawrence Baum. 1992. "Supreme Court Authority in the Judiciary: A Study of Remands." *American Politics Quarterly* 20:169–91.

Peltason, J. W. 1961. *Fifty-Eight Lonely Men: Southern Federal Judges and School Desegregation.* New York: Harcourt Brace.

Perry, H. W., Jr. 1991. *Deciding to Decide: Agenda Setting in the U.S. Supreme Court.* Cambridge, Massachusetts: Harvard University Press.

Petty, Richard E., and John T. Cacioppo. 1981. *Attitudes and Persuasion: Classic and Contemporary Approaches.* Dubuque, Iowa: Wm. C. Brown Company.

Posner, Richard A. 1990a. *Cardozo: A Study in Reputation.* Chicago: University of Chicago Press.

1990b. *The Problems of Jurisprudence.* Cambridge, Massachusetts: Harvard University Press.

1995. *Overcoming Law.* Cambridge, Massachusetts: Harvard University Press.

Pritchett, C. Herman. 1948. *The Roosevelt Court: A Study in Judicial Politics and Values 1937–1947.* New York: Macmillan.

Reddick, Malia, and Sara C. Benesh. 2000. "Norm Violation by the Lower Courts in the Treatment of Supreme Court Precedent: A Research Framework." *The Justice System Journal* 21:117–42.

Rohde, David W., and Harold J. Spaeth. 1976. *Supreme Court Decision Making.* San Francisco: Freeman.

Richman, William M., and William L. Reynolds. 1996. "Elitism, Expediency, and the New Certiorari: Requiem for the Learned Hand Tradition." *Cornell Law Review* 81:273.

Romans, Neil T. 1974. "The Role of State Supreme Courts in Judicial Policy Making." *Western Political Quarterly* 27:38–59.

Rowland, C. K., and Robert A. Carp. 1996. *Politics and Judgment in Federal District Courts.* Lawrence: University Press of Kansas.

Sarat, Austin. 1977. "Judging in Trial Courts: An Exploratory Study." *Journal of Politics* 39:368–98.

Schaefer, Walter V. 1966. "Precedent and Policy." *University of Chicago Law Review* 34:3–25.

Scheb, John M., II, Thomas D. Ungs, and Allison L. Hayes. 1989. "Judicial Role Orientations, Attitudes, and Decision Making: A Research Note." *Western Political Quarterly* 42:427–35.

Schick, Marvin. 1970. *Learned Hand's Court*. Baltimore, Maryland: The Johns Hopkins Press.

Suhubert, Glendon. 1962. "The 1960 Term of the Supreme Court: A Psychological Analysis." *American Political Science Review* 56:90–107.

———. 1965. *The Judicial Mind: Attitudes and Ideologies of Supreme Court Justices, 1946–1963*. Evanston, Illinois: Northwestern University Press.

Segal, Jeffrey A. 1984. "Predicting Supreme Court Cases Probabilistically: The Search and Seizure Cases, 1962–1984." *American Political Science Review* 78:891–900.

———. 1986. "Supreme Court Justices as Human Decision Makers: An Individual-Level Analysis of the Search and Seizure Cases." *Journal of Politics* 48: 938–55.

Segal, Jeffrey A., and Harold J. Spaeth. 1993. *The Supreme Court and the Attitudinal Model*. New York: Cambridge University Press.

Shapiro, Martin. 1965. "Stability and Change in Judicial Decision-Making: Incrementalism or Stare Decisis." *Law in Transition Quarterly* 2:134–57.

———. 1970. "Decentralized Decision Making in the Law of Torts." In S. Sidney Ulmer, ed., *Political Decision-Making*. New York: Van Nostrand.

Sheehan, Reginald S., Mark S. Hurwitz, and Malia Reddick. 1998. "A Longitudinal View of Decision Making on the United States Courts of Appeals." Paper presented at the 1998 Conference of the Southern Political Science Association, Atlanta, Georgia.

Songer, Donald R. 1987. "The Impact of the Supreme Court on Trends in Economic Policy Making in the United States Courts of Appeals." *Journal of Politics* 49:830–41.

Songer, Donald R., and Susan Haire. 1992. "Integrating Alternative Approaches to the Study of Judicial Voting: Obscenity Cases in the U.S. Courts of Appeals." *American Journal of Political Science* 36:963–82.

Songer, Donald R., Jeffrey A. Segal, and Charles M. Cameron. 1994. "The Hierarchy of Justice: Testing a Principal-Agent Model of Supreme Court–Circuit Court Interactions." *American Journal of Political Science* 38:673–96.

Songer, Donald R., and Reginald S. Sheehan. 1990. "Supreme Court Impact on Compliance and Outcomes: *Miranda* and *New York Times* in the United States Courts of Appeals." *Western Political Quarterly* 43:297–319.

Spaeth, Harold J. 1997. United States Supreme Court Judicial Database, 1953–1995 Terms. 7th ICPSR version. East Lansing: Michigan State University, Dept. of Political Science [producer]. Ann Arbor, Michigan: Inter-university Consortium for Political and Social Research [distributor].

Spaeth, Harold J., and Jeffrey A. Segal. 1999. *Majority Rule or Minority Will*. New York: Cambridge University Press.

Stidham, Ronald, and Robert A. Carp. 1982. "Trial Courts' Responses to Supreme Court Policy Changes: Three Case Studies." *Law and Policy Quarterly* 4:215–34.

Swinford, Bill. 1991. "A Predictive Model of Decision Making in State Supreme Courts: The School Financing Cases." *American Politics Quarterly* 19: 336–52.

Tanenhaus, Joseph, Marvin Schick, Matthew Muraskin, and Daniel Rosen. 1963. "The Supreme Court's *Certiorari* Jurisdiction: Cue Theory." In Glendon Schubert, ed., *Judicial Decision Making*. New York: Free Press.

Tarr, G. Alan. 1977. *Judicial Impact and State Supreme Courts*. Lexington, Massachusetts: D.C. Heath and Company.

Tate, Albert, Jr. 1959. " 'Policy' in Judicial Decisions." *Louisiana Law Review* 20:62–75.

Tate, C. Neal, and Roger Handberg. 1991. "Time Binding and Theory Building in Personal Attribute Models of Supreme Court Voting Behavior, 1916–88." *American Journal of Political Science* 35:460–80.

Tomz, Michael, Jason Wittenberg, and Gary King. 1998. CLARIFY: Software for Interpreting and Presenting Statistical Results. Version 1.2. Cambridge, Massachusetts: Harvard University, September 16. http://gking.harvard.edu/

Ulmer, S. Sidney. 1984. "The Supreme Court's Certiorari Decisions: Conflict as a Predictive Variable." *American Political Science Review* 78:901–11.

Unah, Isaac. 1998. *The Courts of International Trade: Judicial Specialization, Expertise, and Bureaucratic Policy-making*. Ann Arbor: University of Michigan Press.

Van Winkle, Steven R. 1997. "Dissent as a Signal: Evidence from the U.S. Courts of Appeals." Unpublished manuscript.

Wahlbeck, Paul J. 1997. "The Life of the Law: Judicial Politics and Legal Change." *Journal of Politics* 59:778–802.

Wahlbeck, Paul J., James F. Spriggs II, and Forrest Maltzman. 1998. "Marshalling the Court: Bargaining and Accommodation on the United States Supreme Court." *American Journal of Political Science* 42:294–315.

Wald, Patricia M. 1992. "Some Real-Life Observations About Judging." *Indiana Law Review* 26:173–86.

Walsh, David J. 1997. "On the Meaning and Pattern of Legal Citations: Evidence from State Wrongful Discharge Precedent Cases." *Law and Society Review* 31:337–60.

Index

179